T0211307

Lecture Notes in Computer Science 10567

Commenced Publication in 1973
Founding and Former Series Editors:
Gerhard Goos, Juris Hartmanis, and Jan van Leeuwen

More information about this series at http://www.springer.com/series/7408

Tibor Csöndes · Gábor Kovács
György Réthy (Eds.)

SDL 2017: Model-Driven Engineering for Future Internet

18th International SDL Forum
Budapest, Hungary, October 9–11, 2017
Proceedings

Editors
Tibor Csöndes
Ericsson Hungary
Budapest
Hungary

György Réthy
Ericsson Hungary
Budapest
Hungary

Gábor Kovács
Budapest University of Technology
and Economics
Budapest
Hungary

ISSN 0302-9743   ISSN 1611-3349   (electronic)
Lecture Notes in Computer Science
ISBN 978-3-319-68014-9   ISBN 978-3-319-68015-6   (eBook)
DOI 10.1007/978-3-319-68015-6

Library of Congress Control Number: 2017953428

LNCS Sublibrary: SL2 – Programming and Software Engineering

Printed on acid-free paper

This Springer imprint is published by Springer Nature
The registered company is Springer International Publishing AG
The registered company address is: Gewerbestrasse 11, 6330 Cham, Switzerland

Preface

The System Design Languages Forum (SDL Forum) is an international conference held every two years and is one of the most important open events in the calendar for anyone from industry and academia involved in system design languages and modelling technologies. Originally focusing on the Specification and Description Language – standardized and further developed by the International Telecommunications Union (ITU) over a period of nearly four decades – the SDL Forum has broadened its topics in the course of time. It is a primary conference for the presentation and discussion of the most recent innovations, trends, experiences, and concerns in system and software modelling, specification, and analysis of distributed systems, embedded systems, communication systems, and real-time systems.

The SDL Forum Society that runs the SDL Forum conferences series is a non-profit organization established in 1995 by language users and tool providers to promote the ITU Specification and Description Language (SDL) and related system design languages including, for instance, Message Sequence Charts (MSC), Abstract Syntax Notation One (ASN.1), Testing and Test Control Notation (TTCN-3), Systems Modeling Language (SysML), Unified Modeling Language (UML), and User Requirements Notation (URN). The aim of the society is to provide and disseminate information on the development and use of the languages, to support education on the languages, and to plan and organize the "SDL Forum" series and events to promote the languages.

The 18th edition of the SDL Forum conference (SDL 2017) was held in Budapest, Hungary, October 9–11, 2017. The co-organizers of conference were the Budapest University of Technology and Economics, Ericsson Hungary Ltd., and the Scientific Association for Infocommunications Hungary (HTE). The special focus of SDL 2017 was on the model-driven engineering for the future Internet. In the past few years, we have witnessed a new level of convergence in the networked digital ecosystem. A large variety of embedded devices are becoming connected. The ever-growing number of heterogeneous devices connected demands highly available, scalable, secure, and mobile services from the telecommunications and computer networks side. The complexity of network services on the other side is increasing at the same time. There are several emerging standards on this field, followed by numerous implementations. This results in time pressure both in standard implementations and product development cycles. Therefore, specification, design, validation, configuration, deployment, and maintenance of such products are complex tasks, and thus high-quality modeling of these new systems with system design languages is essential.

This volume contains the papers selected for presentation at SDL 2017: 10 high-quality papers selected from 17 submissions. Each paper was peer reviewed by at least three Program Committee members and discussed during the online Program Committee meeting. The selected papers cover a wide spectrum of topics related to system design languages ranging from: the System Design Language usage to UML and GRL models; model-driven engineering of database queries, network service design and regression testing; and modelling for Internet of Things (IoT) data processing. The papers are grouped into four technical sessions. The first section focuses on software technology aspects, the seconds section targets IoT, the third section provides an insight into model-driven engineering, and the fourth section discusses system design language development.

The 18th edition of the SDL Forum was made possible by the dedicated work and contributions of many people and organizations. We thank the authors of submitted papers, the 41 members of the Program Committee, and the members of the SDL Forum Society Board. We are grateful for the organization and conference services of HTE and the infrastructure and information technology services of Ericsson. The submission and review process was run with the EasyChair conference system (http://www.easychair.org). We thank the sponsors of SDL 2017, the Budapest University of Technology and Economics, Ericsson, and HTE.

October 2017
Tibor Csöndes
Gábor Kovács
György Réthy

SDL Forum Society

The SDL Forum society is a nonprofit organization that in addition to running the System Design Languages Forum (SDL Forum) conference series of events once in every two years also:

- Runs the System Analysis and Modelling (SAM) workshop series, organized every two years between SDL Forum years
- Is a body recognized by ITU-T as co-developing System Design Languages in the Z.100 series (Specification and Description Language), Z.120 series (Message Sequence Chart), Z.150 series (User Requirements Notation), and other language standards
- Promotes the ITU-T System Design Languages

For more information on the SDL Forum Society, please visit http://www.sdl-forum.org.

Organization

Chairs

Tibor Csöndes	Ericsson, Hungary
Gábor Kovács	Budapest University of Technology and Economics, Hungary
György Réthy	Ericsson, Hungary

SDL Forum Society

Reinhard Gotzhein (Chairman)	University of Kaiserslautern, Germany
Jens Grabowski (Treasurer)	Georg-August-Universität Göttingen, Germany
Ferhat Khendek (Secretary)	Concordia University, Canada
Rick Reed (Non-voting board member)	TSE, UK

Program Chairs

Tibor Csöndes	Ericsson, Hungary
Gábor Kovács	Budapest University of Technology and Economics, Hungary
György Réthy	Ericsson, Hungary

Program Committee

Shaukat Ali	Simula Research Laboratory, Norway
Daniel Amyot	University of Ottawa, Canada
Árpád Beszédes	University of Szeged, Hungary
Francis Bordeleau	Ericsson, Canada
Rolv Braek	Norwegian University of Science and Technology, Norway
Reinhard Brocks	HTW des Saarlandes, Germany
Joachim Fischer	Humboldt University of Berlin, Germany
Pau Fonseca I Casas	Universitat Politècnia de Catalunya, Spain
István Forgács	4D Soft, Hungary
Emmanuel Gaudin	PragmaDev, France
Abdelouahed Gherbi	Université du Quebec, Canada
Reinhard Gotzhein	University of Kaiserslautern, Germany
Jens Grabowski	University of Göttingen, Germany
Jameleddine Hassine	KFUPM, Saudi Arabia
Øystein Haugen	Østfold University College, Norway

Steffen Herbold	University of Göttingen, Germany
Peter Herrmann	NTNU Trondheim, Norway
Dieter Hogrefe	University of Göttingen, Germany
Khendek, Ferhat	Concordia University, Canada
Attila Kovács	Eötvös Loránd University, Hungary
Alexander Kraas	University of Bamberg, Germany
Finn Kristoffersen	Cinderella ApS, Denmark
Bruno Legeard	Smartesting, France
Anna Medve	University of Pannonia, Hungary
Zoltán Micskei	Budapest University of Technology and Economics, Hungary
Birger Møller-Pedersen	University of Oslo, Norway
Gunter Mussbacher	McGill University, Canada
Ileana Ober	University of Toulouse, France
Iulian Ober	University of Toulouse, France
Dorina Petriu	Carleton University, Canada
Andrej Pietschker	Giesecke & Devrient, Germany
Rick Reed	TSE, UK
Manuel Rodríguez	University of Valladolid, Spain
Markus Scheidgen	Humboldt University of Berlin, Germany
Ina Schieferdecker	FOKUS, Germany
Edel Sherratt	University of Wales Aberystwyth, UK
Maria Toeroe	Ericsson, Canada
Andreas Ulrich	Siemens AG, Germany

Contents

Interactive Visualization of Software

Markus Scheidgen$^{(\boxtimes)}$, Nils Goldammer, and Joachim Fischer

Department of Computer Science, Humboldt Universität zu Berlin,
Unter den Linden 6, 10099 Berlin, Germany
{scheidge,goldammer,fischer}@informatik.hu-berlin.de

Abstract. To understand more and more complex software systems and
the rules that govern their development, software visualization uses more
and more complex, but static visual representations (charts) to allow
computer scientists to analyze complex multi-modal, multi-variant, and
potentially temporal data gathered from software artifacts. Data scien-
tist however, use interactive visual analysis to not only visualize data
but to explore and understand data via interactive visualizations.

In this paper, we present a language that allows us to quickly create
such interactive visualizations for software. We present a process to measure software and gather data, a common data meta-model, four principal
ways to combine individual charts into an interactive visualization, the
language constructs needed to specify interactive visualizations, and a
working implementation and examples for this language.

1 Introduction

Understanding software systems and learning the underlying rules that govern
their development is an important goal of many software engineering related
fields such as software re-engineering, software evolution, or mining software
repositories. Furthermore understanding their own software systems becomes a
more and more relevant problem for software engineering practitioners as the
systems they develop become more and more complex.

One way to tackle these problems is to govern complexity with data that comprises abstractions such as component hierarchies, dependencies between components, and software metrics. The resulting data is complex and covers different
sources (e.g. different artifacts and different components; multi-modal data), covers many properties (e.g. different dependency types and metrics; multi-variant
data), and in case of evolving software covers multiple revisions (temporal data).

Traditionally, we use *software visualization* to visualize such data about a
software system with static charts, diagrams, and graphs. The goal is to facilitate
the human eye's broad bandwidth pathway into the mind to gain knowledge from
complex data intuitively [2,11]. While simple visualizations are only capable to
carry information that might cover an isolated aspect of a software systems, visualizations of different types and of different parts of an investigated system can
be combined to form complex visualizations that allow to explore complex relations and greater knowledge from otherwise isolated pieces of information [30].

© Springer International Publishing AG 2017
T. Csöndes et al. (Eds.): SDL 2017, LNCS 10567, pp. 1–17, 2017.
DOI: 10.1007/978-3-319-68015-6_1

While researches in software visualization already try to show relations in complex data-sets with more and more complex visualizations [17], the static nature of visualizations limits the effectiveness of software visualization.

In other fields, data scientists use a process called *visual analytics* [14] to explore complex (multi-modal, multi-variant, temporal) data-sets with tasks executed alternately by machine and human via *interactive visual analysis* and *interactive visualizations*. Interactive visual analysis [20] (sometimes described as the seeable iceberg tip of visual analytics) allows users to not only see, but to explore and understand data. One particular form of interaction is machines allowing users to select data-points in one representation and highlighting or showing them related data-points in different representations. This is known as *brushing* (creating a selection) and *linking* (establishing a visual connection between representations) [20].

In this paper, we want to bring interactive visual analysis and especially brushing and linking to software visualization. Users should be able to explore the relations between data represented in different traditional software visualizations (i.e. charts) through interaction. This paper is not about measuring software, but about the interactive analysis of respective measurements. We therefore separate the process of gathering data (i.e. the automated analysis of software artifacts) from the visualization of this data (i.e. the interactive analysis of software measurements). While we briefly address the measuring step in Sect. 3, we generally assume that this process is well researched within the fields of reverse engineering [9], knowledge discovery models [24], software metrics, and mining software repositories [13].

We formally defined and implemented a language that allows users to build interactive visualizations from existing chart types. The language entails a common data meta-model as an interface to the data gathering process, an extendable set of predefined chart types, and the language constructs necessary to combine charts and to show relations through interaction. We designed the language around four principal ways to combine charts through brushing and linking.

Figure 1 shows an example for an interactive software visualization build with this language. This visualization shows package-class composition, class dependencies, and different class metrics with 7 different charts in 5 different chart types. The example allows us to perform an interactive visual analysis in three steps/tasks. First, you can select interesting packages based on package dependencies and relative complexity. Then you filter classes based on their metrics and dependency patterns to remove outlier and unusual classes. And finally, you explore the relations between different class metrics. The language implementation, in the form of a web-component library and a browser-based UI called *d3ng* (pronounced: dee-three-en-gee) as well as all examples can be found and tried in [28].

Throughout the paper, we use the following nomenclature. A *chart* refers to all visual data representations that cannot be separated into multiple visualizations in a meaningful manner. A *visualization* refers to either a chart or a combination of charts (i.e. *complex visualization*). All systematic machine responses

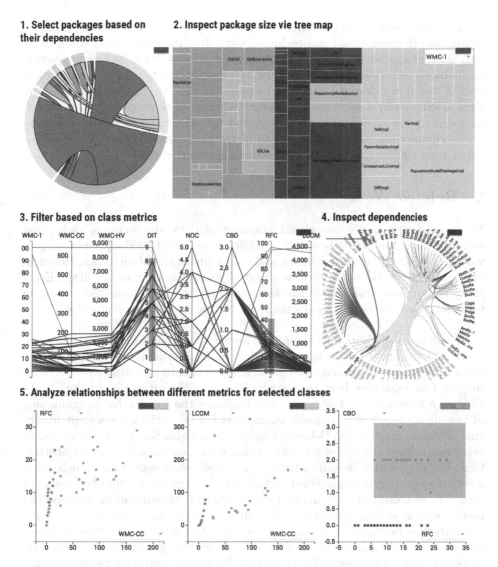

Fig. 1. An example of an interactive and complex software visualization based on different chart types depicting different aspect of the software on different levels of abstraction.

to events caused by human users are referred to as *interactions*. The terms data *meta-models* or *data structures* are used to refer to the definition of possible *data models* or simply *data* (instances of meta-models) by means of classifiers and properties. We often use the word *type* to refer to a class of similar instances, like in charts of the same chart type or combinations of the same combination type.

The paper is organized as follows. In the following section on related work, we summarize the conceptual and technical work that our approach is based on as well as other approaches to visualizing software systems. We then briefly describe methods for gathering data from software systems (i.e. measuring software) in Sect. 3, before we describe the data meta-model that we use to organize data. This is followed by a section on the identified types of chart combination as well as a description of the abstract syntax and formal semantics of our language. Section 6 describes our implementation of the proposed language. We close the paper with conclusions and a set of points for future work.

2   Related Work

Munzner describes a conceptional language of data abstractions, tasks, and actions to describe concrete visual analytics processes [19]. She focuses on providing the vocabulary to document and reason about visual analytics. However, our language can be interpreted as a partial implementation of her ideas. Especially actions like *brushing* and *linking* (as described by Hauser [20]) to aid in tasks such as *understanding relationships* can be technically realized with our work.

There are a plethora of frameworks, libraries, languages, and other forms of tools that facilitate the technical realizations of data analytics and visualizations (independent from a certain domain, e.g. software visualization). We want to give four examples here to describe four possible categories of such tools. First, we have low level libraries that facilitate the imperative programming of visualizations. A very popular example is D3 [4] itself, a Javascript library that allows to generate SVG-based graphics from data. Second, we have declarative description languages for data visualizations on various levels of abstraction. Vega [1], which describes itself as a *visualization grammar* is such a low level language (incidentally build on top of D3). Vega draws from the *grammar* idea [31]: visualizations are made from certain well known and understood elements, such as scales, axis, marks, etc. On top of Vega for example, we have the more abstract language Vega-lite [25], that operates on the assumption of reasonable customizable defaults for visualization elements (e.g. standard configuration of axis, legends, and scales). Based on this, Vega-lite is more restrictive but also allows more concise visualization descriptions. Vega-Lite also introduces interactivity between charts, including brushing and linking [25,26]. In this sense, Vega-Lite does for Vega, what we try to achieve for D3. Beyond tools that focus on visualization only, there are also tools that accommodate complete analytics workflows including data (pre-)processing, transformation, and reasoning. Here, we can also find tools on different abstraction levels. Third example: Caleydo [30] based on the Eclipse platform. Caleydo assumes that visualization data already exists and concentrates on describing the relationship between data sets and on linking respective visualizations. In Caleydo, clients can model their analysis process and Caleydo produces corresponding complex visualizations. Caleydo aims for all possible visual analytics tasks and idioms. It therefore works on a rather low level of abstraction and requires intensive programming work to create concrete visualizations, but allows for a very high degree of freedom. Examples for complex visualizations with this approach can be found in the domains of clinical [18,22] and biological [23] data analysis. As a last example, KNIME [3], also an Eclipse based framework, KNIME operates on a high-level of abstraction, including a formal data analytics workflow language and a library of predefined chart types.

The work of Khan et al. [15] applies KNIME to software visualization. Similar to our work, they identified structure (hierarchies), dependencies, and metrics as the most important aspects to visualize. Unfortunately, interactivity is limited to chart configuration and therefore does not allow to visually reason about relations via charts being connected through tasks like brushing and linking. While all these approaches are independent from the used source artifact language, there are no processes that allow to use these approaches in a language independent manner. All existing implementations for these approaches are implemented for a certain programming language or require otherwise acquired data sets.

As software visualization is an established research field many visualizations and chart types for different requirements and goals have been proposed. Ball et al. [2] and Gracanin et al. [11] provide an overview over the field. Some of the work in software visualization targets visualizations that combine multiple data dimensions and aspects into single static charts with goals similar to ours. Lanza for example introduced the concept of *polymetric views* [17]. Polymetric views depict structural information with trees and graphs, where the nodes encode metrical data with node dimensions or colors. Holten et al. [12] extends this approach to explore the limits of human comprehensibility by adding shades and textures as possible dimensions. Of course this polymetric view approach can be used in 3D [6,8] or even virtual reality [7]. These 3D visualizations lead to the often used metaphor of *software maps* [16] with software components taking the shape of geographic features like buildings or mountains. Extreme forms of this metaphor use real world events to depict certain conditions in a software system, e.g. use fire to visualise problematic components [32].

Regarding model-based development of software visualization, a couple of approaches comparable to ours exist. The framework ELVIZ [21] uses model queries in source artifacts to acquire metrics data that can be visualized in a fixed set of statistics charts. The use of queries limits this approach to metrical data and it also only supports a fixed meta-model for such data. Therefore, ELVIZ is a rather monolithic approach that is hard to extend with other visualization types and that does not allow to combine visualizations. In [10] the authors describe the framework SAMPLER that allows to create abstractions from model-based source artifacts. SAMPLER allows to implement and use filters that reduces source artifacts to those elements that are instances of certain meta-model classes and features. SAMPLER uses traditional means for representing models graphically (e.g. graphs and trees) to visualize the filtered models. MoDisco [5] provides a similar approach for MoDisco models.

3   Measuring Software

When we say measuring software, we actually want to measure the artifacts that constitute or otherwise represent a piece of software or some static or dynamic aspects of this piece of software. Common artifact types include source-code files (compilation units), all kinds of software models, execution traces, or revision histories (e.g. in source-code repositories).

In order to measure those artifacts, we need formally defined *measures*. The most commonly known type of such measures are *software metrics*: well defined abstractions that assign numbers (metric values) to a piece of software or a software component. Metrics are calculated based on the artifacts that describe the measured software or component. Depending on the metric, either instances of formal language constructs of the artifact language (e.g. programming or modeling language) or language independent artifact properties (e.g. lines of code) are used.

Besides metrics, one should also be interested in information about the structure of a piece of software by means of software components and their *relationships*. The most important of these relationships are composition *hierarchies* and *dependencies*. Note that these relationships can either be directly found within a software artifact by means of a corresponding language construct (e.g. a method call represents a dependency between two classes) or can be derived from the relationships of contained components (e.g. two package are depended when they have depended classes). Furthermore, such relationships can have their own metrics. We distinguish between relationships that form trees (e.g. containment or inheritance hierarchies) and those that form graphs (e.g. call graphs, general dependency graphs).

The technical application of measures depends on the corresponding artifacts and artifact languages. A well understood, researched, and standardized approach that can be used to measure software in a generalized manner is *reverse engineering*. The goal of reverse engineering is to gain knowledge about existing software by deriving models on a higher and higher level of abstraction. Beginning with language dependent models that represent software artifact as a direct one-to-one model (usually in the form of abstract syntax trees/graphs), ending with language independent models solely comprised of highly aggregated structures and metrics (e.g. knowledge discovery models or software metric models). Model transformation and query languages can be used to describe the applied measures in a formal manner.

To create example data and corresponding visualizations, we use the MoDisco reverse engineering framework to derive AST-models from existing Java source-code. We use an OCL inspired internal DSL in Xtend to describe and execute software measures based on MoDisco models. We use this approach to measure the McCabe and Halstead complexity for all methods, the set of CK-metrics for all classes, all method-call and field-access based dependencies between classes, corresponding aggregations for all packages, and all containment's between packages, classes, and methods. The measured data is then represented in a model based on the data meta-model described in the next section. We describe details about this process for gathering data from the Eclipse source code and its full revision history in [27,29].

4   A Meta-Model for Software Data

In the previous section, we established certain types of measures: metrics, hierarchies, and dependencies. This leaves us with data in the form of tables, trees, and graphs. We refer to the entirety of all data to be analyzed as *data-set*; to all data that represents an individual software component (e.g. package, class, or method) as a *data-point*; and to a single datum that represents a certain characteristic of a software component as a *property*. Properties are either *attributes* with a nominal, ordinal, or metric value or they describe a *reference* to other data-points. References are either compositions (they form trees) or not (they can form graphs). Data-points have a type and a label. Types are used to identify data-points that exhibit the same properties (e.g. all classes have values for the same metrics attached).

Figure 2 (a) shows the meta-model that we use for the measured data. Figure 2 (b) depicts a sample data-set comprising a hierarchy of packages (M), classes (C), and methods (M) with metrics for classes and methods and dependencies (with metrics) between classes. We omitted constraints here, but it is reasonable to assume that rules for type consistency, composition are trees, etc. can be formally defined by means of OCL or similar languages.

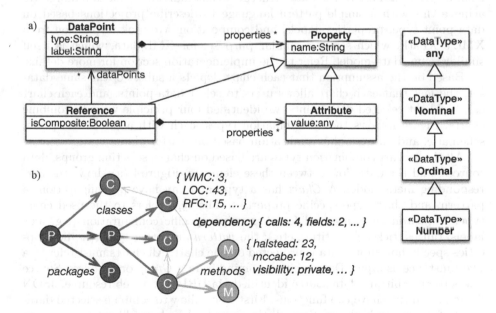

Fig. 2. Common data meta-model (a) and an example data-set comprised of packages, classes, and methods, their metrics and dependencies (b).

5   A Language for Interactive Visualizations

In the last sections, we described how software can be measured and how the resulting data can be organized. In this section, we want to describe a language that can be used to create interactive visualizations for the gathered data. There are three things that we need to address: (1) the set of chart types that can be used as building blocks, (2) how to project parts of our data to individual charts, (3) how to combine charts and let users interact with the relations between charts. Due to space restrictions, we will only briefly address the first two points, and we will focus on the combination of charts, which constitute the larger contribution of this paper.

Figure 5 shows types of charts (simple visualizations) that can be used to describe common software data such as composition hierarchies, dependencies between components, and software metrics. The type of used charts does not really matter for the combination of charts, as long as each of the following is available for all chart types. First, a clear definition of the data structure that charts can visualize, e.g. pairs of metric values for scatter plots, or trees with a metric values on each leaf for tree maps. Second, the user can interact with all charts by means of selecting visualized data-points (brushing). Third, each chart can highlight selected data-points based on shared styles (e.g. colors or symbols). Refer to the implementation section for more details.

Since each chart type expects data in a different structure, a structure that is usually distinct from the data-set as a whole, we need a way to project data from a given data-set to the data structures that individual charts require. We achieve this with a simple pattern language to describe projections based on data-point type, properties, labels, and composition. We took inspiration from XML's XPath, which serves a similar purpose, for XML-data, which is itself similar to our data-model. Refer to the implementation section for more details.

Based on the assumption that each chart depicts a subset of the same data-set, the fact that each chart allows users to select data-points, and each chart can highlight selected data-points, we identified four principle ways to combine charts. Figure 3 shows these combination types, each with a brief description, schematic, and an example visualization based on scatter plots.

All these chart combination types are based on charts, selection groups, data sources, and the data flow between these elements. Figure 4 (a) shows the corresponding meta-model. A *Chart* has a type and can have a configuration, a pattern, and chart type specific properties. The *type* refers to the used chart type; *configuration* is reserved for chart type specific configuration (e.g. axis labels, ranges, ticks, chart titles, etc.); the *pattern* and other type specific properties specify how input data is projected on the chart. All charts must refer to a *Data* instance as input. Data is either coming from a *Group* or a *Source*. Source refers to an arbitrary data source identified via URI (e.g. a web resource, JSON file, etc.). Groups have two functions. First, they allow to combine selected data-points from multiple charts. Second, they can feed such combined selections to other charts as input data. Each group comes with a certain style (i.e. color). The derived property *all input groups* denotes all groups that provide the input

a) Selection Group: Interactive selection in one chart is reflected in the selection of other charts. Charts that interact via selections form selection groups.

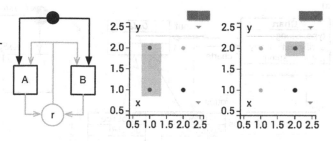

b) Overlapping Selection Groups: Each selection group is associated with a color to distinguish selection groups and selections belonging to different groups.

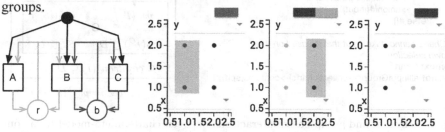

c) Mixed Hierarchy Levels: If data is hierarchical, charts might represent data on different hierarchy levels. In this case, a data point (parent) in one chart can represent multiple data points (children) in another chart.

d) Input from Selections: Often we want to use a chart or selection group to select the input data for other charts.

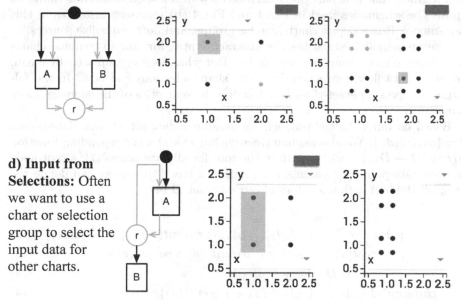

Fig. 3. Informal depiction of the four chart combination types based on selections and selection groups.

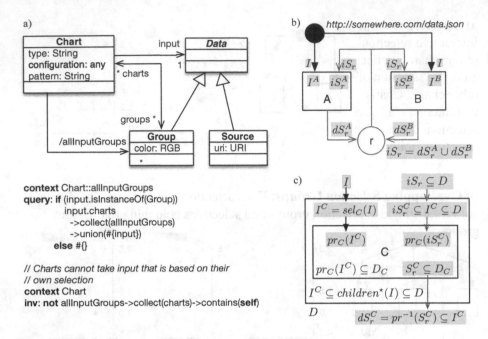

Fig. 4. Selection and group based interactions between charts: meta-model with constraints (a) and data flow depiction for simple charts (b) and charts with projection (c).

either directly or indirectly (via other groups). A chart must not get input data from a group that it is part of. Otherwise its own selection would determine its input. The schematics used in Fig. 3 and Fig. 4 (b) represent instances of this meta-model. Boxes depict charts, circles groups, and dots symbolize sources.

The meta-model establishes the abstract syntax for how to combine charts and groups to more complex visualization. But what does a group actually mean, how does data flow, and when do charts share selections and how? In the following, we use simple set-theory to describe the semantics of the language more formally.

Based on our data meta-model, we assume a data-set D with data-points $D = \{d_1, \ldots, d_n\}$. We also assume trees within D and a corresponding function $parent\colon D \to D \cup \{\epsilon\}$ with a path to the root for all data-points (1); a root node for each data-point (2); parents form indeed a tree (3); and we can define the set of all children within a subset of our data-set D (4):

$$parent^\star(d_1) = \{d_n | \exists d_2, \ldots, d_{n-1}\colon parent(d_i) = parent(d_{i+1})\} \quad (1)$$

$$root(d) = r \text{ with } r \in parent^\star(d) \wedge parent(r) = \epsilon \quad (2)$$

$$\forall d \in D\colon d \notin parent^\star(d) \quad (3)$$

$$children^\star(I \subseteq D) = \{e | \exists d \in I\colon e \in parent^\star(d)\} \quad (4)$$

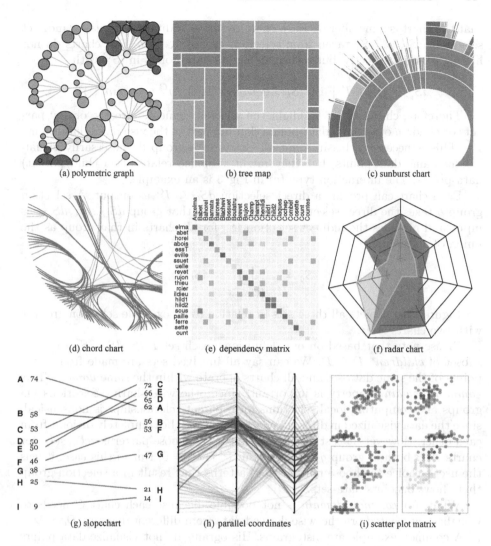

Fig. 5. Suitable chart types for hierarchies (a,b,c), dependencies (d,e,f), and metrics (g,h,i).

Each chart C gets some $I \subseteq D$ as input. Each chart can define a pattern that specifies two functions: a selection function and a projection function. A selection function $sel_C : I \rightarrow \mathcal{P}(D)$ selects a set of data-points $I^C = \bigcup_{i \in I} sel_C(i) \subseteq D$ within the children of the input I: $I^C \subseteq children^\star(I)$. Charts do not visualize their input I directly, but rather the selected data-points in I^C. A chart without pattern implicitly gets the identity $id(d) = d$ as its selection function.

Each chart can be part of a selection group and therefore can highlight data-points selected within itself (direct selection) or selected within other charts of the same group (indirect selection). There are different selections for each group that the chart is a member of. Each chart can have additional inputs for indirect selections $iS_1, \ldots, iS_n$ taken from selection groups $1, \ldots, n$. But charts do not highlight all iS_i directly, but rather highlights data-points in iS_i^C with

$$iS_i^C = \{i^C \in I^C | \exists i \in iS_i : i \in parent^\star(i^C) \vee i^C \in parent^\star(i)\}$$

Therefore, charts either highlight the selected elements directly, or any parents or children of selected data-points that are part of the visualized data-points I^C. This is necessary, because not all charts in a group do necessarily visualize the same data-points, but they might visualize related (via child/parent) data-points. The interaction type (c) in Fig. 3 is an example.

Each chart can provide a direct selection $dS_C \subseteq I^C$ as output. A selection group g takes the direct selections of all charts in that group $dS_{C_1}, \ldots, dS_{C_n}$ as input and provides the indirect selection iS_g for all charts in that group as the union of all inputs:

$$iS_g = \bigcup_{C \in \{C_1, \ldots, C_n\}} dS_C$$

Figure 4 (b) depicts all these sets in relation to an example selection group r with two charts A, B.

Please note that based on our definitions, each set $I, I^C, dS_C, iS_g, iS_g^C$ is a subset of $children^\star(I) \subseteq D$. We can say all involved sets are made from data-points of the same data-set and all charts operate within the same *domain*. This *common domain* property is important, since otherwise sharing selections via groups and computing local selections form parent relationships is nonsensical, since the data visualized in different charts might well be completely disjoint from each other. However, it is still possible that users choose patterns sel_A, sel_B for charts A, B both in group g that result in $I^A \cap I^B = \emptyset$. But in this case, it was the user's choice to choose nonsensical patterns that result in a selection group that shows disjoints data-sets.

What if a *common domain* is not possible, because each chart C needs to visualize aggregated or otherwise derived data from different domains $D_C \cap D = \emptyset$? A common example are histograms. Histograms do not visualize data-points directly; they aggregate data-points in bins and visualize the amount of data-points in each bin. These bins represent data-points that are not part of D and therefore cannot be highlighted in any other chart directly.

In these cases, each chart needs to define a projection function $pr_C : \mathcal{P}(D) \rightarrow \mathcal{P}(D_C)$. The function pr_C operates on subsets of D rather than on elements of D to allow aggregation, i.e. the mapping of multiple elements of the co-domain D to one element of the domain D_C. Since the projections pr_A, pr_B of multiple charts A, B (e.g. within the same group) can be independent, we have to assume $D_A \cap D_B = \emptyset$. Since each chart shows data-points from $pr_C(I^C)$ rather than I^C the projected user's selection prS_C can be $prS_C \subseteq pr_C(I^C)$ and $prS_C \not\subseteq I^C$. To maintain $dS_C \subseteq I^C$, each chart needs to define the reverse projection $pr_C^{-1} : \mathcal{P}(D_C) \rightarrow \mathcal{P}(D)$ in order to define $dS_C = pr^{-1}(prS_C)$ and maintain $dS_C \subseteq I^C$. Furthermore, charts also need to apply the projection function to indirect selections from each group in order to display the selected elements within the projection domain. Similar to pattern functions, we can assume $id(d) = d$ as the default projection for each chart. Figure 4 (c) depicts the data-flow with respect to distinct selection and projection functions.

In practice, we can mostly find projection functions that depend only on the chart type (e.g. histograms) and many chart types do not need a real projection (e.g. scatter plots). Therefore, projections can be encapsulated within the implementation of chart types and users usually only have to describe selections. Such selections can be described with before mentioned pattern language. Projection can be more difficult (especially the reverse projections). There are best implemented in a general purpose programming language, hidden from language users. Their reverse can be realized via traces or similar techniques.

6   Implementation

A typical implementation platform would be a combination of Eclipse, EMF, and a Java/SWT-based chart library, such as JChart. Other frameworks, like Caleydo, went this route. But, the problem with typical chart libraries is that they treat charts as write/generate only entities, where provided data is simply *drawn* as graphical elements and then forgotten about. As a result, support for selecting data-points is limited. Even if one would implement such functionality, there are no traces between data and graphical elements, hence reversing projections is difficult.

The web-based library D3.js works differently. Instead of a simple drawing tool, D3.js is a transformation language that allows us to transform data models into document object models (DOM). Graphical elements are not simply drawn on a canvas, but rather kept within a DOM tree. Furthermore, traces between data-points and representing DOM-elements are kept. Therefore, projections are easily reversible. Additionally, each DOM-element allows to handle user events and stylization of graphical elements with a unified programming interface. Therefore, common tasks, such as highlighting elements or reacting to selection events, can be handled uniformly and independent from chart types or concrete graphical elements. Figure 6 depicts the interplay between data, DOM, and graphical elements.

We implemented the previously described language as a library of web-components within the Angular-2 framework. We provide an abstract component for charts, with concrete derivations for scatter plots, parallel coordinates, tree maps, collapsible trees, force graphs, chord diagrams, edge bundled dependency charts, simple list, and histograms. Of course this list is growing and users can provide their own chart components. We furthermore have components to specify input patterns and groups. We use Angular-2's double data-bindings to describe the data-flow between charts and groups. Therefore, users do not have to handle selection events themselves. The different chart-components are realized with D3.js. If users want to create their own chart components, they have to implement three things. First, the projection from selected data-points to the DOM.

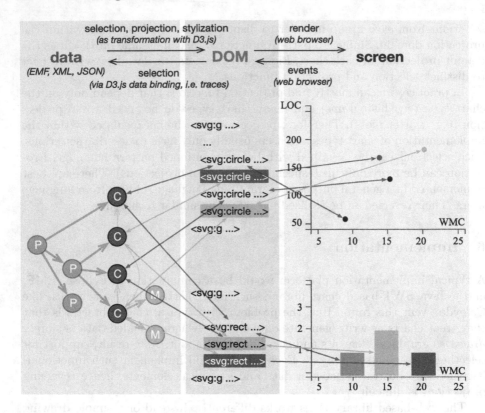

Fig. 6. Realization of chart interactions with web technologies: D3.js, DOM, events, and styles.

Second, the highlighting of directly or indirectly selected data-points. Third, a selection mechanism that is suitable to the chart type and fires corresponding selection events.

If users want to create an interactive visualization, they can describe it with HTML using our components (components can be instantiated via HTML-tags). Our library also provides a workbench, that allows users to compose visualization via a web-UI interactively.

7   Conclusions

We conceptualized, specified, and implemented a language for interactive software visualizations that focuses on the combination of known chart types rather than inventing new chart types. The relationship between data visualized in different charts can be explored through interactions that are based on selecting data-points in one chart and observing corresponding changes in other charts. Users can compose complex visualizations from existing chart types via simple HTML-code or interactively via UI. In contrast to other frameworks, users can create visualization without many programming efforts. The relationships between charts are established via simple patterns over a common data model. Programming effort is required however, if new chart types or more complex projections are needed. We only focus on interactive visualizations and not on other tasks, such as gathering data, cleaning data, aggregating data, conduction statistical tests, etc.

The presented work has some limitations that should be addressed in future work. First, we allow users to specific selection functions with a simple pattern language. Since we use hierarchical JSON data in a standard way and our data meta-model is compatible with many other data representations (e.g. XML), it should be possible to replace this pattern language with an existing more complex and feature rich pattern/query language. Second, we only use parent/child relationships to highlight indirectly selected data-points. Users might want to customize this for their visualizations, especially when more complex projections are involved. Third, selection groups always form the union over all direct selections to form the set of indirect selections. Users might want to customize this behavior. Fourth, we assume that projections only depend on the chart type, but it might be possible that users want to use two different projections for the same type. Custom projections would also increase the re-usability of chart types. Fifth, we always represent data in the form of collections over data-points. Each selection, group, chart maintains its own collections and produces the associated memory consumption. Instead of representing sets as collections of data-points, in many cases, we should describe sets with predicates and expressions. When one uses a scatter plot to select all data-points within some boundaries, we can represent this set via those boundaries instead of a collection with a possibly very large number of data-points. This would also allow to work with partial data. The browser only needs to maintain the data that is currently visualized. If user interaction requires additional children to be loaded, some client-server architecture could be facilitated to query the respective additional data from a server.

References

1. Vega: A visualization grammar, November 2016. https://vega.github.io/vega/
2. Ball, T., Eick, S.G.: Softw. Vis. Large. East **29**(4), 33–43 (1996)
3. Berthold, M.R., et al.: KNIME: the Konstanz information miner. In: Preisach, C., Burkhardt, H., Schmidt-Thieme, L., Decker, R. (eds.) Data Analysis, Machine Learning and Applications. Studies in Classification, Data Analysis, and Knowledge Organization, pp. 319 326. Springer, Heidelberg (2008). doi:10.1007/978-3-540-78246-9_38
4. Bostock, M., Ogievetsky, V., Heer, J.: D3 data-driven documents. IEEE Trans. Visual Comput. Graphics **17**(12), 2301–2309 (2011). http://dx.doi.org/10.1109/TVCG.2011.185
5. Bruneliere, H., Cabot, J., Jouault, F., Madiot, F.: Modisco: a generic and extensible framework for model driven reverse engineering. In: Proceedings of the IEEE/ACM International Conference on Automated Software Engineering, pp. 173–174. ASE 2010, NY (2010). http://doi.acm.org/10.1145/1858996.1859032

6. Dal Sasso, T., Minelli, R., Mocci, A., Lanza, M.: Blended, not stirred: multi-concern visualization of large software systems. In: 2015 IEEE 3rd Working Conference on Software Visualization (VISSOFT), pp. 106–115. IEEE (2015)
7. Fittkau, F., Krause, A., Hasselbring, W.: Exploring software cities in virtual reality. In: 2015 IEEE 3rd Working Conference on Software Visualization (VISSOFT), pp. 130–134. IEEE (2015)
8. Gall, H., Jazayeri, M., Riva, C.: Visualizing software release histories: the use of color and third dimension. In: Proceedings IEEE International Conference on Software Maintenance 1999 (ICSM 1999). 'Software Maintenance for Business Change' (Cat. No. 99CB36360) (1999)
9. Gannod, G.C., Cheng, B.H.: A framework for classifying and comparing software reverse engineering and design recovery techniques. In: 1999 Proceedings of the Sixth Working Conference on Reverse Engineering, pp. 77–88. IEEE (1999)
10. Garmendia, A., Jim, A., Lara, J.D.: Scalable model exploration through abstraction and fragmentation strategies. In: BigMDE 2015 Workshop at STAF 2015 (2015)
11. Gračanin, D., Matković, K., Eltoweissy, M.: Software visualization. Innovations Syst. Softw. Eng. $\mathbf{1}$(2), 221–230 (2005)
12. Holten, D., Vliegen, R., Van Wijk, J.J.: Visual realism for the visualization of software metrics. In: Proceedings of VISSOFT 2005: 3rd IEEE International Workshop on Visualizing Software for Understanding and Analysis, pp. 27–32 (2005)
13. Kagdi, H., Collard, M.L., Maletic, J.I.: Towards a taxonomy of approaches for mining of source code repositories. In: ACM SIGSOFT Software Engineering Notes, vol. 30, pp. 1–5. ACM (2005)
14. Keim, D., Andrienko, G., Fekete, J.-D., Görg, C., Kohlhammer, J., Melançon, G.: Visual analytics: definition, process, and challenges. In: Kerren, A., Stasko, J.T., Fekete, J.-D., North, C. (eds.) Information Visualization. LNCS, vol. 4950, pp. 154–175. Springer, Heidelberg (2008). doi:10.1007/978-3-540-70956-5_7
15. Khan, T., Barthel, H., Ebert, A., Liggesmeyer, P.: Visual analytics of software structure and metrics. In: 2015 IEEE 3rd Working Conference on Software Visualization (VISSOFT), pp. 16–25, September 2015
16. Kuhn, A., Loretan, P., Nierstrasz, O.: Consistent layout for thematic software maps. In: Proceedings of Working Conference on Reverse Engineering, WCRE, pp. 209–218 (2008)
17. Lanza, M., Ducasse, S.: Polymetric views - a lightweight visual approach to reverse engineering. IEEE Trans. Software Eng. $\mathbf{29}$(9), 782–795 (2003)
18. Lex, A., Streit, M., Schulz, H.J., Partl, C., Schmalstieg, D.: StratomeX: visual analysis of large-scale heterogeneous genomics data for cancer subtype characterization. Comput. Graph. Forum $\mathbf{31}$(3pt3), 1175–1184 (2012). http://doi.wiley.com/10.1111/j.1467-8659.2012.03110.x
19. Munzner, T.: Visualization Analysis and Design. CRC Press, Boca Raton (2014)
20. Oeltze, S., Doleisch, H., Hauser, H., Weber, G.: Interactive visual analysis of scientific data. Tutorial at the IEEE VisWeek, October 2012. http://www.vismd.de/lib/exe/fetch.php?media=teaching_tutorials:ieeevisweektutorial_2012_iva_proposal.pdf
21. Ostendorp, M.C., Jelschen, J., Winter, A.: Elviz: a query-based approach to model visualization. In: Modellierung, pp. 105–120 (2014)
22. Partl, C., Lex, A., Streit, M., Strobelt, H., Wassermann, A., Pfister, H., Schmalstieg, D.: ConTour: data-driven exploration of multi-relational datasets for drug discovery. IEEE Trans. Vis. Comput. Graph. $\mathbf{20}$(12), 1883–1892 (2014)

23. Partl, C., Kalkofen, D., Lex, A., Kashofer, K., Streit, M., Schmalstieg, D.: EnRoute: dynamic path extraction from biological pathway maps for in-depth experimental data analysis. In: Proceedings of IEEE Symposium on Biological Data Visualization 2012, BioVis 2012, pp. 107–114 (2012)
24. Pérez-Castillo, R., De Guzman, I.G.R., Piattini, M.: Knowledge discovery metamodel-iso/iec 19506: a standard to modernize legacy systems. Comput. Stand. Interfaces **33**(6), 519–532 (2011)
25. Satyanarayan, A., Moritz, D., Wongsuphasawat, K., Heer, J.: Vega-lite: a grammar of interactive graphics. IEEE Trans. Vis. Comp. Graph.(Proc. InfoVis) **23**(1), 341–350 (2017). http://idl.cs.washington.edu/papers/vega-lite
26. Satyanarayan, A., Wongsuphasawat, K., Heer, J.: Declarative interaction design for data visualization. In: ACM User Interface Software & Technology (UIST) (2014). http://idl.cs.washington.edu/papers/reactive-vega
27. Scheidgen, M., Fischer, J.: Model-based mining of source code repositories. In: Amyot, D., Fonseca i Casas, P., Mussbacher, G. (eds.) SAM 2014. LNCS, vol. 8769, pp. 239–254. Springer, Cham (2014). doi:10.1007/978-3-319-11743-0_17
28. Scheidgen, M., Goldammer, N.: D3ng: D3 and angular2 based interactive visualizations of complex data (2017). http://github.com/markus1978/d3ng
29. Scheidgen, M., Schmidt, M., Fischer, J.: Creating and analyzing source code repository models - a model-based approach to mining software repositories. In: Proceedings of the 5th International Conference on Model-Driven Engineering and Software Development MODELSWARD, vol. 1, pp. 329–336 (2017)
30. Streit, M., Schulz, H.J., Lex, A., Schmalstieg, D., Schumann, H.: Model-driven design for the visual analysis of heterogeneous data. IEEE trans. vis. comput. graph. **18**(6), 998–1010 (2012). http://www.ncbi.nlm.nih.gov/pubmed/21690642
31. Sugimoto, A.: Vega: a visual modeling language for digital systems. IEEE Des. Test Comput. **3**(3), 38–45 (1986)
32. Würfel, H., Trapp, M., Limberger, D., Döllner, J.: Natural phenomena as metaphors for visualization of trend data in interactive software maps. In: CGVC, pp. 69–76 (2015)

Static Syntax Validation for Code Generation with String Templates

Dorian Weber[✉] and Joachim Fischer

Institut für Informatik, Humboldt-Universität zu Berlin, Berlin, Germany
{weber,fischer}@informatik.hu-berlin.de

Abstract. Many applications of model-based techniques ultimately require a model-to-text transformation to make practical use of the information encoded in meta-model instances. This step requires a code generator that has to be validated in order to ensure that the translation doesn't alter the semantics of the model. Validation is often test-based, i.e. the code generator is executed on a wide range of inputs in order to verify the correctness of its output. Unfortunately, tests generally only prove the presence of errors, not their absence. This paper identifies the common core of string template implementations that are often used in the description of code generators, deriving a formal model that is suitable for mathematical reasoning. We provide a formal proof of the equivalence in expressiveness between string templates and context free grammars, thereby allowing the application of formal results from language theory. From there, we derive a scheme that would allow the verification of syntactical correctness for generated code before the translation of any model-instance is attempted, at the expense of freedom in the variability of the description.

Keywords: Code generation · Language theory · String template · Meta language · Domain-specific language

1 Introduction

The core tenet of model-driven engineering is the use of domain models to represent abstract knowledge about a particular application domain. These models are used to connect different problem sets through a shared information base which helps to reduce redundancy, increase modularity and facilitate the creation of less verbose programs through the use of domain-specific languages. In order to use a domain model for a particular problem set, it is often necessary to vary its representation, e.g. by applying a model-to-model or model-to-text transformation. The focus of this paper is on model-to-text transformations using string templates and it deals with the sub-problem on how to ensure the syntactical correctness of the generated text as a sentence of the output language. In other words, prior to seeing any meta-model instance under which circumstances can we guarantee that a string template will expand to syntactically correct code?

© Springer International Publishing AG 2017
T. Csöndes et al. (Eds.): SDL 2017, LNCS 10567, pp. 18–29, 2017.
DOI: 10.1007/978-3-319-68015-6_2

```
1     """
2     <body>
3       <h2>«module.name»</h2>
4       «FOR expr: module.member»
5         <h3>«expr.name»</h3>
6         <dl>
7           «FOR it: expr.member»
8             «IF it.univerval»
9               <dt>«it.name»</dt>
10              <dd>=«it.value»</dt>
11            «ELSEIF it.extensible»
12              <dt/>
13              <dd><i>Enumeration is extensible</i></dd>
14            «ENDIF»
15          «ENDFOR»
16        </dl>
17      «ENDFOR»
18    </body>
19    """
```

Listing 1. *Xtend* string template for generating *HTML* code from an *ASN.1* meta-model instance.

The ability to guarantee the syntactical correctness for generated code has applicability in a wide range of related topics, e.g. in traditional compiler construction for specification-type languages (e.g. *ASN.1*), languages featuring syntax extension mechanisms (e.g. *SLX*), or languages that support string templates for code generation (e.g. *Xtend*). As a result, this area has been studied extensively with promising theoretical results but severe technological prerequisites. The goal of this paper is to provide a formal foundation for novel techniques addressing this problem with the expectation that the derived solutions will be simpler in terms of implementation and maintenance.

The paper is organized as follows. We begin by providing an instance of the problem we are attempting to solve, followed by taking a look at related work and discussing the relationship to this paper. We continue in Sect. 2 by formally defining string templates and providing a proof establishing their equivalence to context free grammars. Section 3 outlines a potential solution that would allow automatic proof-based verification for syntax of the generated language. Finally, Sect. 4 contains conclusion and outlook.

1.1 Brief Example

Listing 1 shows an example of a string template in *Xtend* that seems to generate *HTML* code. In line 10, we notice that the opening **<dd>** is closed by **</dt>** . Therefore, without knowing the concrete value of module, we deduce that the output can be invalid *HTML*. We can do so by analyzing the algorithm used to generate the code. Compare and contrast with listing 2 that seems to generate an enumeration in *C*. Here, the output looks like it should be syntactically valid, but we cannot be sure since we don't know whether for example expr.name in line 2 will expand into a valid identifier or not.

Given the context free grammar for the syntax of a target language (e.g. *HTML*, *C*), this paper attempts to identify the circumstances under which it would be possible to decide whether all value configurations (i.e. meta-model instances) lead to syntactically correct code.

```
1      '''
2          typedef enum «expr.name» {
3              «FOR it: expr.member»
4                  «IF it.univerval»
5                      «it.name» = «it.value»,
6                  «ELSEIF it.extensible»
7                      /*
8                       * Enumeration is extensible
9                       */
10                 «ENDIF»
11             «ENDFOR»
12         } e_«expr.name»;
13     '''
```

Listing 2. *Xtend* string template for generating an enumeration in *C* from an *ASN.1* meta-model instance.

1.2   Related Work

Parr discusses the relationship between string templates and context free languages in a semi-formal manner that includes an informal sketch for a proof [6]. Our paper provides formal answers for that topic.

Wachsmuth describes an algorithm to mechanically derive a *code template language* based on the grammar of an output language that guarantees syntax correctness [9]. While the paper contains a complete syntax and semantics description, no proof of correctness is offered. Dynamically evaluated expressions embedded in string templates fall outside of the scope of the paper as well.

Arnoldus deals with *syntax safe templates* in his PhD thesis [1], which constitute a language that is the result of augmenting a specific notation for string templates with the grammar of the target language, providing a proof-of-concept for the aforementioned paper by Wachsmuth. Using a parser for that grammar, the static parts of an interconnected set of string templates can be verified to be syntactically correct fragments of the output language. In order to guarantee full syntax correctness, one must also ensure that dynamic expressions embedded within the string template are validated, for which the author proposes a runtime scheme. This step changes the validation from proof to test based. The advantages are tangible nonetheless, since the static parts of string templates can be verified statically. The author makes no attempt to identify common features with other kinds of string template languages beyond his own. Our paper attempts to derive more general truths about this issue, as well as proposing a mechanism to capture dynamic expressions in the automated proof.

2 Relationship between Context Free Grammars and String Templates

In this section, we provide a formal proof showing that string template languages are alternative notations of context free grammars. This allows us to conclude that the general problem of deciding whether a set of string templates generate a subset of a context free language is undecidable. We begin by defining mathematical structures for the representation of context free grammars and string templates, outlining the latter's connection to the string template notation featured in *Xtend* as a representation of string template notations used in industrial strength languages. We continue with a constructive proof that maps context free grammars to string templates and vice versa while preserving the generated language. Finally, we discuss the consequences of this result.

2.1 Basic Definitions

Definition 1. *A* Context Free Grammar (**CFG**) *is defined by the tuple* (V, Σ, P, V_0) *where*

- V *is a finite set of meta characters,*
- Σ *is a finite set of symbols, disjoint from* V,
- $P \subseteq V \times (\Sigma \cup V)^*$ *is a finite relation,*
- $V_0 \in V$ *is the start symbol.*

We denote the production rule $(S, \alpha) \in P$ *as* $S \to \alpha$.

Definition 2. *A* Context Free Language (**CFL**) *is the set of all strings that can be produced by a CFG through application of a sequence of production rules via substitution of a meta character by the rule's right-hand-side.*

For $\mu, \nu \in (\Sigma \cup V)^*$ *we write that* $\mu \underset{C}{\Rightarrow} \nu$ *iff* $\mu = \mu_1 S \mu_2$ *and* $\nu = \mu_1 \alpha \mu_2$ *and* $S \to \alpha$. *Let* $\mu \underset{C}{\overset{*}{\Rightarrow}} \nu$ *denote that operation's reflexive, transitive closure. Then* $L = \left\{ \omega \in \Sigma^* \,\middle|\, V_0 \underset{C}{\overset{*}{\Rightarrow}} \omega \right\}$ *defines the context free language.*

Example 1. A CFG (V, Σ, P, V_0) for arithmetic expressions can be defined by

- $V = \{E, T, F\}$
- $\Sigma = \{\oplus, \odot, (,), f\}$
- $V_0 = E$
- P defined as

$$E \to T \oplus E$$
$$E \to T$$
$$T \to F \odot T$$
$$T \to F$$
$$F \to (E)$$
$$F \to f$$

An example for a valid sentence is $(f \oplus f) \odot f \oplus f$.

Definition 3. *A* String Template System (**STS**) *can be defined as a tuple* (T, Σ, R, T_0) *where*

- T *is a finite set of string templates,*
- Σ *is a finite set of symbols, disjoint from* T,
- $R : T \rightarrow (\Sigma \cup T \cup \mathcal{P}(T))^*$ *is a function with* $\mathcal{P}(T) = \{U \,|\, U \subseteq T\}$ *being the power set,*
- $T_0 \in T$ *is the expanded string template.*

The symbol $\mathcal{E}$ *is used to denote a string template with an empty right-hand-side, i.e.* $R(\mathcal{E}) = \varepsilon$. *We denote the mapping* $R(A) = \alpha$ *as* $A \mapsto \alpha$.

Definition 4. *A* String Template Language (**STL**) *is the set of all strings that can be produced by a STS through recursive substitution of string templates with their mapping. For sets of string templates, any member may be expanded.*
For $A \in T, \alpha \in \mathcal{P}(T), \beta, \mu, \nu \in (\Sigma \cup T \cup \mathcal{P}(T))^*$ *we write*

$$\mu \underset{S}{\Rightarrow} \nu \Leftrightarrow (\mu = \mu_1 A \mu_2 \wedge \nu = \mu_1 \beta \mu_2 \wedge A \mapsto \beta)$$

$$\vee\, (\mu = \mu_1 \alpha \mu_2 \wedge \nu = \mu_1 B \mu_2 \wedge B \in \alpha)$$

We denote applications of the first alternative as $\mu \overset{1}{\underset{S}{\Rightarrow}} \nu$, *of the second alternative* $\mu \overset{2}{\underset{S}{\Rightarrow}} \nu$ *and the reflexive, transitive closure as* $\mu \overset{*}{\underset{S}{\Rightarrow}} \nu$. *Then* $L = \left\{ \omega \in \Sigma^* \,|\, T_0 \overset{*}{\underset{S}{\Rightarrow}} \omega \right\}$ *denotes the string template language.*

Example 2. A STS (T, Σ, R, T_0) for tuples can be defined by

- $T = \{S, F, C, E, D\}$
- $\Sigma = \{p, |, (,)\}$
- $T_0 = S$
- R defined as

$$S \mapsto (F)$$
$$F \mapsto E \{C, \mathcal{E}\}$$
$$C \mapsto |F$$
$$E \mapsto \{S, D\}$$
$$D \mapsto p$$

An example for a valid sentence is $(p|((p|p)|p))$.

Remark 1. The key difference between the structures for CFG and STS is found in the notation of alternatives. CFGs allow alternative definitions for meta symbols, but only a single definition on the right-hand-side of a rule, while STSs allow only a single definition for each string template but with multiple possible expansions.

```
1    def S() // S ↦ (F)
2        '''(«F»)'''
3
4    def F() // F ↦ E {C, 𝓔}
5        '''«E»«IF c₁»«C»«ENDIF»'''
6
7    def C() // C ↦ |F
8        '''|«F»'''
9
10   def E() // E ↦ {S, D}
11       '''«IF c₂»«S»«ELSE»«D»«ENDIF»'''
12
13   def D() // D ↦ p
14       '''p'''
```

Listing 3. *Xtend* string template for generating the tuple STS from example 2.

$$S \mapsto \texttt{<body><h2>}D_1\texttt{</h2>} \{T_1, \mathcal{E}\} \texttt{ </body>}$$
$$T_1 \mapsto \texttt{<h3>}D_2\texttt{</h3><dl>} \{T_2, \mathcal{E}\} \texttt{ </dl>} \{T_1, \mathcal{E}\}$$
$$T_2 \mapsto \{T_3, T_4, \mathcal{E}\} \{T_2, \mathcal{E}\}$$
$$T_3 \mapsto \texttt{<dt>}D_3\texttt{</dt><dd>=}D_4\texttt{</dt>}$$
$$T_4 \mapsto \texttt{<dt/><dd><i>Enumeration is extensible</i></dd>}$$

Listing 4. STS for listing 1 from the introduction. This rendering doesn't account for whitespace and has no mappings defined for the dynamic expansions D_1 to D_4.

2.2 Relation to Real-World String Templates

String templates typically feature embedded control structures for branching, looping and recursion as well as embedded variable references in expressions. During interpretation, the textual output is determined by evaluating the dynamic expressions and inserting their string representations into the output stream in sequence. Conditions attached to the control structures are evaluated as well and used to adjust the control flow accordingly. Examples for string template engines that function as described include *String Template* [7], rich strings in *Xtend* [2], and *Cheetah* for *Python* [8]. Both the evaluation of dynamic expressions and the selection of the applicable expansion are done referencing a meta-model instance.

Since the point of static analysis is to abstract from meta-model instances, Definition 3 captures the control structures with the power set for string templates and Definition 4 allows the control flow to pass to any of the included string templates within a power set. This arrangement allows the modeling of control structures as well as arbitrary other forms of selecting alternative expansions. Loops are a special case of recursion (tail-recursion) and can therefore also be expressed within the structure. The mathematical structure doesn't capture dynamic expressions; we will disregard them until the relationship to context free grammars is understood more clearly.

Listings 3 and 4 provide examples for mapping between the specific *Xtend* notation for string templates and the structure from Definition 3. In the set of string template mappings in listing 4 all whitespace is omitted for brevity. The attribute references represented by D_1 to D_4 cannot be expressed as STS yet and therefore have an undefined mapping. We revisit dynamic expressions in Sect. 3.

2.3   Mappings

With the definitions in place, we can now ask the formal question: given a CFG $G = (V, \Sigma, P, V_0)$ describing the target language and a STS $S = (T, \Sigma, R, T_0)$ describing the code generator, can we decide if $L_S \subseteq L_G$?

Definition 5. *STS $\mapsto$ CFG can be defined as follows: Define a function that takes the right-hand-side of a string template definition and expands it into a set of right-hand-sides with no alternatives. Use it for the definition of productions, since these allow multiple definitions but no alternative expansions.*

Formally, let $f : (\Sigma \cup T \cup \mathcal{P}(T))^* \to \mathcal{P}\left((\Sigma \cup T)^*\right)$ be

$$f(\omega) = \begin{cases} \{\varepsilon\} & \text{for } \omega = \varepsilon \\ \{\omega\} & \text{for } \omega \in \Sigma \cup T \\ \{S \in \omega\} & \text{for } \omega \in \mathcal{P}(T) \\ \{\sigma b|\, b \in f(\beta)\} & \text{for } \omega = \sigma\beta, \sigma \in \Sigma \cup T, \beta \in (\Sigma \cup T \cup \mathcal{P}(T))^+ \\ \{Ab|\, A \in \alpha, b \in f(\beta)\} & \text{for } \omega = \alpha\beta, \alpha \in \mathcal{P}(T), \beta \in (\Sigma \cup T \cup \mathcal{P}(T))^+ \end{cases}$$

Then $(V, \Sigma, P, V_0) = (T, \Sigma, \{S \to \alpha|\, S \in T, \alpha \in f(R(S))\}, T_0)$.

Lemma 1. *Every STS can be expressed as a CFG such that their respective languages are equal.*

Proof. Let L_S be the language of the STS $S = (T, \Sigma, R, T_0)$ and L_G the language of the CFG $G = (V, \Sigma, P, V_0)$ defined as outlined in Definition 5.

$L_S \subseteq L_G$ Let $T_0 \overset{*}{\underset{S}{\Rightarrow}} \omega$, i.e. there is a sequence $T_0 \underset{S}{\Rightarrow} \omega_1 \underset{S}{\Rightarrow} \ldots \underset{S}{\Rightarrow} \omega_n = \omega$ with $\omega_1, \ldots, \omega_n \in (\Sigma \cup T \cup \mathcal{P}(T))^*$. Without loss of generality, let the sequence be ordered such that for every application of the form $\mu_1 S \mu_2 = \omega_i \overset{1}{\underset{S}{\Rightarrow}} \omega_{i+1} = \mu_1 \alpha \mu_2$, there is an immediate sequence of derivation steps $\omega_{i+1} \overset{2}{\underset{S}{\Rightarrow}} \ldots \overset{2}{\underset{S}{\Rightarrow}} \omega_{i+j} = \mu_1 \alpha' \mu_2$ with $\alpha' \in (\Sigma \cup T)^*$. We can now rewrite the sequence as

$$T_0 \overset{1}{\underset{S}{\Rightarrow}} \omega_1 \overset{2}{\underset{S}{\Rightarrow}} \ldots \overset{2}{\underset{S}{\Rightarrow}} \underset{\|}{\omega_{j_2}} \overset{1}{\underset{S}{\Rightarrow}} \ldots \overset{2}{\underset{S}{\Rightarrow}} \underset{\|}{\omega_{j_3}} \overset{1}{\underset{S}{\Rightarrow}} \ldots \overset{2}{\underset{S}{\Rightarrow}} \underset{\|}{\omega_{j_k-1}} \overset{1}{\underset{S}{\Rightarrow}} \underset{\|}{\omega_{j_k}} = \omega$$
$$\quad \chi_1 \overset{*}{\underset{S}{\Rightarrow}} \qquad\qquad \chi_2 \overset{*}{\underset{S}{\Rightarrow}} \qquad\quad \chi_3 \overset{*}{\underset{S}{\Rightarrow}} \cdots\cdots \; \chi_{k-1} \overset{1}{\underset{S}{\Rightarrow}} \chi_k$$

Selecting an arbitrary step $\chi_i \overset{*}{\underset{S}{\Rightarrow}} \chi_{i+1}$, we reason:

$$\Rightarrow \chi_i = \mu_1 S \mu_2 \wedge \chi_{i+1} = \mu_1 \alpha' \mu_2 \wedge S \overset{1}{\underset{S}{\Rightarrow}} \alpha \overset{2}{\underset{S}{\Rightarrow}} \ldots \overset{2}{\underset{S}{\Rightarrow}} \alpha'$$

$$\Rightarrow \alpha' \in f(R(S))$$

$$\Rightarrow S \to \alpha'$$

$$\Rightarrow \chi_i \underset{C}{\Rightarrow} \chi_{i+1}$$

We conclude that $T_0 \overset{*}{\underset{C}{\Rightarrow}} \omega$.

$L_S \supseteq L_G$ Let $T_0 \overset{*}{\underset{C}{\Rightarrow}} \omega$, i.e. there is a sequence $T_0 = \chi_1 \underset{C}{\Rightarrow} \cdots \underset{C}{\Rightarrow} \chi_n = \omega$ with $\chi_1, \ldots, \chi_n \in (\Sigma \cup T)^*$. Selecting an arbitrary step $\mu_1 S \mu_2 = \chi_i \underset{C}{\Rightarrow} \chi_{i+1} = \mu_1 \alpha \mu_2$, we conclude that $S \to \alpha$. Therefore $\alpha \in f(R(S))$ and $S \overset{*}{\underset{S}{\Rightarrow}} \alpha$. It follows that $\chi_i \overset{*}{\underset{S}{\Rightarrow}} \chi_{i+1}$. Since all steps have analogous derivations, we conclude $T_0 \overset{*}{\underset{S}{\Rightarrow}} \omega$.

Example 3. Given the STS (T, Σ, R, T_0) defined in Example 2 and following the construction in Definition 5, an equivalent CFG (V, Σ, P, V_0) is

- $V = T$
- $V_0 = T_0$
- P defined as

$$S \to (F)$$
$$F \to E$$
$$F \to EC$$
$$C \to |F$$
$$E \to S$$
$$E \to D$$
$$D \to p$$

Definition 6. *CFG $\mapsto$ STS can be defined as follows: Define a function that takes a meta character from the left-hand-side of a production rule and defines the set of all possible expansions. Use it to add an indirection to the rules in R, using the mechanism of selecting an alternative during an expansion and adding new string templates as targets.*

Formally, let $g : V \to P\left((\Sigma \cup V)^*\right)$ be defined as $g(S) = \{\alpha | S \to \alpha\}$. Then (T, Σ, R, T_0) can be defined as

- $T = V \cup \{A_{S_i} | S \in V, i \in \{1, \ldots, |g(S)|\}\}$
- $T_0 = V_0$
- $R = \{S \mapsto \{A_{S_i}\}, A_{S_i} \mapsto \alpha | i \in \{1, \ldots, |g(S)|\}, \alpha \in g(S)\}$

Lemma 2. *Every CFG can be expressed as a STS such that their respective languages are equal.*

Proof. Let L_G be the language of the CFG (V, Σ, P, V_0) and L_S the language of the STS (T, Σ, R, T_0) defined according to Definition 6.

$L_G \subseteq L_S$ Let $T_0 \overset{*}{\underset{C}{\Rightarrow}} \omega$, i.e. there is a sequence $T_0 \underset{C}{\Rightarrow} \omega_1 \underset{C}{\Rightarrow} \ldots \underset{C}{\Rightarrow} \omega_n = \omega$ with $\omega_1, \ldots, \omega_n \in (\Sigma \cup V)^*$. Selecting an arbitrary step $\mu_1 S \mu_2 = \omega_i \underset{C}{\Rightarrow} \omega_{i+1} = \mu_1 \alpha \mu_2$, we conclude $S \to \alpha$. By construction, the derivation sequence $S \overset{1}{\underset{S}{\Rightarrow}} \{A_{S_i}\} \overset{2}{\underset{S}{\Rightarrow}} A_{S_j} \overset{1}{\underset{S}{\Rightarrow}} \alpha$ is possible. Therefore $\omega_i \overset{*}{\underset{S}{\Rightarrow}} \omega_{i+1}$ is valid as well. Since all steps have analogue derivation steps, we can conclude that $T_0 \overset{*}{\underset{S}{\Rightarrow}} \omega$.

$L_G \supseteq L_S$ Let $T_0 \overset{*}{\underset{S}{\Rightarrow}} \omega$, i.e. there is a sequence $T_0 \underset{S}{\Rightarrow} \omega_1 \underset{S}{\Rightarrow} \ldots \underset{S}{\Rightarrow} \omega_n = \omega$ with $\omega_1, \ldots, \omega_n \in (\Sigma \cup T \cup \mathcal{P}(T))^*$. By construction of R, we observe that the sequence for expanding any $S \in V$ must be $S \overset{1}{\underset{S}{\Rightarrow}} \{A_{S_i}\} \overset{2}{\underset{S}{\Rightarrow}} A_{S_j} \overset{1}{\underset{S}{\Rightarrow}} \alpha$. This sub-sequence has an analogue in $S \underset{C}{\Rightarrow} \alpha$. Since $T_0 \in V$ and $\omega \in \Sigma^*$, i.e. all symbols have been expanded, we conclude $T_0 \overset{*}{\underset{C}{\Rightarrow}} \omega$.

Example 4. Given the CFG (V, Σ, P, V_0) defined in Example 1 and following the construction in Definition 6, an equivalent STS is

- $T = V \cup \{A_{E_1}, A_{E_2}, A_{T_1}, A_{T_2}, A_{F_1}, A_{F_2}\}$
- $T_0 = V_0$
- R defined as

$$E \mapsto \{A_{E_1}, A_{E_2}\}$$
$$A_{E_1} \mapsto T \oplus E$$
$$A_{E_2} \mapsto T$$
$$T \mapsto \{A_{T_1}, A_{T_2}\}$$
$$A_{T_1} \mapsto F \odot T$$
$$A_{T_2} \mapsto F$$
$$F \mapsto \{A_{F_1}, A_{F_2}\}$$
$$A_{F_1} \mapsto (E)$$
$$A_{F_2} \mapsto f$$

Corollary 1. *Given Lemmas 1 and 2, STS and CFG are interchangeable notations for the same set of languages.*

Theorem 1. *Given an arbitrary STS S and an arbitrary CFG G, the problem $L_S \subseteq L_G$ is undecidable.*

Proof. The containment-problem is undecidable for context free languages [3]. Since the two formalisms have the same expressive power, this result applies.

Corollary 2. *Given an arbitrary CFG G, we can derive an equivalent STS S with $L_S = L_G$. Any subset $S' \subseteq S$ fulfills $L_{S'} \subseteq L_G$.*

3   Discussion

The equivalence in expressiveness between context free grammars and string templates established in Corollary 1 helps to explain the latter's popularity within the domain of code generation, since string templates are essentially context free grammars with imperative execution semantics and code generators are typically written in an imperative programming style.

Theorem 1 of the previous section also shows that even though arbitrary problem instances are undecidable, we can guarantee the syntactical correctness of the generated language by restricting the allowed set of string templates to subsets and language invariant transformations of the target language's associated STS (see Corollary 2). This provides a formal explanation for the results in Wachsmuth's paper [9] and their subsequent adaptation as part of Arnoldus' PhD thesis [1].

3.1   Capturing Dynamic Expressions

In order to capture dynamic expressions we can extend the structure in Definition 3 to support variable references with an associated mapping into strings. The interpretation from Definition 4 can then be adjusted to evaluate these newly allowed expressions through substitution with their image. This prompts the following changes to Definitions 3 and 4:

Definition 7. *A String Template System with Expressions* (**STSE**) *can be defined as a tuple* $(T, E, \Sigma, F, R, T_0)$ *where*

- T *is a finite set of string templates,*
- E *is a finite set of expressions, disjoint from* T,
- Σ *is a finite set of symbols, disjoint from* T *and* E,
- $F : E \to \Sigma^*$ *is a function,*
- $R : T \to (\Sigma \cup T \cup E \cup \mathcal{P}(T))^*$ *is a function,*
- $T_0 \in T$ *is the expanded string template.*

Definition 8. *A String Template Language with Expressions* (**STLE**) *is the set of all strings that can be produced by a STSE through recursive substitution of string templates with their mapping and substitution of expressions with their mapping. For sets of string templates, any member may be expanded.*

For $A \in T, \alpha \in \mathcal{P}(T), \beta, \mu, \nu \in (\Sigma \cup T \cup E \cup \mathcal{P}(T))^*$ *we write*

$$\mu \underset{S}{\Rightarrow} \nu \Leftrightarrow (\mu = \mu_1 A \mu_2 \wedge \nu = \mu_1 \beta \mu_2 \wedge R(A) = \beta)$$

$$\vee (\mu = \mu_1 E \mu_2 \wedge \nu = \mu_1 \gamma \mu_2 \wedge F(E) = \gamma)$$

$$\vee (\mu = \mu_1 \alpha \mu_2 \wedge \nu = \mu_1 B \mu_2 \wedge B \in \alpha)$$

Then $L = \left\{ \omega \in \Sigma^* \,|\, T_0 \underset{S}{\overset{*}{\Rightarrow}} \omega \right\}$ *denotes the string template language with expressions.*

Unfortunately, as Parr points out in [6], this makes the interpretation much more expressive, allowing for the generation of type 0 languages since F essentially introduces a Turing machine and is therefore impossible to verify statically [4]. In other words, allowing arbitrary strings in the image of F can invalidate any formal syntax.

However, restricting the image to regular expressions instead of arbitrary strings would continue to allow for static validation. In addition, unlike for context free grammars the containment problem is decidable for regular expressions, allowing us to assign arbitrary regular expressions to dynamic components without losing the ability to statically verify their correctness.

We would like to propose the addition of a dedicated regular expression type to the type system of domain-specific languages for code generation as a subclass of the generic string type in order to allow the static type-checker to verify the correctness of a dynamic expression with regards to the syntax of the target language in the context of a string template. Since grammars for real-world languages typically describe their terminals using regular expressions already, it would be feasible to support dynamic expressions at exactly these points in the associated STSE without sacrificing any static guarantees.

4   Conclusions and Outlook

We have formally defined sets of interconnected string templates and have shown their equivalence to context free grammars using a constructive proof that maps one onto the other. From this, we were able to conclude the undecidability of the general version of the problem to statically decide whether the language generated by a set of string templates is a subset of the target language. However, the construction has also allowed us to identify the conditions under which a static guarantee for syntactical correctness can be provided: if we prevent arbitrary sets of string templates to be used in the code generation and instead only allow those that can be proven to have an analogue derivation for the grammar of the target language. We have connected these results to previous literature and outlined a scheme to include support for dynamically evaluated expressions as well.

It remains to be seen if the proposed restrictions with regards to allowing typed dynamic expressions only at specific points in string templates will be acceptable to programmers or not. If not, an easy workaround for programmers would be a dynamic cast from an unrestricted string into a string with a compatible regular expression, restoring the test-based verification outlined by Arnoldus [1].

References

1. Arnoldus, B.J.: An illumination of the template enigma: software code generation with templates. Ph.D. thesis, Technische Universiteit Eindhoven (2010)
2. Bettini, L.: Implementing Domain-Specific Languages with Xtext and Xtend. Packt Publishing, Birmingham (2013)

3. Hopcroft, J.E., Ullman, J.D.: Introduction to Automata Theory, Languages, and Computation, Chap. 8, p. 203. In: [5] (1979)
4. Hopcroft, J.E., Ullman, J.D.: Introduction to Automata Theory, Languages, and Computation, Chap. 8, pp. 185–192. In: [5] (1979)
5. Hopcroft, J.E., Ullman, J.D.: Introduction to Automata Theory, Languages, and Computation. Addison-Wesley (1979)
6. Parr, T.J.: Enforcing strict model-view separation in template engines. In: Proceedings of the 13th International Conference on World Wide Web, pp. 224–233. ACM (2004)
7. Parr, T.J.: A functional language for generating structured text (2006). http://www.cs.usfca.edu/~parrt/papers/ST.pdf
8. Rudd, T., Orr, M., Bicking, I., Esterbrook, C.: Cheetah: the python-powered template engine. In: 10th International Python Conference-2002 (2007)
9. Wachsmuth, G.: A formal way from text to code templates. In: Chechik, M., Wirsing, M. (eds.) FASE 2009. LNCS, vol. 5503, pp. 109–123. Springer, Heidelberg (2009). doi:10.1007/978-3-642-00593-0_8

On the Impact of the SDL Forum Society Conferences on Academic Research

Daniel Amyot[1(✉)], Abdelwahab Hamou-Lhadj[2],
and Jameleddine Hassine[3]

[1] University of Ottawa, Ottawa, ON, Canada
damyot@uottawa.ca
[2] Concordia University, Montréal, Québec, Canada
wahab.hamou-lhadj@concordia.ca
[3] King Fahd University of Minerals and Petroleum,
Dhahran, Kingdom of Saudi Arabia
jhassine@kfupm.edu.sa

Abstract. The SDL Forum Society exists since the early 1990's and has led the organization of numerous conferences and workshops over the years. This paper performs a citation analysis of 491 papers published in 22 SDL/SAM proceedings published between 1991 and 2016 in order to assess the impact of these events on academic research. Through the use of common metrics, the most influential papers and authors are identified. Common languages and topics discussed in the papers are also highlighted. This paper finally identifies several strengths and challenges of the SDL Forum Society as a research community.

Keywords: SDL forum · SAM · Publications · Researchers · Citations · Metrics

1 Introduction

The SDL Forum Society [41] is a not-for-profit organization that aims to promote *System Design Languages*, especially those developed by the International Telecommunication Union (ITU-T). In addition to providing information on the development, use, and education of System Design Languages, the Society helps organizing conferences and workshops that lead to proceedings containing scientific contributions. The Society was formally established in 1995 as a not-for-profit organization, but it has existed informally since June 1990. Many researchers and practitioners from academic and industrial organizations around the world have contributed to the Society's success over the years. Many Society members have led the standardization and revisions of ITU-T languages, and the Society has created a community of academic and industrial experts that shared their experiences using these languages and their supporting tools.

From an academic research perspective, it is also important to reflect on the impact of the events organized by an organization such as the SDL Forum Society. This paper attempts to do so by answering questions about:

© Springer International Publishing AG 2017
T. Csöndes et al. (Eds.): SDL 2017, LNCS 10567, pp. 30–45, 2017.
DOI: 10.1007/978-3-319-68015-6_3

1. Which *papers* published at events organized by the Society had the highest academic impact?
2. Which *authors* of papers published at events organized by the Society had the highest academic impact and the largest number of contributions?
3. What are the *topics* and system design *languages* explored in the Society's papers?

Answering such questions is often done using *citation analysis* [32], which refers to systematic methods for measuring the importance of authors, articles, conferences, journals, and institutions by counting citations in the published literature. Citation analysis has the benefit of being simple to perform and is well supported by tools and common publication search engines. As this approach is known to be imperfect (e.g., the semantics of the citations in a paper is seldom taken into account [43]), often several metrics are used to provide different perspectives during the impact assessment.

This paper hence contributes a citation-based assessment of the impact of the SDL Forum Society on academic research since the beginning of its informal existence, 27 years ago. Section 2 describes the methodology used to collect papers, authors, and citations, and to support their analysis. Sections 3 and 4 report on our findings regarding the most influential papers and authors, respectively. Section 5 provides simple observations on common topics and languages studied in these papers. Then, Sect. 6 discusses limitations of this study and some observations about the community as a whole, while Sect. 7 provides conclusions.

2   Methodology

The methodology involves selecting the relevant event proceedings, selecting the relevant papers, collecting citation counts, and computing relevant metrics.

2.1   Selection of Event Proceedings

The first event that was organized by the SDL Forum Society is the 5th SDL conference, in 1991, where "SDL" at the time referred (and refers in the rest of this paper) to ITU-T's *Specification and Description Language* (Rec. Z.100) [20]. The first four conferences on SDL are hence outside the scope of this study. In 1998, a workshop called SAM (for *SDL and MSC*, where MSC referred to ITU-T's *Message Sequence Chart* language, Rec. Z.120 [22]) was introduced. SAM was later renamed *System Analysis and Modeling*, to become more encompassing. In addition, in 2014, SAM became a full conference of its own.

Table 1 lists the events that are within the scope of the current study. Note that there was no SAM workshop in 2008. More informal one-day workshops such as the *Integrated-reliability with Telecommunications and UML Languages (ISSRE04: WITUL)*[1] in Rennes in 2004 and the *Joint ITU-T and SDL Forum Society workshop on "ITU System Design Languages"*[2] in Geneva in 2008 were also excluded. The former

---

[1] http://sdl-forum.org/issre04-witul/.

[2] http://www.itu.int/ITU-T/worksem/sdlsmc/2008/programme.html.

workshop had its papers resubmitted to a journal [17] while the latter workshop had no peer-reviewed publications. Finally, journal special issues such as [6, 17, 37] are also not included because they were not directly under the control of the Society.

Table 1. Selected conferences and workshops.

Year	SDL/SAM	Title	Editors	Location
1991	5th SDL	Evolving Methods	O. Færgemand, R. Reed	Glasgow, Scotland
1993	6th SDL	Using Objects	O. Færgemand, A. Sarma	Darmstadt, Germany
1995	7th SDL	With MSC in CASE	R. Bræk, A. Sarma	Trondheim, Norway
1997	8th SDL	Time for Testing, SDL, MSC and Trends	A.R. Cavalli, A. Sarma	Evry, France
1998	1st SAM	SDL and MSC	Y. Lahav, A. Wolisz, J. Fischer, E. Holz	Berlin, Germany
1999	9th SDL	The Next Millennium	R. Dssouli, G. von Bochmann, Y. Lahav	Montréal, Canada
2000	2nd SAM	SDL and MSC	S. Graf, C. Jard, Y. Lahav	Grenoble, France
2001	10th SDL	Meeting UML	R. Reed, J. Reed	Copenhagen, Denmark
2002	3rd SAM	Telecommunications and beyond: The Broader Applicability of SDL and MSC	E. Sherratt	Aberystwyth, Wales
2003	11th SDL	System Design	R. Reed, J. Reed	Stuttgart, Germany
2004	4th SAM	System Analysis and Modeling	D. Amyot, A.W. Williams	Ottawa, Canada
2005	12th SDL	Model Driven	A. Prinz, R. Reed, J. Reed	Grimstad, Norway
2006	5th SAM	Language Profiles	R. Gotzhein, R. Reed	Kaiserslautern, Germany
2007	13th SDL	Design for Dependable Systems	E. Gaudin, E. Najm, R. Reed	Paris, France
2009	14th SDL	Design for Motes and Mobiles	R. Reed, A. Bilgic, R. Gotzhein	Bochum, Germany
2010	6th SAM	About Models	F.A. Kraemer, P. Herrmann	Oslo, Norway
2011	15th SDL	Integrating System and Software Modeling	I. Ober, I. Ober	Toulouse, France
2012	7th SAM	Theory and Practice	Ø. Haugen, R. Reed, R. Gotzhein	Innsbruck, Austria
2013	16th SDL	Model-Driven Dependability Engineering	F. Khendek, M. Toeroe, A. Gherbi, R. Reed	Montréal, Canada
2014	8th SAM	Models and Reusability	D. Amyot, P. Fonseca i Casas, G. Mussbacher	Valencia, Spain
2015	17th SDL	Model-Driven Engineering for Smart Cities	J. Fischer, M. Scheidgen, I. Schieferdecker, R. Reed	Berlin, Germany
2016	9th SAM	Technology-Specific Aspects of Models	J. Grabowski, S. Herbold	Saint-Malo, France

Note that the years in Table 1 reflect the years when the events where held; several SAM workshops had post-event proceedings published early the following year.

2.2   Selection of Relevant Papers

The proceedings of the 22 events in Table 1 contain several types of papers. This study focuses on scientific and industrial contributions. Several categories of short papers such as prefaces and extended abstracts (for posters, tool demos, and tutorials) were excluded from the dataset. This resulted in a collection of 491 papers, whose list and other raw details from this study are available online at https://goo.gl/ZFNfhc.

In order to minimize having multiple author entries for the same author, names were cleaned up by removing all dots, dashes, and extra spaces, leading to a uniform representations uniform. For example, "Bochmann GV", "V Bochmann G", and "van Bochmann G" were all replaced by "von Bochmann G", "Haugen O" was replaced by "Haugen Ø", etc. One name, "Ober I", was handled manually as two different people share the same name and initial. 790 unique authors were identified for these papers.

2.3   Collection of Citation Counts

In order to collect citations, three main sources were exploited over two days (June 22–23, 2017). First, Google Scholar[3] was used for all 491 papers. Harzing's *Publish or Perish* tool [16] was used as a front end to facilitate the collection of most citations. This tool was reliable for proceedings published by Springer (since 2001), but for older proceedings published by Elsevier (before 2000) or simply made available online (2000), this was supplemented by manual searches on Google Scholar based on paper titles. When there were two reference counts reported (e.g., because a citing paper made a mistake on the year of a reference), these were simply summed up as there was no overlap in the lists of citing papers.

As a second source of citations, Elsevier's Scopus[4], a comprehensive engine that indexes 67 million records, was used for Springer's proceedings. Scopus indexes high-quality publications and excludes non-peer-reviewed papers, theses, white papers, and low-quality papers (e.g., from so-called predatory publishers). The number of citations for a paper is lower with Scopus than with Google Scholar, as the later does not discriminate papers based on quality, leading to some questionable citations.

Unfortunately (and surprisingly), Scopus did not have citation counts for the SDL Forum proceedings prior to 2000. We hence used a third comprehensive engine, namely Clarivate Analytics's Web of Science (WoS)[5], which stores 100 million records. This enabled the gathering of citation counts from high-quality publications for the SDL papers between 1991 and 1999. Note however that the SAM 1998 and SAM 2000 workshops were neither covered by Scopus nor by WoS because their proceedings were not provided by a recognized publisher.

2.4   Computation of Metrics

For each paper, we have two basic citation counts: one from Google Scholar, and another one from Scopus (2001–2016) or WoS (1991–1997 and 1999). Having two sources allows us to reason about each individually, but also in combination. Some of our metrics use, for instance, a *combined* count for each paper that is the sum of the two basic counts. Such combined count can be used to rank papers and authors by placing more weight on high-quality citations (essentially counted twice) while not forgetting other less reliable citations (counted only once). The next sections provide more details about the nature of the concrete metrics used, with answers to our research questions.

3   Most Influential Papers

The first results of our analysis, which answer the first question in the introduction, are reported in the next three tables.

---

[3] https://scholar.google.com/.

[4] https://www.elsevier.com/solutions/scopus/content.

[5] http://clarivate.com/?product=web-of-science.

Table 2. Fifteen most influential papers according to combined citation counts, Google Scholar citation counts, and combined citations per year, with corresponding global ranks for each.

Authors	Title	Year	Combined	Combined Rank	Scholar	Scholar Rank	Combined/Year	Combined/Year Rank
Mauw S, Reniers MA	High-level Message Sequence Charts	1997	145	1	137	1	7.25	6
Eichner C, Fleischhack H, Meyer R, et al.	Compositional semantics for UML 2.0 sequence diagrams using Petri nets	2005	124	2	84	5	10.33	1
Grabowski J, Hogrefe D, Nahm R	Test Case Generation with Test Purpose Specification by MSCs	1993	110	3	110	2	4.58	17
Graubmann P, Rudolph E, Grabowski J	Towards a Petri Net Based Semantics Definition for Message Sequence Charts	1993	109	4	109	3	4.54	18
Amyot D, Farah H, Roy JF	Evaluation of development tools for domain-specific modeling languages	2006	94	5	69	8	8.55	3
Bozga M, Fernandez JC, Ghirvu L, Graf S, et al.	IF: An intermediate representation for SDL and its applications	1999	90	6	87	4	5.00	12
Amyot D, Mussbacher G	URN: Towards a new standard for the visual description of requirements	2002	87	7	68	9	5.80	9
Kerbrat A, Jeron T, Groz R	Automated test generation from SDL specifications	1999	84	8	78	6	4.67	16
Roy JF, Kealey J, Amyot D	Towards integrated tool support for the User Requirements Notation	2006	81	9	60	12	7.36	4
Baker P, Bristow P, Jervis C, King D, et al.	Automatic generation of conformance tests from message sequence charts	2002	80	10	63	11	5.33	11
Katoen JP, Lambert L	Pomsets for message sequence charts	1998	73	11	73	7	3.84	31
Miga A, Amyot D, Bordeleau F, et al.	Deriving message sequence charts from use case maps scenario specifications	2001	69	12	52	14	4.31	22
Algayres B, Lejeune Y, Hugonnet F	GOAL: Observing SDL behaviors with GEODE	1995	66	13	66	10	3.00	41
Bozga M, Graf S, Mounier L, et al.	Timed extensions for SDL	2001	63	14	50	15	3.94	30
Haugen Ø	Comparing UML 2.0 interactions and MSC-2000	2004	56	15	47	17	4.31	23
Mauw S, van Wijk M, Winter T	A Formal semantics of Synchronous Interworkings	1993	55	16	55	13	2.29	61
Mansurov N, Zhukov D	Automatic synthesis of SDL models in use case methodology	1999	53	17	50	15	2.94	47
Kraemer FA, Bræk R, Herrmann P	Synthesizing components with sessions from collaboration-oriented service specifications	2007	48	20	36	24	4.80	15
Lúcio L, Mustafiz S, Denil J, et al.	FTG+PM: An integrated framework for investigating model transformation chains	2013	37	30	21	55	9.25	2
Genon N, Amyot D, Heymans P	Analysing the cognitive effectiveness of the UCM visual notation	2010	35	36	23	49	5.00	12
Fleurey F, Haugen Ø, Møller-Pedersen B et al.	Standardizing variability - Challenges and solutions	2011	29	52	17	75	4.83	14
Denil J, Jukss M, Verbrugge C, et al.	Search-based model optimization using model transformations	2014	22	74	16	81	7.33	5
Hackenberg G, Campetelli A, et al.	Formal technical process specification and verification for automated production systems	2014	19	91	12	118	6.33	7
Haugen Ø, Øgård O	BVR – better variability results	2014	18	99	12	118	6.00	8
Duran MB, Mussbacher G, et al.	On the reuse of goal models	2015	11	162	8	168	5.50	10

Table 2 identifies the 25 papers that represent the 15 most influential papers according to three different metrics: combined citation counts (where more weight is given to high-quality citations), Google Scholar-based citation counts, and combined citation counts per year (as older publications are more likely to have more citations). For each paper, the table shows the values for each metrics as well as the corresponding

Table 3. Most cited paper(s) per year, excluding 2016.

Year	Authors	Title	Scopus / WoS	Scholar	Combined
2015	Duran MB, Mussbacher G, Thimmegowda N, Kienzle J	On the reuse of goal models	3	8	11
2014	Denil J, Jukss M, Verbrugge C, Vangheluwe H	Search-based model optimization using model transformations	6	16	22
2013	Lúcio L, Mustafiz S, Denil J, Vangheluwe H, Jukss M	FTG+PM: An integrated framework for investigating model transformation chains	16	21	37
2012	Schneider M, Großmann J, Tcholtchev N, et al.	Behavioral fuzzing operators for UML sequence diagrams	8	13	21
2011	Perrotin M, Conquet E, Delange J, Schiele A, Tsiodras T	TASTE: A real-time software engineering tool-chain overview, status, and future	6	20	26
2011	Fleurey F, Haugen Ø, MøllerPedersen B, et al.	Standardizing variability - Challenges and solutions	12	17	29
2010	Genon N, Amyot D, Heymans P	Analysing the cognitive effectiveness of the UCM visual notation	12	23	35
2009	Mussbacher G, Amyot D	Extending the User Requirements Notation with aspect-oriented concepts	12	20	32
2007	Kraemer FA, Bræk R, Herrmann P	Synthesizing components with sessions from collaboration-oriented service specifications	12	36	48
2006	Amyot D, Farah H, Roy JF	Evaluation of development tools for domain-specific modeling languages	25	69	94
2005	Eichner C, Fleischhack H, Meyer R, Schrimpf U, Stehno C	Compositional semantics for UML 2.0 sequence diagrams using Petri nets	40	84	124
2004	Haugen Ø	Comparing UML 2.0 interactions and MSC-2000	9	47	56
2003	Petriu D, Amyot D, Woodside M	Scenario-based performance engineering with UCMNAV	9	25	34
2003	He Y, Amyot D, Williams AW	Synthesizing SDL from use case maps: An experiment	11	23	34
2002	Amyot D, Mussbacher G	URN: Towards a new standard for the visual description of requirements	19	68	87
2001	Miga A, Amyot D, Bordeleau F, Cameron D, Woodside M	Deriving message sequence charts from use case maps scenario specifications	17	52	69
2000	Hélouët L, Le Maigat P	Decomposition of Message Sequence Charts	0	38	38
2000	Bozga M, Graf S, Kerbrat A, Mounier L, Ober I, Vincent D	SDL for real time: What is missing ?	0	37	37
2000	Schmitt M, Grabowski J, Ebner M	Test Generation with Autolink and Testcomposer	0	37	37
1999	Bozga M, Fernandez JC, Ghirvu L, Graf S, Krimm JP, et al.	IF: An intermediate representation for SDL and its applications	3	87	90
1998	Katoen JP, Lambert L	Pomsets for message sequence charts	0	73	73
1997	Mauw S, Reniers MA	High-level Message Sequence Charts	8	137	145
1995	Algayres B, Lejeune Y, Hugonnet F	GOAL: Observing SDL behaviors with GEODE	0	66	66
1993	Grabowski J, Hogrefe D, Nahm R	Test Case Generation with Test Purpose Specification by MSCs	0	110	110
1993	Graubmann P, Rudolph E, Grabowski J	Towards a Petri Net Based Semantics Definition for Message Sequence Charts	0	109	109
1991	Luo G, Das A, von Bochmann G	Test selection based on SDL specifications with save	1	12	13

rank amongst the 491 papers. The work of Mauw and Reniers on High-level Message Sequence Charts in 1997 [31] and of Eichner et al. on a Petri net-based composition semantics for UML 2.0 sequence diagrams in 2005 [7] are certainly the most influential papers from the Society's community on academic research so far.

Table 4. Proceeding-level metrics for each year, with best values highlighted.

Year	Sum of Scopus/WoS	Sum of Scholar	Sum of Combined	Number of Papers	Citations per Paper	Citations per Paper / Year	H-index (Scholar)	H-index / Year	Reference
1991	11	126	137	38	3.32	0.13	7	0.27	[8]
1993	0	462	462	37	12.49	0.52	8	0.33	[9]
1995	8	241	249	30	8.03	0.37	9	0.41	[3]
1997	45	517	562	35	14.77	0.74	13	0.65	[4]
1998	0	228	228	27	8.44	0.44	8	0.42	[30]
1999	37	443	480	30	14.77	0.82	11	0.61	[5]
2000	0	307	307	23	13.35	0.79	11	0.65	[14]
2001	102	348	450	26	13.38	0.84	12	0.75	[38]
2002	81	264	345	15	17.60	1.17	9	0.60	[42]
2003	102	235	337	23	10.22	0.73	11	0.79	[39]
2004	68	201	269	19	10.58	0.81	9	0.69	[2]
2005	138	352	490	24	14.67	1.22	10	0.83	[36]
2006	82	244	326	14	17.43	1.58	8	0.73	[12]
2007	74	179	253	17	10.53	1.05	8	0.80	[11]
2009	62	119	181	15	7.93	0.99	8	1.00	[40]
2010	61	115	176	15	7.67	1.10	7	1.00	[29]
2011	66	127	193	18	7.06	1.18	6	1.00	[35]
2012	40	82	122	14	5.86	1.17	6	1.20	[15]
2013	50	79	129	16	4.94	1.23	5	1.25	[27]
2014	42	80	122	21	3.81	1.27	5	1.67	[1]
2015	8	23	31	19	1.21	0.61	3	1.50	[10]
2016	0	3	3	15	0.20	0.20	1	1.00	[13]
TOTAL	1077	4775	5852	491	9.73	—	32	—	—

Table 3 reports on the most influential papers for each of the selected proceedings between 1991 and 2015. Year 2016 is not included as only three papers had one citation each, so it is too soon to identify any trend for the SAM'2016 papers.

Table 3 reports on the two individual citation counts (Scopus/WoS and Google Scholar) and their sum (Combined). A clear leader was easily identifiable for most years; however, years 2003, 2000, and 1993 include multiple papers each as the scores were very close (i.e., a difference of 0 or 1 citation).

In terms of the academic impact of the proceedings themselves, Table 4 reports on the citation counts (Scopus/WoS, Scholar, Combined) for the papers of each proceedings. The table also reports on common metrics such as the number of citations per paper (on average), this average per year since the publication of the proceedings, the H-index (the number n of papers in the proceedings that have at least n citations), and the H-index per year. The best value for each of these metrics is highlighted in the table. The last row reports on the same metrics, but for the 22 proceedings taken together. The 491 papers resulted in 4775 citations on Google Scholar so far, including over a thousand citations in Scopus or Web of Science. Collectively, these papers have a global H-index of 32.

4 Most Influential Authors

In order to answer the second research question from the introduction, citations were also counted of each of the 790 unique authors of research papers identified in the proceedings. Table 5 identifies the 20 authors with the highest numbers of combined citation (where more weight is given to citations from high-quality peer-reviewed papers). The citation counts for Google Scholar are also included to document that additional perspective.

Table 5. Top-20 authors with the highest numbers of combined citations.

Author	Combined Citations	Scholar Citations	Author	Combined Citations	Scholar Citations
Amyot D	675	489	Fischer J	197	147
Grabowski J	516	485	Bozga M	190	174
Gotzhein R	330	257	Mounier L	190	174
Mauw S	290	271	Graubmann P	185	175
Hogrefe D	251	236	Baker P	183	140
Bræk R	250	178	Khendek F	161	135
Graf S	243	216	Reniers MA	161	153
Rudolph E	241	223	Mansurov N	154	133
Roy JF	227	168	Haugen Ø	150	119
Mussbacher G	200	142	Kerbrat A	148	139

Another interesting answer to the most influential author question comes from a simple measure: the number of papers published. Table 6 shows the 20 authors with the highest numbers of publications in the 22 SDL/SAM proceedings used in this study. The remaining authors all had 6 or fewer papers. In particular, 588 authors, i.e., 74.4% of the 790 unique authors, had only one paper each.

Table 6. Top-20 authors with the highest numbers of publications in SDL/SAM proceedings.

Author	Count	Author	Count
Fischer J	22	Mansurov N	9
Gotzhein R	22	Rudolph E	9
Amyot D	19	Mauw S	8
Grabowski J	19	Møller-Pedersen B	8
Khendek F	18	Mussbacher G	8
Bræk R	13	Scheidgen M	8
Haugen Ø	12	Weigert T	8
Prinz A	12	Christmann D	7
Hassine J	10	Floch J	7
Hogrefe D	9	Graubmann P	7

5   Observations on Languages and Topics

Peripheral to the impact on academic research, the third question in the introduction targets the identification of system design languages and related topics addressed in the 491 papers of the selected 22 proceedings. A systematic literature review or a systematic literature mapping could be used to inspect each paper, collect keywords and concepts, infer appropriate categories, and report on frequencies and trends over time [28]. However, as this would require work well beyond a typical citation analysis, a simpler, alternative approach is used here, based on word frequencies in *titles* and *keywords* only. Although this could be seen as a gross approximation of the reality, we believe that SDL/SAM authors tend to choose their titles and keywords carefully, especially in terms of technologies they cover. The keywords were obtained automatically from Scopus and Web of Science. However, only 133 out of 491 papers had user-provided keywords, especially in the more recent proceedings.

Regarding languages, each of the 491 titles and keyword sets were automatically searched in Microsoft Excel for the following system and design languages (see the spreadsheets in https://goo.gl/ZFNfhc for details):

- "SDL" or "Specification and Description Language" [20].
- "MSC" or "Message Sequence Chart" [22]. This covers High-level MSCs as well.
- "TTCN" or "Testing and Test Control Notation" or "Tree and Tabular Combined Notation" [25]. We made no attempt to distinguish TTCN-3 from its predecessors.
- "ASN.1" or "Abstract Syntax Notation One" or "ASN 1". There was no ASN1 in the titles [19].
- "ODL" or "Object Description Language". This covers eODL as well [23]. Note that eODL is no longer an ITU-T Recommendation.
- "CHILL", for the ITU-T CHILL programming language [26].
- "UML" or "Unified Modeling Language" [34]. This was sufficient to cover class, sequence, state, activity, and use case diagrams as well (as UML was next to them whenever they were used).
- "OCL" or "Object Constraint Language" [33].
- "Petri", for Petri nets [18].
- "Profil", to cover UML profiles and profiling approaches [21].
- For the User Requirements Notation [24], which contains two sub-languages, we counted three sets of terms:
  - "GRL" or "Goal-oriented Requirement Language"
  - "UCM" or "Use Case Map"
  - "URN" or "User Requirements Notation" or one of the four above terms.

Finally, an "Others" category was used to count the number of papers that had none of the above terms in their title or user-provided keywords.

The word cloud in Fig. 2 graphically shows which language categories (represented by their acronyms) were the most frequent among the 491 papers. Unsurprisingly, SDL was the most common language with 51% of the papers mentioning it, followed by Others (25%) and MSC (16%).

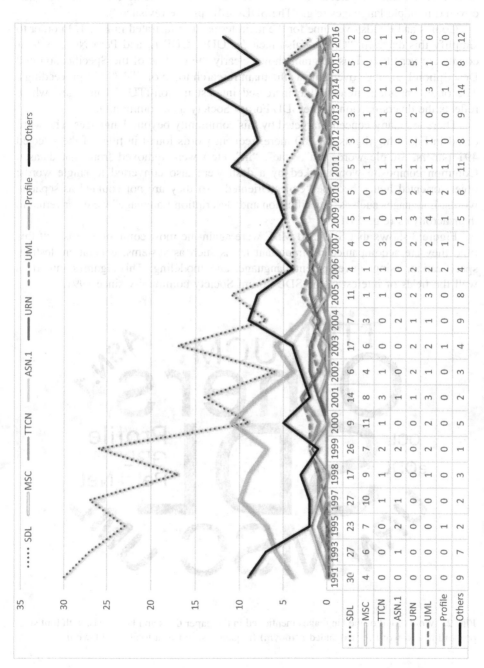

Fig. 1. Languages mentioned in the paper titles and keywords over the years.

All of the other terms had less than 7%, and the lowest count was 1 for CHILL. Note that the sum of percentages is higher than 100% as some titles and keywords covered multiple languages (e.g. "The SDL-UML profile revisited").

Counts and trends over time for the main terms are illustrated in Fig. 1. In order to simplify this diagram, "Others" also includes ODL, CHILL, and Petri Nets, as their counts are very low. This diagram shows clearly the decline of the Specification and Description Language over time as the main research topic of SDL/SAM proceedings. The other important trend is the increased interest in non-ITU-T languages, which reflects the diversification of the SDL Forum Society as a community.

There are many concepts targeted by this community beyond languages. The word cloud in Fig. 3 highlights the 100 more frequent words found in titles of the selected 491 papers. Simple words ("a", "the", "in", etc.) were removed from that dataset. Common composite words linked by a dash were also converted to single words; object-oriented hence became "ObjectOriented", so they are not counted as separate words. Languages such as "Specification and Description Language" were converted to their acronyms (e.g., SDL).

Figure 3 shows that SDL and MSC were again the most common words, but this time they are accompanied by important terms such as systems, generation, testing, specification, using, development, language, and modeling. This figure summarizes well the fields of interest of the SDL Forum Society community since 1991.

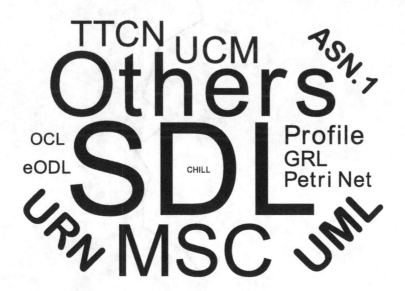

Fig. 2. Word cloud of the languages mentioned in the paper titles and keywords, with font sizes proportional to word (or expanded acronym) frequencies, out of a total of 611 words.

Fig. 3. Top-100 most frequent words in paper titles, with sizes proportional to the square root of word frequencies.

6 Discussion

This section provides some observations about the Society's community and discusses several limitations and threats to the validity of this work.

6.1 Observations

Sections 3 and 4 report on many success stories of individual authors and publications. The Society can indeed be proud of its champions and their impact on academic research. As a whole, Table 4 highlights that over 4775 citations (on Google Scholar) resulted from these 22 proceedings, and this does not even cover the impact of other publications in which the Society had a role, albeit more modest (e.g., [6, 17, 37]). With an average of nearly 278 citations per year, an average 9.7 citations per paper, and a global H-index of 32, the SDL Forum and SAM conferences continue to deliver impactful research results.

What is less obvious from the data presented so far is that 91 out of the 491 papers (18.6%) have not been cited at all. These include 12 papers from 2016 without citations (the latter had little opportunity to get cited at this time). This means that the Society's conference organizers still accept a sizable proportion of papers that have little measurable impact on academic research. These papers come from 119 authors out of 790 (15%) who have no citations. It would be interesting to study the topics of these papers and other potential causes for this situation, and perhaps to consider potential correlations with acceptance rates.

Another major concern visible in Table 4 relates to the numbers of papers published per year, where all proceedings in the last decade have fewer papers than the average (22.7), with a clear negative trend whatever the regression model used. On the other hand, the same table suggests that the popularity of these papers is higher as the H-index per year is consistently higher than the average (0.84) since 2009, and consistently lower before that.

From Sect. 5 we observe that ITU-T's Specification and Description Language is by far the most popular topic of the 22 events. However, Fig. 1 shows that this language's popularity as a paper topic has been steadily declining since the beginning of the new millennium. Similarly, papers on ITU-T's Message Sequence Charts have basically disappeared in the past decade, in part because most of their concepts have been integrated to UML 2. On the other hand, the SDL Forum and SAM conferences have shown their openness to other system design languages; on average 24% of the 491 papers are about "other" languages and concepts, with 2004 being a pivotal point ("others" vary between 3% and 21% before 2004, and between 25% and 75% since 2004).

6.2   Threats to Validity

There are several threats to the validity of our analysis. Citation analysis measures only one type of impact on academic research. Others could be studied in the future, including impact on research projects, on academia-industry partnerships, and on course content. Citations themselves have often been criticized as a means of measuring impact, especially as not all citations are equal (some are core to a paper's topic whereas others are just mentioned in passing or convey a negative sentiment) [43]. The sources of citations themselves have different levels of quality and research value, and Google Scholar is unfortunately known to index many of them. This last threat was mitigated in part by using two large, comprehensive, and reputable search engines (Scopus and Web of Science) in order to put more weight on citations coming from quality sources. Still, involving other search engines could influence some of the rankings and metrics.

As mentioned previously, other threats target the completeness of the dataset, limited to a subset of the papers influenced by the Society (e.g., journal special issues were not included in the analysis). Also, neither Scopus nor WoS had indexed SAM 1998 and 2000, so only Google Scholar citations were counted for their papers. This was however anticipated as proceedings of these workshops were published by Humboldt University Berlin (SAM 1998 [30]) and by Verimag/IRISA and the SDL Forum Society (SAM 2000 [14]).

Other threats also exist with regards to the construction and conclusions related to the third research question, addressed in Sect. 5. As we did not have the resources to perform a rigorous systematic literature review of the selected 491 papers, we relied on frequency analysis based on words found in titles and keywords, whenever available. Although this analysis was automated, the conclusions certainly lack precision. In particular, the "others" category likely contains several papers that focus on some of the other categories. Yet, although we believe the score of the "others" category to be higher than it should be, even a strong correction would not invalidate the trends we have observed about the popularity of the SDL and MSC languages.

To help minimize the risks of mistakes and to help avoid bias and opacity, we have also made our datasets freely available online as Excel spreadsheets.

7 Conclusion

It is important for a research community such as the SDL Forum Society to be able measure its success and reflect on its impact. This paper used citation analysis to answer two important questions:

1. Which *papers* published at events organized by the Society had the highest academic impact? This was answered with Table 2 for the fifteen most influential papers according to three different metrics. In addition, the most influential papers for each event between 1991 and 2015 were reported in Table 3, for three types of citation counts. Finally, Table 4 reports on the impact of the event proceedings themselves through 8 different metrics.
2. Which *authors* of papers published at events organized by the Society had the highest academic impact and the largest number of contributions? The first part of this question is answered by Table 5, which reports the top-20 authors according to two types of citation counts. The second part is answered by Table 6, which lists the top-20 authors in terms of contributed papers.

The third question was answered with an analysis of word frequencies based on paper titles and keywords:

3. What are the *topics* and system design *languages* explored in the Society's papers? The answer to the language part is provided in Fig. 2 with a global ranking visualized as a word cloud, and in Fig. 1 with trends for different languages over time. The topic part is simply shown as another word cloud (based on titles) in Fig. 3.

These contributions, together with the discussion in Sect. 6.1, represent evidence-based metrics and observations that we hope will trigger a reflection about who the Society is, what its successes are (so they can be built on), and where it could go from here to address emerging challenges.

In terms of future work, many limitations discussed in Sect. 6.2 can be turned into action or research items so that remaining threats can be further mitigated. In addition, a similar exercise could be envisioned beyond the scope of "academic research" in order to assess the impact of the SDL Forum Society on industry, on tool development, and on standards development.

References

1. Amyot, D., Fonseca i Casas, P., Mussbacher, G. (eds.): SAM 2014. LNCS, vol. 8769. Springer, Cham (2014). doi:10.1007/978-3-319-11743-0
2. Amyot, D., Williams, A.W. (eds.): SAM 2004. LNCS, vol. 3319. Springer, Heidelberg (2005). doi:10.1007/b105884

3. Bræk, R., Sarma, A.: SDL'95 with MSC in Case. Elsevier, Amsterdam (1995)
4. Cavalli, A.R., Sarma, A.: SDL'97 Time for Testing, SDL, MSC and Trends. Elsevier, Amsterdam (1997)
5. Dssouli, R., von Bochmann, G., Lahav, Y.: SDL'99 the Next Millennium. Elsevier Science, Amsterdam (1999)
6. Dssouli, R., Lahav, Y.: MSC and SDL in project life cycles. Comput. Netw. **35**(6), 611–612 (2001)
7. Eichner, C., Fleischhack, H., Meyer, R., Schrimpf, U., Stehno, C.: Compositional semantics for UML 2.0 sequence diagrams using petri nets. In: Prinz, A., Reed, R., Reed, J. (eds.) SDL 2005. LNCS, vol. 3530, pp. 133–148. Springer, Heidelberg (2005). doi:10.1007/11506843_9
8. Færgemand, O., Reed, R.: SDL'91 Evolving Methods. North Holland, Amsterdam (1991)
9. Færgemand, O., Sarma, A.: SDL'93 Using Objects. North Holland, Amsterdam (1993)
10. Fischer, J., Scheidgen, M., Schieferdecker, I., Reed, R. (eds.): SDL 2015. LNCS, vol. 9369. Springer, Cham (2015). doi:10.1007/978-3-319-24912-4
11. Gaudin, E., Najm, E., Reed, R. (eds.): SDL 2007. LNCS, vol. 4745. Springer, Heidelberg (2007). doi:10.1007/978-3-540-74984-4
12. Gotzhein, R., Reed, R. (eds.): SAM 2006. LNCS, vol. 4320. Springer, Heidelberg (2006). doi:10.1007/11951148
13. Grabowski, J., Herbold, S. (eds.): SAM 2016. LNCS, vol. 9959. Springer, Cham (2016). doi:10.1007/978-3-319-46613-2
14. Graf, S., Jard, C., Lahav, Y.: 2nd Workshop on SDL and MSC. VERIMAG, IRISA, and SDL Forum (2000). https://goo.gl/11S5Jn
15. Haugen, Ø., Reed, R., Gotzhein, R. (eds.): SAM 2012. LNCS, vol. 7744. Springer, Heidelberg (2013). doi:10.1007/978-3-642-36757-1
16. Harzing, A.-W.: The Publish or Perish Book – Your Guide to Effective and Responsible Citation Analysis. Tarma Software Research Pty Ltd., Melbourne (2010)
17. Hogrefe, D., Reed, R.: Telecommunications and UML languages. Comput. Netw. **49**(5), 622–626 (2005)
18. ISO/IEC: ISO/IEC 15909-1:2004 Systems and software engineering - High-level Petri nets - Part 1: Concepts, definitions and graphical notation (2004). https://www.iso.org/standard/38225.html
19. ITU-T: Rec. X.680-X.693 (08/2015) Information Technology - Abstract Syntax Notation One (ASN.1) & ASN.1 encoding rules (2015). https://www.itu.int/rec/T-REC-X.680/
20. ITU-T: Rec. Z.100 (04/16) Specification and Description Language - Overview of SDL-2010 (2016). https://www.itu.int/rec/T-REC-Z.100/
21. ITU-T: Rec. Z.119 (02/07) Guidelines for UML profile design (2007). https://www.itu.int/rec/T-REC-Z.119/
22. ITU-T: Rec. Z.120 (02/11) Message Sequence Chart (MSC) (2011). https://www.itu.int/rec/T-REC-Z.120/
23. ITU-T: Rec. Z.130 (07/03) Extended Object Definition Language (eODL): Techniques for distributed software component development - Conceptual foundation, notations and technology mappings; (deleted standard) (2003). https://www.itu.int/rec/T-REC-Z.130
24. ITU-T: Rec. Z.151 (10/12) User Requirements Notation (URN) - Language definition (2012). https://www.itu.int/rec/T-REC-Z.151/
25. ITU-T: Rec. Z.161 (10/16) Testing and Test Control Notation version 3: TTCN-3 core language (2016). https://www.itu.int/rec/T-REC-Z.161/
26. ITU-T: Rec. Z.200 (11/99) CHILL - The ITU-T Programming Language (1999). https://www.itu.int/rec/T-REC-Z.200/
27. Khendek, F., Toeroe, M., Gherbi, A., Reed, R. (eds.): SDL 2013. LNCS, vol. 7916. Springer, Heidelberg (2013). doi:10.1007/978-3-642-38911-5

28. Kitchenham, B., Brereton, O.P., Budgen, D., Turner, M., Bailey, J., Linkman, S.: Systematic literature reviews in software engineering – a systematic literature review. Inf. Softw. Technol. **51**(1), 7–15 (2009)
29. Kraemer, F.A., Herrmann, P. (eds.): SAM 2010. LNCS, vol. 6598. Springer, Heidelberg (2011). doi:10.1007/978-3-642-21652-7
30. Lahav, Y., Wolisz, A., Fischer, J., Holz, E.: Proceedings of the 1st Workshop of the SDL Forum Society on SDL and MSC. Informatik-Bericht, Nr. 104, Humboldt University Berlin, Germany (1998). https://goo.gl/pevzJZ
31. Mauw, S., Reniers, M.A.: High-level message sequence charts. In: SDL'97 Time for Testing, SDL, MSC and Trends, pp. 291–306. Elsevier (1997)
32. Meho, L.I.: The rise and rise of citation analysis. Phys. World **20**(1), 32 (2007)
33. Object Management Group: Object Constraint Language (OCL) Version 2.4. Formal/2014-02-03 (2014). http://www.omg.org/spec/OCL/2.4/PDF
34. Object Management Group: Unified Modeling Language (OMG UML) Version 2.5. Formal/15-03-01 (2015). http://www.omg.org/spec/UML/2.5/PDF
35. Ober, I., Ober, I. (eds.): SDL 2011. LNCS, vol. 7083. Springer, Heidelberg (2012). doi:10.1007/978-3-642-25264-8
36. Prinz, A., Reed, R., Reed, J. (eds.): SDL 2005. LNCS, vol. 3530. Springer, Heidelberg (2005). doi:10.1007/b137793
37. Reed, R.: ITU-T System Design Languages (SDL). Comput. Netw. **42**(3), 283–284 (2003)
38. Reed, R., Reed, J. (eds.): SDL 2001. LNCS, vol. 2078. Springer, Heidelberg (2001). doi:10.1007/3-540-48213-X
39. Reed, R., Reed, J. (eds.): SDL 2003. LNCS, vol. 2708. Springer, Heidelberg (2003). doi:10.1007/3-540-45075-0
40. Reed, R., Bilgic, A., Gotzhein, R. (eds.): SDL 2009. LNCS, vol. 5719. Springer, Heidelberg (2009). doi:10.1007/978-3-642-04554-7
41. SDL Forum Society. http://sdl-forum.org. Accessed 24 June 2017
42. Sherratt, E. (ed.): SAM 2002. LNCS, vol. 2599. Springer, Heidelberg (2003). doi:10.1007/3-540-36573-7
43. Zhu, X., Turney, P.D., Lemire, D., Vellino, A.: Measuring academic influence: not all citations are equal. JASIST **66**(2), 408–427 (2015)

Intelligent Resilience in the IoT

Edel Sherratt[(✉)]

Department of Computer Science, Aberystwyth University,
Aberystwyth, UK
eds@aber.ac.uk
http://users.aber.ac.uk/eds

Abstract. Failing or hostile elements are normal in the public Internet of Things (IoT). Resilient IoT systems are engineered to fail safely and recover gracefully in the face of challenges presented by their environment. Approaches to ensuring resilient behaviour include intrusion detection, redundancy and self-healing. Adaptive, anomaly-based defence mechanisms are particularly well-suited to systems that are deployed in the public internet. This paper discusses the use of SDL+ (SDL with MSC and ASN.1) to generate simulation results for training anomaly-based defence mechanisms for smart systems. It outlines an approach based on the SDL+ methodology to create resilient IoT systems.

Keywords: SDL (Z.100) · Internet of Things (IoT) · Resilience · Anomaly detection · Machine learning

1 Introduction

When new systems are deployed on the public Internet, they are subject to a variety of accidental and deliberate threats [1]. A resilient smart system deals with these threats safely, and quickly recovers to provide normal service. Self-healing systems go further, not only recovering normal behaviour, but also addressing the vulnerability that led to faulty behaviour [2].

Because IoT systems share the public Internet with so many different systems, new kinds of threat emerge frequently and unpredictably [1]. Resilience is essential to any new smart IoT system where reliable behaviour is important, and anomaly detection is key to achieving resilience.

Anomaly detection based on machine learning has the potential to identify new kinds of event that have not previously been encountered, which makes it particularly suitable for IoT systems. However, obtaining useful data to train and evaluate machine learning systems can be problematic [3–5].

SDL-2010 and MSC, with ASN.1 [6], collectively known as SDL+, with their well-established modelling and simulation tools[1,2,3], represent a highly promising source of training data for anomaly detection in new smart, connected systems.

---

[1] PragmaDev Studio.
[2] Cinderella.
[3] IBM Rational Tau.

© Springer International Publishing AG 2017
T. Csöndes et al. (Eds.): SDL 2017, LNCS 10567, pp. 46–60, 2017.
DOI: 10.1007/978-3-319-68015-6_4

Following a brief overview of anomaly detection, this paper outlines some IoT scenarios in which anomaly detection would be beneficial. A methodological approach adds anomaly detection to each activity in the SDL+ methodology [7], showing how those activities are well suited to the task of engineering intelligent resilience in IoT systems. An important element of this approach is the extraction of training data as a by-product of the SDL+ process, leading to a practical approach to creating intelligent IoT systems that can recognise previously unknown threats, and mount an effective response to those threats.

2 Anomaly Detection

Anomaly detection means identifying unexpected patterns in data [3]. Anomaly detection has applications in many fields, including detection of behaviour in networked computer systems that may indicate security violations [8]. This is of particular concern with the emergence of the Internet of Things, where smart systems are vulnerable to a variety of accidental and deliberate threats [1].

Techniques for detecting anomalies in distributed systems include statistical approaches, support vector machines, Bayesian networks, neural networks and more [3]. Classification based anomaly detection uses labelled training data to learn to distinguish between normal and anomalous behaviour, and then to classify live data as normal or anomalous. This approach, based on machine learning, has the potential to identify the new kinds of threat that are likely to be encountered in the Internet of Things. However, obtaining data sets for training and subsequent evaluation can present a significant challenge [3,5].

To address this challenge, several data sets have been made publicly available for evaluation of intrusion detection. Some of the best known are the DARPA Intrusion Detection Data Sets[4]. Several more recent datasets are listed on Quora by Scully[5].

Amongst the many benefits offered by public data sets is the ability to compare the relative effectiveness of different learning and classification algorithms. However, because new kinds of threat are emerging all the time, it is essential to supplement existing data sets with new information. Moreover, for new kinds of system, high quality data typifying normal behaviour is needed.

The following sections explore the potential of SDL simulation to deliver training data for new IoT systems. The aim is to create smart systems with inbuilt anomaly detection, and so to lay the foundation for effective response and overall resilience.

3 Anomaly Detection in IoT Systems

How and where anomaly detection takes place depends on the kind of system that is developed. The following three scenarios outline how anomaly detection

---

[4] https://www.ll.mit.edu/ideval/data/.

[5] https://www.quora.com/Where-can-I-get-the-latest-dataset-for-a-network-intrusion-detection-system.

may be a subsystem of an IoT system, or may be external to the IoT system, how the data available for anomaly detection is constrained by the IoT system, and how requirements for anomaly detection depend on potential threats to the IoT system.

3.1   Environmental Monitoring

Figure 1 illustrates an environmental monitoring system, similar to that developed by [9]. The system comprises a number of devices that collect sensor data and send it to a central location for analysis. Threats to the system include data contamination and failure of the devices themselves. Battery life is limited, so processing in the field is limited to data collection and transmission.

A machine-learning based anomaly detection system is likely to be co-located with the central analysis software. Data available to the anomaly detection system is the same sensor data as is available to the analysis system. The content of the data, together with its pattern of arrival form patterns that enable classification into normal and anomalous activity.

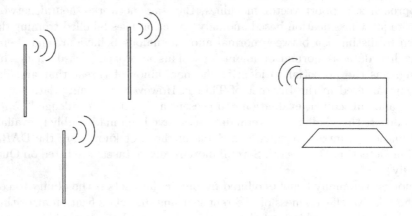

Fig. 1. Remote sensors transmit environmental data to central system for analysis

3.2   Smart Fridge

A smart fridge [10] captures information about fridge contents and uploads that information to a website. The website sends messages to the fridge owner recommending recipes based on fridge content and reminding them when items need to be re-stocked (Fig. 2). Threats to the website and threats to the integrity of the data that is sent from the fridge should be addressed by the anomaly detection system.

Data for anomaly detection consists of the data arriving from the fridge and the requests and responses that form the pattern of website usage. Anomaly detection is likely to consist of generic anomaly detection for the web server, with a bespoke system to classify the content of the fridge data as normal or anomalous.

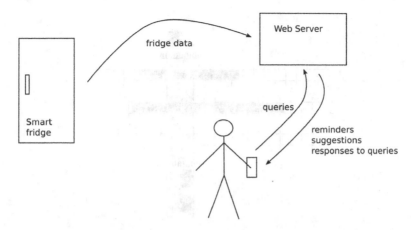

Fig. 2. Smart fridge sends data to website; web server sends recipes and suggestions to fridge owner.

3.3 Railway Crossing

The railway crossing scenario [11], is more complex than the previous two systems. It involves tracks, trains, a variety of sensors and signals, and a public highway, with signals and the crossing gates all managed by a central controller.

Threats to the system include failure of any of the components, deliberate injection of false sensor data, and malicious manipulation of gates or signals. Various problem scenarios are considered in [11] with detailed documentation available on the SDL forum website[6].

Anomaly detection is likely to form part of the central controller for the railway crossing. It has access to sensor data from which it can infer patterns of road and rail traffic, as well as patterns of usage for opening and closing the crossing gates and for activating the crossing signals.

4   Building Intelligent Resilience into Smart Systems

SDL [6], with its established track record in telecommunications and embedded systems, and its emphasis on modelling and simulation, has the potential to support development of robust, reliable IoT systems [1]. This section discusses how the SDL+ methodology [7] can be used to create smart systems with the capacity to identify and respond to previously unknown threats (Fig. 3).

Before proceeding, it is reasonable to ask how an IoT system differs from any other distributed, embedded system, and, if there is any significant difference, whether or not the existing SDL+ methodology is also suitable for developing an IoT system? An IoT system is a distributed embedded system, but with the key feature that an IoT system typically exposes low level elements, such as

---

[6] http://www.sdl-forum.org/SAM_contest/Li_Probert_Williams/Railway_doc.pdf.

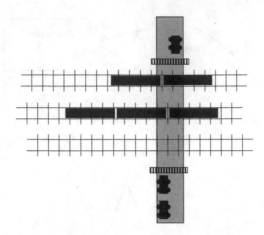

Fig. 3. Railway crossing challenge

sensors, to the public Internet. An IoT system is also likely to include elements that collect raw, un-validated data via the public Internet. As a distributed, embedded system, an IoT system is amenable to development using the SDL+ methodology [7]. As a system whose internal communications are exposed to unwanted external interference, an IoT system needs the kind of resilience that an integral anomaly detection system can provide.

The following sections present the SDL+ methodology [7] and indicate how each of the different SDL+ activities can be adapted to include anomaly detection as an integral component of the emerging IoT system. Of particular interest is the opportunity to use the results of simulation to accelerate initial training of bespoke anomaly detection systems for new networked smart things.

4.1 The SDL+ Methodology

SDL-2010 [6] refers to the ITU system design language documented in the Z.100 series of recommendations. SDL-2010 is normally used in conjunction with ASN.1 for describing data[7] and the message sequence chart (MSC) notation (Recommendation Z.120 from [6].) SDL+ refers to the use of SDL-2010 with ASN.1 and the MSC notation.

The SDL+ methodology [7] focuses on three core activities: analysis, design and formalization, illustrated in Fig. 4. The three core activities interact with four further activities: requirements capture, validation, documentation and implementation. The SDL+ methodology is not restricted to any particular software development process, but its activities can be included in different plan-driven or agile processes.

If the proposed system is to include an anomaly detection system, then that fact should be recorded in the classified requirements, and formalized in the SDL+ description.

---

[7] https://www.itu.int/en/ITU-T/asn1/Pages/introduction.aspx.

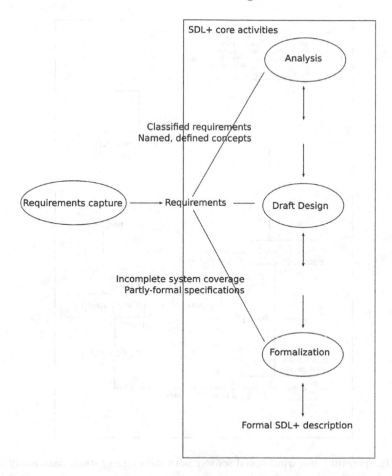

Fig. 4. Requirements for resilience are included amongst the requirements used by the SDL+ core activities

4.2   Resilience and the SDL+ Core Activities

Requirements capture results in a statement of requirements, preferably expressed using the User Requirements Notation (URN) [12]. If resilience is important, then requirements for resilient behaviour should be included with the other requirements on the proposed system.

Analysis results in a model of concepts with names and definitions. This essentially ontological structure facilitates discovery of similar concepts in previous systems whose components can be reused. This means that it also supports discovery of previous threats and countermeasures that also apply to the current system.

Draft design results in partial specifications that explore different designs for the proposed system. Draft design for a resilient IoT system includes exploration of different options for anomaly detection, diagnosis and recovery. This activity

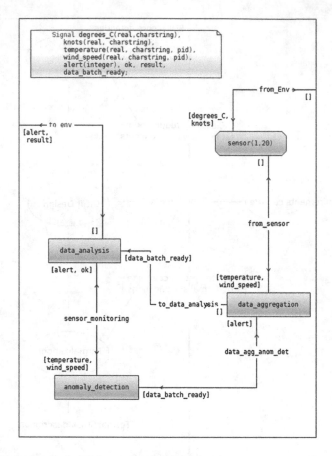

Fig. 5. Temperature and wind-speed sensors with data aggregation, data analysis and anomaly detection.

is also where vulnerabilities associated with different system designs can be explored, and costs and relative effectiveness of different countermeasures can be evaluated.

Formalization results in a formal SDL+ definition, expressed in SDL-2010 with MSC and ASN.1. The behaviour specified by the formal specification is fully specified by the SDL formal semantics. If, as is likely, an external anomaly detection system is used, the formal SDL+ specification will include calls to the external system. For example, the system illustrated in Fig. 5 includes anomaly_detection.

The anomaly detection block contains a process which calls an externally defined procedure to perform anomaly detection, illustrated in Fig. 6. The system also includes signals to indicate detection of anomalous behaviour. To complete the description, the actions taken by the system to respond to threats and to make itself more resistant to future threats should also be specified. This is why

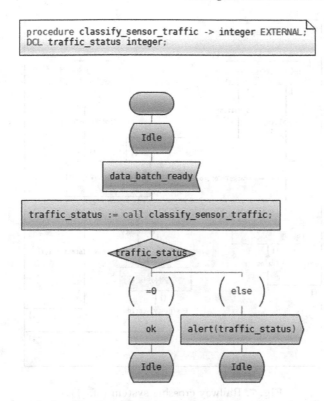

Fig. 6. An external classification (machine learning) procedure signals an alert when it detects abnormal traffic conditions.

alerts are made available to the data aggregation and data analysis blocks in Fig. 5.

Anomaly detection in the smart fridge system is modelled in a similar way.

For the railway crossing, a more complex model, reflecting the variety and distribution of the different sensors, as well as the physical actuation involved in changing the states of gates and light signals would be needed. An outline SDL system diagram, derived from [11], is illustrated in Fig. 7.

Anomaly detection could be incorporated in the controller, but there would also be benefits in providing different system elements with their own anomaly detection and recovery systems.

4.3 Validation, Testing and Anomaly Detection

Model validation aims to determine whether or not a simulation model provides and adequate representation of a system being modelled [15], where adequacy depends on the purpose of the model. A formal SDL+ model is usually created with the ultimate aim of generating code that will behave correctly when it is deployed in a live embedded system.

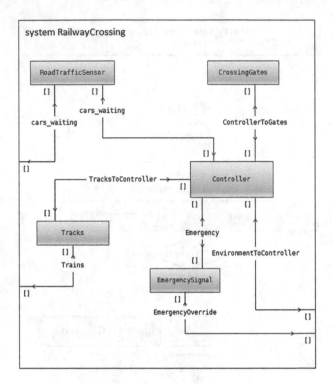

Fig. 7. Railway crossing system (cf. [11])

In the context of the SDL+ methodology, the formal SDL+ definition is subject to validation and testing (Fig. 8) with a view to correcting mistakes and omissions in the specification before any code is generated or deployed. This is necessary because specifications are created by people, and people make mistakes, even when working at the level of specifications rather than code [7].

Validation is like test execution, with similar test cases being used for both activities. The main difference between validation and testing is that validation compares the SDL+ model with the classified requirements and concepts produced by analysis, while testing compares the SDL+ specification with an executable implementation.

Validation entails checking the syntax and semantic consistency of the SDL+ description, and checking that requirements are met by the proposed system. While different strategies are available for validating a simulation model [15], validating an SDL+ description against requirements is typically achieved by executing the SDL+ description in different environmental contexts. Environmental conditions are represented as combinations of events that are specified using TTCN-3 [13], or MSC ([6], Z.120) or SDL-2010. Validation is performed with the help of automated tool support, which also makes it possible to extract training data for anomaly detection.

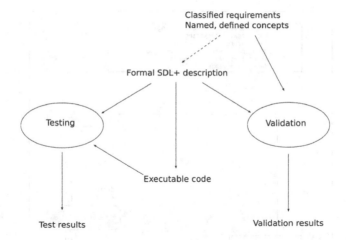

Fig. 8. Validating and testing a formal SDL+ description

Validation makes use of a formal validation model, which models parts of the environment. For example, the validation model for the environmental sensing application, illustrated in Fig. 8, and specified in SDL-2010, includes a special process, RTDS_env, used by PragmaDev Studio[8] to simulate different environmental conditions, and so to explore the behaviour of a new system in the context of different combinations of external events.

While the primary purpose of validation is to provide reasonable confidence that a validated system will meet its requirements when it is deployed in a live environment, the products of simulation also have the potential to serve as data sets to train classification systems to recognize normal behaviour and to identify abnormal behaviour. That is, SDL simulation has the potential to provide high-quality, labelled data for training an anomaly detection system.

4.4 Training the Anomaly Detection System

The results of validation depend on the kinds of simulation performed. Typical validation results from Cinderella[9] and PragmaDev Studio (see Footnote 8) consist of execution traces in the form of message sequence charts. These results can be used to train a classification system as illustrated in Fig. 10. In other words, training data for anomaly detection can be generated as a by-product of system development with SDL+.

Before validation results can be used in this way, they must be transformed to form usable by a machine-learning classification system. This is not difficult. The textual form of an execution trace [14], is readily expressed as an XML document, which in turn can be transformed, for example, to Attribute Relation File Format (ARFF) or any other input format required by a classification system.

---

[8] http://pragmadev.com/product/index.html.

[9] http://www.cinderella.dk/.

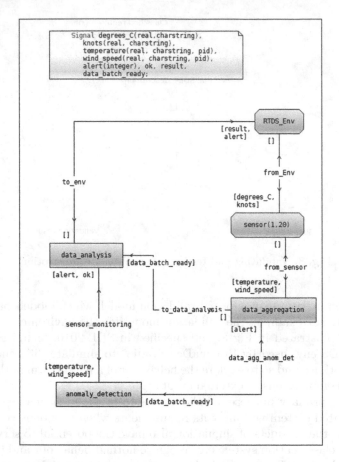

Fig. 9. The SDL+ validation model includes a special tool-dependent process, RTDS_Env, to simulate different environmental conditions.

Execution traces that show acceptable system behaviour, without unwanted interference by other systems or other problems, represent normal behaviour, and traces representing unacceptable behaviour, or including unwanted interference, represent anomalous behaviour.

As well as execution traces, signal payloads can also be analysed. This is important for systems such as the environmental monitoring system described above, where contamination of the sensor data has the potential to lead to incorrect inferences and poor policy decisions. It is critical for safety in the case of the railway crossing. Again, the formality of the data definitions means that it is relatively straightforward to re-cast signal content in a form that is accessible to machine-learning based classification systems.

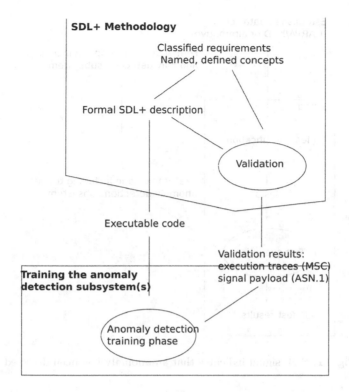

Fig. 10. Execution traces and signal payload are converted to training data for anomaly detection

4.5   Testing the Anomaly Detection System

The anomaly detection subsystem is tested as part of the overall testing process (Fig. 11). An established data set, such as one of the well established DARPA/KDD data sets or more recent data sets such as the CSIC 2010 HTTP Dataset or the ECML/PKDD 2007 data set, is re-framed as events to be fed in to the system under simulation. Test results in the form of execution traces can be then be evaluated for effectiveness and accuracy of anomaly detection.

Responses to threats are tested in a similar way, to increase confidence in the resilience of the system before it is deployed.

Post deployment monitoring should also be performed, particularly if the anomaly detection system includes the capacity to learn from events encountered in the target environment. Post deployment monitoring can also feed back to model validation, revealing new kinds of situation to be simulated, and so improving future simulations of new systems (Fig. 9).

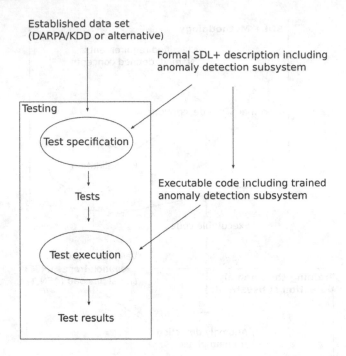

Fig. 11. SDL signal indicates that an anomaly has been detected

4.6   Summary of the Methodological Approach

The SDL+ methodology supports design, modelling and simulation of IoT systems that include adaptive anomaly detection and intelligent response to varied and previously unknown threats.

Requirements capture provides a statement of the expected behaviour of the proposed IoT system, including behaviour in the face of threats caused by failure or malicious agents.

Analysis results in an ontology that names and defines the concepts embodied in the requirements. This facilitates discovery of usable components, and also discovery of threats to the proposed system.

Draft design is where different options can be explored. Amongst these options are different anomaly detection systems. There are several key factors involved in choosing software to identify anomalous behaviour. These include

- the questions the classification will be expected to resolve;
- the data that will be available;
- whether the data will be batched or streamed;
- the kind of adaptive behaviour that will be needed to deal with new kinds of threat;
- scalability in terms of the number and kinds of component in the IoT system and the quantity of data the anomaly detection system will have to process.

Formalization results in a formal SDL+ description that can be simulated and validated. Validation has the well-established purpose of helping ensure that a new system meets its requirements, but the execution traces produced in the course of SDL+ validation can also serve as labelled training data for an integral anomaly detection system.

The trained system is tested using one or more of the established data sets, possibly leading to further development or modification.

Documentation should also include decisions about choice of anomaly detection system, and about various validation and test activities that the IoT system has undergone.

5   Next Steps

SDL+ with its associated tools provides a promising source of training data for anomaly detection. An engineering process for developing IoT systems with integral anomaly detection provides a secure foundation for creating smart systems that will be resilient in the face of the many and varied threats they will encounter in the public Internet.

The SDL+ methodology provides a framework that readily includes activities related to creating intelligent IoT systems with in-build anomaly detection, response and recovery. In particular, SDL+ validation results in execution traces that provide a source of training data for machine-learning based anomaly detection.

Further work is needed to specify the kinds of questions an anomaly detection system should resolve in a resilient IoT system. The starting point is to use execution traces from SDL+ simulation to represent normal behaviour, and to classify other behaviour as abnormal. But more investigation is needed to identify, for example, what represents an acceptable level of false positives.

Appropriate response to threats is also an area that needs work. Distributing threat detection and resolution presents a promising approach to creating reliable, resilient IoT systems. However, the nature of fault resolution, and the scalability of self-healing systems is an area of ongoing research [2].

Investigative development is also needed to recreate existing IoT systems, but this time with inbuilt adaptive anomaly detection, and to evaluate their behaviour in the field.

This paper discusses the case for incorporating anomaly detection into new IoT systems, and outlines how SDL+ provides a promising way to make that a practicable proposition. In particular, its validation activity provides training data for anomaly detection as a by-product. Given the pressing need for intelligent, adaptive, resilient IoT systems, and the fact that the SDL+ activities are adaptable to different software engineering processes, this approach is likely to deliver significant value to IoT systems developers.

References

1. Sherratt, E., Ober, I., Gaudin, E., Fonseca i Casas, P., Kristoffersen, F.: SDL - the IoT language. In: Fischer, J., Scheidgen, M., Schieferdecker, I., Reed, R. (eds.) SDL 2015. LNCS, vol. 9369, pp. 27–41. Springer, Cham (2015). doi:10.1007/978-3-319-24912-4_3
2. Scully, P.M.D.: CARDINAL- Vanilla: immune system inspired prioritisation and distribution of security information for industrial networks, Aberystwyth University, Ph.D. thesis (2014). http://cadair.aber.ac.uk/dspace/handle/2160/43304
3. Chandola, V., Banerjee, A., Kumar, V.: Anomaly detection: a survey. ACM Comput. Surv. **41**(3), 58 (2009). Article 15. ACM. http://doi.acm.org/10.1145/1541880.1541882
4. García-Teodoro, P., Díaz-Verdejo, J., Maciá-Fernándeza, G., Vázquez, E.: Add to E-shelf anomaly-based network intrusion detection: techniques, systems and challenges. Comput. Secur. **28**(1–2), 18–28 (2009). Elsevier
5. Ahmed, M., Mahmood, A.N., Hu, J.: A survey of network anomaly detection techniques. J. Netw. Comput. Appl. **60**, 19–31 (2016). Elsevier. http://dx.doi.org/10.1016/j.jnca.2015.11.016
6. ITU-T: Z.100 series Recommendations for SDL 2010, International Telecommunications Union 2011–2016. ITU-T (2011–2016). https://www.itu.int/rec/T-REC-Z/en
7. ITU-T: Z-series Recommendations Supplement 1, International Telecommunications Union 2015 (2015). https://www.itu.int/rec/T-REC-Z.Sup1/en
8. Song, J., Zhu, Z., Scully, P., Price, C.: Selecting features for anomaly intrusion detection: a novel method using fuzzy C means and decision tree classification. In: Wang, G., Ray, I., Feng, D., Rajarajan, M. (eds.) CSS 2013. LNCS, vol. 8300, pp. 299–307. Springer, Cham (2013). doi:10.1007/978-3-319-03584-0_22
9. Blanchard, T.: Endocrine inspired control of wireless sensor networks: deployment and analysis. Aberystwyth University, Ph.D. thesis (2016)
10. Alolayan, B.: Toward sustainable households: passive context-aware intervention to promote reduction in food waste. Aberystwyth University, Ph.D. thesis (2016)
11. Williams, A.W., Probert, R.L., Li, Q., Kim, T.-H.: The winning entry of the SAM 2002 design contest. In: Reed, R., Reed, J. (eds.) SDL 2003. LNCS, vol. 2708, pp. 387–403. Springer, Heidelberg (2003). doi:10.1007/3-540-45075-0_23
12. ITU-T: Recommendation ITU-T Z.151, User Requirements Notation (URN) Language definition ITU-T (2012). https://www.itu.int/rec/T-REC-Z.150-201102-I/en
13. TTCN-3 standards, ETSI - European Telecommunications Standards Institute. http://www.ttcn-3.org/index.php/downloads/standards
14. ITU-T: Recommendation ITU-T Z.120, Message Sequence Chart (MSC). ITU-T (2011). https://www.itu.int/rec/T-REC-Z.120-201102-I/en
15. Sargent, R.G.: Verification and Validation of Simulation Models. In: Henderson, S.G., Biller, B., Hsieh, M.-H., Shortle, J., Tew, J.D., Barton, R.R. (eds.) Proceedings of WSC 2007, Winter Simulation Conference (2007). http://www.informs-sim.org/wsc07papers/014.pdf

An Ontology-Based Approach for IoT Data Processing Using Semantic Rules

Ahmed Bali$^{(\boxtimes)}$, Mahmud Al-Osta, and Gherbi Abdelouahed

Department of Software and IT Engineering,
École de technologie supérieure, Montreal, Canada
{ahmed.bali.1,mahmud.al-osta.1}@ens.etsmtl.ca,
abdelouahed.gherbi@etsmtl.ca

Abstract. Internet of Things (IoT) applications rely on a network of heterogeneous devices including sensors and gateways. These devices are endowed with the capacity to continuously sense the environment and collect data, which can be further transfered through gateway devices to the cloud. The generated data by IoT systems is often massive. Therefore, the communication gateways might become a bottleneck affecting the system performance due to their resources constraints. This is further exacerbated in the case of bandwidth limitation. The huge amount of data generated increases also the cost associated with data storage and processing at the cloud level. Edge computing, which is a recent IoT trend can contribute to addressing these issues by delegating data processing task to the edges (e.g. gateway devices). In this paper, we propose an approach, which aims at supporting the data processing and minimizes the size of the transferred data to the cloud side. To this end, our approach is based on the notion of rules used to filter the collected data. In order to support the principle of sharing and reusing the rules and the domain knowledge, we propose a Platform Independent Model (PIM) to specify this knowledge independently from the used platform (gateway node). In particular, we define a rule meta-model to support the creation of the model that captures the domain rules. Furthermore, we use Web semantic techniques to represent the knowledge at the semantic level. This representation facilitates the instantiation of these rules and domain knowledge to obtain the Platform Specific Model (PSM) at the gateway level to process and filter the data.

Keywords: Semantic web · Internet of Things · Ontology · Semantic rules · Platform independent model · Platform specific model

1 Introduction

Internet of Things (IoT) is an emerging paradigm that promotes the integration between objects in the real world and services in the digital world. This integration paves the way toward the development of innovative applications, which have an impact on many aspects of our life. According to Cisco [1], tens of billions of devices are anticipated to connect to the Internet by 2020. These devices

© Springer International Publishing AG 2017
T. Csöndes et al. (Eds.): SDL 2017, LNCS 10567, pp. 61–79, 2017.
DOI: 10.1007/978-3-319-68015-6_5

will be deployed to observe the surroundings and collect data that represent real world phenomenas. These data will be further transmitted to diverse cloud platforms for aggregation, analyze, and storage processes. Typically, the data generated by IoT systems is massive and heterogeneous. Consequently, the task of IoT applications in interpreting and efficiently using this data is increasingly complex. To reap the value from this data, conveying it to high-level knowledge is a vital step, which in turn, promotes the development of interoperable and smarter IoT applications [1,2].

In addition to the heterogeneity of data generated by IoT systems, in this paper we target another challenge, which is the huge amount of data transmitted from IoT gateway devices to the cloud platforms. Although, the latter have the potential to handle such amount of data, this process requires a considerable amount of resources, where in some cases users would have to expand their infrastructure to cope with the increasing amount of data. Furthermore, continually transferring data forth and back between the cloud and IoT gateways has lead to network traffic overloading and latency issues that might influence time-sensitive services [3].

Inspired by success that Semantic Web (SW) technologies have conveyed to the data integration process on the Web, a recent trend to extend them to the IoT domain have been widely accepted. SW technologies have the potential to alleviate the data heterogeneity issue and promote interoperability between IoT systems [4]. This could be achieved by modeling IoT data based on shared vocabularies that can be interpreted by different software agents. This process is called semantic annotation, which requires using several SW standards such as: OWL, RDFs, and RDF to construct conceptual models (i.e. Ontology) to describe the application domain concepts and the relationships between them [5]. Resource Definition Framework (RDF) is a standard language for representing information about Web resources as XML format. It provides a unified framework for exchanging information between applications without loss of meaning. Data in RDF are stored in the form of triples; each triple is consisted of (subject, property, and object).

In order to reduce the volume of data uploaded to the cloud, gateway devices can be increasingly used to perform data processing at the edge level. Recently, these devices have witnessed a significant improvement in terms of computing and communication capabilities, which enable them to carry out data processing algorithms taking in consideration the limited number of sensor nodes connected to them. Since the gateway nodes work closely to sensor nodes, it could achieve faster response times, and provide processing capabilities for filtering out useless data. Thus reducing the amount of data volumes transferred to the cloud, which in turn, enhances the network performance and minimizes the latency. Also, it provides more flexibility since it could be deployed everywhere. Moreover, networks and cloud platforms could benefit from edge devices by reducing the results delivery time; which in turn, save the bandwidth [6].

In this paper, we propose a semantic-based approach, to support at the edge side, the data processing and minimizes the size of the transferred data to the cloud side. To this end, our approach is based on the notion of rules used to filter the collected data. Our approach enables the principle of sharing and reusing the rules and the domain knowledge. For this reason, we propose a Platform Independent Model (PIM) to specify this knowledge independently from the used platform (gateway node). In particular, we define a rule meta-model to support the creation of the model that captures the domain rules. Furthermore, we use Web semantic techniques to represent the knowledge at the semantic level. This representation facilitates the instantiation of these rules and domain knowledge to obtain the Platform Specific Model (PSM) at the gateway level to process and filter the data.

The reminder of this paper is organized as follows: Sect. 2 discusses the related work presenting their advantages and limitations. The overall architecture of our proposed approach is presented in Sect. 3 followed by a detailed description about ontologies and semantic rules metamodel in Sect. 4. A prototype implementation and evaluation are presented in Sect. 5 while Sect. 6 concludes the paper.

2   Related Work

Several research works on IoT related issues using SW technologies are reported in the literature. In this section, we discuss briefly some of these that either integrate SW technologies at the edge of IoT networks or use the semantic rule notion.

In [7], the author designed an architecture to annotate heterogeneous data captured using sensor measurements (sensor gateways) and aggregation gateways which convert sensed data into semantic measurements using semantic web technologies. A sensor measurement ontology (SenMESO) was designed to automatically convert heterogeneous sensor measurement to semantic data. In the same topic, the authors of [8], propose an annotation architecture mainly targeting virtualized wireless sensor networks. The architecture consists of two overlays namely: data annotation and ontology storing. Our approach takes into consideration, the sensors description and it is open to use any sensor ontologies like Semantic Sensor Network ontology (SSN) [9] and SenMESO. The sensor description is used, through the models mapping, to annotate the data using the instantiation of domain ontologies. Moreover, our approach reasons on the annotated data by applying the filtering rules.

In [10] the authors propose an approach for mapping heterogeneous sensor data to a formal (ontology-based) model in Ambient Assisted Living (AAL) environments. A proposed Senior core ontology is divided into Core part (sen_core), which presents the sensor description model and Sense part (sen_sense), which presents the sensor data as instances of the description model. We see that the description model is not sufficient to describe all aspects of data, which are necessary to reason about the data as their filtering. In [11] the authors design a data semantic fusion model based on a smart home domain ontology, to facilitate capturing the domain knowledge by defining a set of concepts that represent different abstraction levels of the data generated in the smart homes. The authors designed the semantic matching rule for user behavior reasoning, in an attempt to provide accurate and personalized home services. The SWRL [12] is used for the representation of the matching rule. In our approach, taking into account the resource constrained gateway, we have proposed a specialized rule model (based on rule metamodel) that requires only limited resource to reason on rather than using of general rule model as SWRL. Moreover, in order to widen the usage of our data filtering, we proposed a rule model in the form of an ontology.

3   The Overall Approach Architecture

The architecture of an IoT system is in general composed of three categories of components, namely the sensor nodes, the gateways, and the cloud platforms. Typically, sensor nodes are the lowest level and consist of a set of resource-constrained sensors. The main task of sensors nodes is only to collect data and send it to the gateways. The Devices in the gateway category have more computing resources compared to the sensor nodes. A gateway device acts as a hub by aggregating sensory data and bridging the connection between sensor nodes and IoT cloud services.

In our work, we focus on the data processing while minimizing the size of the data to be actually sent to the cloud level. Our proposed approach is based on using the ontologies for the annotation of the collected data and the modeling of the rules to be used for their filtering, which is the step required for the data size minimization. This approach, as illustrated in Fig. 1, is organized also around of three levels, namely: Sensor Node, Gateway, and Cloud level.

In our approach the data processing step is agnostic to the type of gateway and sensor used. This is achieved through the semantic description of the knowledge at the cloud level. This allows reusing the knowledge independently from the platform deployed. At the gateway level, specific knowledge instantiations are then used. In our approach, we apply the instantiated rules to minimize the data to be sent by filtering those that are not significant. Moreover, in our approach we take into consideration the resource limitations of the gateway devices as the filtering of rules and concepts for each gateway allows to instantiate only those relevant for the data collected by the sensors connected to the gateway.

The following subsections describe the two main levels of our approach and their structures in more detail.

3.1   Cloud Level

In this level, we have the different domain ontologies that are required for the data modeling at semantic level. The rules of data filtering are defined using the different elements of the domain ontologies (i.e. concepts and properties). The application of these rules allows to judge whether a value of a given data is significant or not. The end-user (i.e. the data consumer) can not only view the data collected but can also configure according to his needs the filtering rules, which are defined by the system administrator.

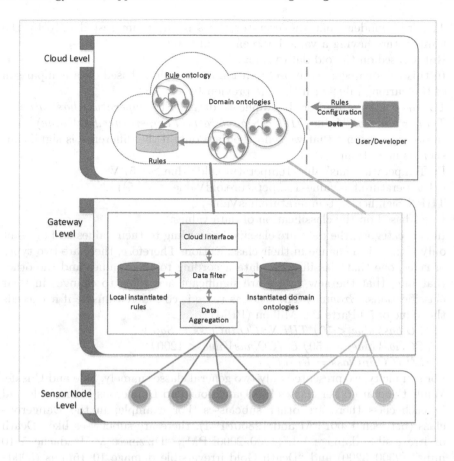

Fig. 1. The proposed gateway architecture.

In the remainder of this subsection, we provide further details about the notion of rules in our approach. We use the rules to identify whether a data value is significant to be sent to the cloud. The general form of a rule is as follows: *IF (Precondition) THEN Postcondition.*

The Precondition(v) presents the condition to apply the rule. It is a conjunction and/or disjunction of the predicates on the data values (v) in order to judge whether the value is significant to be sent. In our approach, we propose three categories of data processing rules, namely:

– Rules based on a specific data value:
  In this category of rules, the preconditions of the rule are based on a basic comparison (i.e., $<, <=, =, >=, >$) of the data value to a predefined specific value (by the user, the administrator or the system).
  Example: IF(Temperature.hasValue $>= 20$) & (Temperature.hasValue < 30) THEN Significatif(Temperature.hasValue)

This rule models that the user (or the system) is interested only by the temperature having a value between 20 and 30 C.

- Rules based on the old data value:

In this rules category, the precondition of the rule is based on a comparison of the current value with the one previously sent.

Example: A rule to filter the duplicate data. $IF(Temperature.hasValue! = Temperature.oldValue)THENSignificatif(Temperature.hasValue)$

In order to specify, that we send the data only if the difference is significant such as more than 5°:

IF(Temperature.hasValue-Temperature.oldValue $>=$ 5) V ((Temperature.hasValue-Temperature.oldValue $<=$ −5))

THEN Significatif(Temperature.hasValue)

- Rules based on the classification of data values:

In this category, the data are classified according to their values and are sent only if there is a change in their classification. Therefore, there are two types of rules, one that classifies the data according to their values and the other that infer that the new values are significant according to changes in their classifications. *Example:* The CO gas value is considered unsafe if it exceeds the value of 50 Parts Per Million (PPM).

$IF(CO.hasValue < 50)$ *THEN* $(CO.inClass = Safe)$
$IF(CO.hasValue >= 50)$ & $(CO.hasValue < 1200)$
THEN $(CO.inClass = Unsafe)$

For simplicity, we presented only two general classes namely, Safe and Unsafe. While there are other classes like Dangerous and Dangerous Flammable and in each class there are other subclasses. For example, in the Dangerous class (between 1200PPM and 12800PPM), there are subclasses like "Death or irreversible damage 1 h"(1200–2000PPM), "Dizziness & Headache 5–10 mins" (2000–3200) and "Death Gold irreversible damage 10–15mins (5000–6400PPM) [13].

Given the high importance of some data such as those presented in the previous example, we have proposed a fourth level of rules concerning the security, performance and maintenance aspects. For example, the system must send the data in a time interval even if the rules of the previous levels are not applicable (e.g. data is duplicated). This makes it possible to distinguish between the case of the failure of a sensor and the case where there is no need to send the data (because of the rules of three previous levels). However, we do not focus on this type of rules in this work because we are interested in data processing by minimizing its sent size.

3.2   Gateway Level

In our approach shown in Fig. 1, the main role of the Gateway is to collect the data from the sensors and send them to the cloud after processing (filtering) in order to minimize their size. The gateway level in our approach consists of three basic modules, namely Cloud Interface, Data Filter and Data Aggregation.

These modules are shown in Fig. 2 in more details. The 'Data aggregation' module collects the raw data from the sensors and passes them to the 'Data filter' module, which filters and sends them to the cloud via the 'Cloud Interface' module. In the following sub-sections, we explain the two modules 'Cloud Interface' and 'Data Filter'.

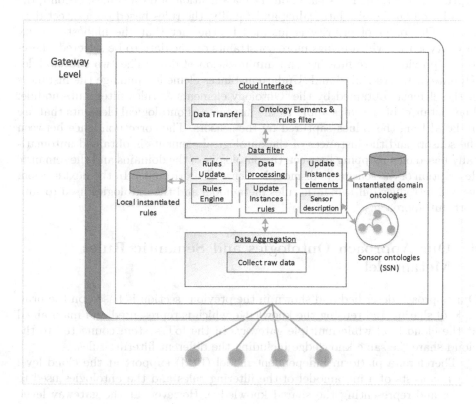

Fig. 2. Gateway level architecture

Cloud Interface Module: This module supports the communication with the cloud. It is further composed of the Data Transfer module, which provides one of the basic functionality of the gateway, namely the data transmission after processing (in our case is filtering). In our approach, we take into account the capacity constraints of gateway. To this end, we propose the 'Ontology Elements & rules filter' module. This module selects only the concepts and properties that have a link to the data types processed by the gateway, and therefore it selects the rules relevant for these elements. In our approach, this module is automatic thanks to the semantic description of the sensors which represent the data source.

Data Filter Module: This module plays the essential role of our proposal, namely data filtering. This functionality is implemented by the sub-module "Data processing", which is based on the sub-module 'Rules engine' in order to know the data having significant new values and therefore it is necessary to send them. The Rules Engine sub-module applies the rules in the following order of priority: First, the rules based on the classification of data values; Second, the rules based on the old data value; and Finally, the rules based on a direct data value. This order of priority is justified by the fact that the highest priority category is that which brings more constraints on the data to be selected, therefore it provides more filtering and minimization of data. The two sub-modules 'Update instances Rules' and 'Update instances elements' manage the instances of the elements obtained by the 'Ontology elements & rules filter' sub-module. The instances of the rules apply to the instances of ontological elements that are updated from the values captured by the sensors. The correspondence between the sensors and the instances of the ontological elements is obtained automatically based on a mapping between the ontologies of the domains and the semantic description of the sensors (sub-module 'Sensor Description'). In the next section, we will introduce our semantic rules metamodel and the ontologies used to support our approach.

4   Our Approach Ontologies and Semantic Rules Metamodel

Our approach described and shown in the previous section is based on the principle of sharing and reusing the knowledge which is represented and maintained at the cloud level while multiple gateways in the IoT system connected to the cloud share the same knowledge including the different filtering rules.

Therefore, a platform independent model (PIM) support at the cloud level which consists of a metamodel of the filtering rules and the ontologies used to model and representing the shared knowledge. However, at the gateway level, we use specific instances of the knowledge relevant for the mission and the types of handled data. This specific representation specific to the gateway can be designated as a Platform specific model (PSM).

In the following subsections, we will explain how we used these two levels of representation.

4.1   Platform Independent Model for the Cloud Level

In our work, the use of a platform independent model (PIM) is motivated by the need to support sharing cloud-based knowledge between different gateways (seen as different platforms). It should be possible to reuse the knowledge by different users and even other clouds. Using this PIM, the description of the domain knowledge (including the rules) will be independent of the gateway level. We propose to use a semantic model of knowledge based on the domain ontologies and an ontology of the rules domain that we have developed. This choice is motivated by the consideration of ontologies as the key to the representation of knowledge at the semantic level. Moreover, the wide use of ontology in several domains such as shared specifications of knowledge offered us a wide variety of different domains modeling, which are ready to be reused.

Using our ontology of rules of data filtering, the rules will also be defined in a semantic way which has the advantage of allowing their independence from any specific use and consequently support also their reuse. In addition, semantic modeling helps to represent all types of rules that will be used.

As shown in Fig. 1 at the cloud level, there are two basic elements, namely domain ontologies and rules. In the following we present their modeling.

Domain Ontologies: The ontology which semantically describes a domain of knowledge defines the concepts of the domain and the different relations between them. Thus, it is widely used for communication, interoperability and reuse [14]. Moreover, to support the machine processing of the ontologies, these should be coded in standard formats and languages such as RDF (S) and OWL. The OWL is characterized by its rich expressiveness. However, the RDF(S) is more appropriate when the modeled knowledge is less complicated.

Example: In approach evaluation section (Sect. 5), we assume to use a domain ontology of gas. This ontology will be used in a scenario of an IoT system that controls the air gases of an area (eg. industrial zone), by using electrochemical sensors connected to the gateways that collect the data captured by these sensors and send them to the cloud. Table 1, for example, shows an extract of the gas domain ontology. The concept CO (Carbon monoxide) is a subclass of the class oxide (which means a chemical compound that contains at least one oxygen atom and one other element).

The unit of measure of the gases is of the Literal type which designates Parts-per notation, for example we will use the PPM (parts-per-million) for the value of CO presented by the hasValue property. For the sake of simplicity, we have not presented these different details and the modeling of the different chemical characteristics of the different types of gas.

Ontology of the Rules: In Sect. 3.1, we have proposed the notion and different categories data processing rules that we use in our approach. Using this notion and categories, we have defined the rule metamodel represented by the class diagram in Fig. 3. This metamodel supports the specification, modeling and validation of the rules. Using this metamodel of the rules, we define the language which we use to describe the filtering rules. The class diagram in Fig. 3 shows that a rule applies to the values of the concept properties relevant for the rule which are described in a domain ontology (the URI property). We specified the cardinality "1–1" for the relations between the two classes Attribute and Value, to express that we are only interested in the old value (hasOldValue) and the new value (hasValue). The old value is the last one sent to the cloud and the new value is the current value received from the sensor. In this way, we avoid recording unnecessary data.

Table 1. Example of gas domain ontology

```
<?xml version=1.0?>
<rdf:RDF
    xmlns:owl ="http://www.w3.org/2002/07/owl#"
    xmlns:rdf ="http://www.w3.org/1999/02/22-rdf-syntax-ns#"
    xmlns:rdfs="http://www.w3.org/2000/01/rdf-schema#"
    xmlns:xsd ="http://www.w3.org/2001/XMLSchema#">
    <owl:Ontology rdf:about="Gaz"/>
    <owl:Class rdf:ID="CO">
        <rdfs:comment>Carbon monoxide</rdfs:comment>
        <rdfs:subClassOf rdf:resource="#oxide"/>
    </owl:Class>
    <owl:DatatypeProperty rdf:ID="hasValue">
        <rdfs:domain rdf:resource="#CO"/>
        <rdfs:range rdf:resource="&xsd;positiveInteger"/>
    </owl:DatatypeProperty>
    <owl:Class rdf:ID="Ci2"/>
    ...
    <owl:Class rdf:ID="Gas">
        <owl:unionOf rdf:parseType="collection">
        <owl:Class rdf:about="#CO"/>
        <owl:Class rdf:about="#Ci2"/>
        ...
    </owl:Class>
    <owl:DatatypeProperty rdf:ID="measureUnit">
        <rdfs:domain rdf:resource="#Gas"/>
      <rdfs:range rdf:resource="&xsd;string"/>
    </owl:DatatypeProperty>
    ...
</rdf:RDF>
```

In addition, the application of the rule updates the value of the 'isSignificant' attribute of the data value. For the application of a rule, its preconditions should be verified. The preconditions are expressed in terms of comparisons which have three types (Direct, Old and Comparative Classification) corresponding to the three types of rules (the DirectValue, OldValue and Classification rule classes). A comparison can be made using conjunction and/or disjunction operations with other comparisons. In addition, a comparison may be composed of other comparisons. We defined a 'Class' class to define different intervals in which the classification comparison is based.

For the specification of the rules model which is an instance of the meta-model (from the modeling point of view), we propose to use a semantic language to ensure their re-use and understanding by the machine. To do this, we transform the meta-model of the rules to an ontology of the rules in order to be instantiated during the description of the rules.

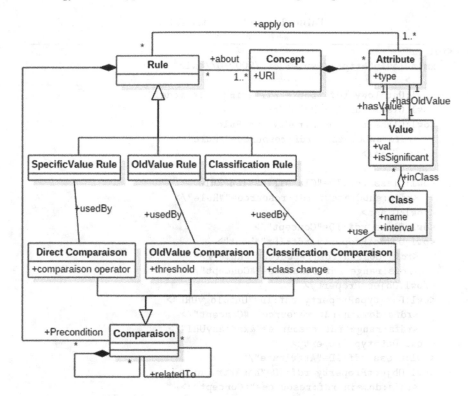

Fig. 3. Metamodel of filtering rules

The level of modeling in which we use this ontology is the metalevel (called also as High Level [15]). Thus, the proposed rules ontology is a meta-ontology type [16] (it can be called also meta-model ontology [17] or foundational ontology [18]) i.e., an ontology that gives the meaning of the meta model elements. Thus, it is a domain independent ontology and it can be seen as representational ontology [19]. The representational feature of our proposed ontology means that it provides the representational primitives of the representation language of knowledge. In our case, the knowledge is the domain rules model which is domain specific (eg. the rules of the gas domain).

Therefore, this ontology of rules is used to describe the rules semantically, by declaring it to the header of the rule description document as a namespace (vocabulary). Table 2 shows an extract from the OWL document of our rules ontology.

In the following subsection, we will present how we use this ontology for the definition of data filtering rules.

Rules Model: We specify the rules also using a semantic model in order to ensure its independence from the platform and to benefit from the advantages of semantic representation, namely the automatic processing of knowledge and

Table 2. Ontology of the rules

```
<rdf:RDF
   xmlns:owl="http://www.w3.org/2002/07/owl#"
   ....>
   <owl:Ontology rdf:about="Filtering Rule model"/>
   <owl:Class rdf:ID="Rule"/>
   <owl:Class rdf:ID="DirectValue Rule">
      <rdfs:subClassOf rdf:resource="#Rule"/>
   </owl:Class>
   ...
   <owl:Class rdf:ID="Classification Rule">
      <rdfs:subClassOf rdf:resource="#Rule"/>
   </owl:Class>
   <owl:Class rdf:ID="Concept"/>
   <owl:ObjectProperty rdf:ID="about">
      <rdfs:domain rdf:resource="#Rule"/>
      <rdfs:range rdf:resource="#Concept"/>
   </owl:ObjectProperty>
   <owl:DatatypeProperty rdf:ID="OntologyURL">
      <rdfs:domain rdf:resource="#Concept"/>
      <rdfs:range rdf:resource="&xsd;anyURI"/>
   </owl:DatatypeProperty>
   <owl:Class rdf:ID="Attribute"/>
   <owl:ObjectProperty rdf:ID="hasAttribut">
      <rdfs:domain rdf:resource="#Concept"/>
      <rdfs:range rdf:resource="#Attribute"/>
   </owl:ObjectProperty>
   <owl:Class rdf:ID="Value"/>
   <owl:ObjectProperty rdf:ID="hasValue">
      <rdfs:domain rdf:resource="#Attribute"/>
      <rdfs:range rdf:resource="#Value"/>
   </owl:ObjectProperty>
   <owl:Restriction>
      <owl:onProperty rdf:resource="#hasValue"/>
      <owl:maxCardinality
         rdf:datatype="&xsd;nonNegativeInteger">1</owl:maxCardinality>
   </owl:Restriction>
   ....
</rdf:RDF>
```

its reuse. Consequently, the semantic description of a rule is an instantiation of our ontology of the rules. In the description of the rule, we also use other domain ontologies to describe the domain elements relevant for the rule. For example, Table 3 presents an extract from the description of the rules (referred to in Subsect. 3.1) that are relevant for the CO concept of the gas domain ontology (referenced by the GasO namespace in the Table 3). This utilization leads

Table 3. Example of rule

```
<rdf:RDF
  xmlns:rdf="http://www.w3.org/1999/02/22-rdf-syntax-ns#"
  xmlns:GasO="http://localhost/GasOntology#"
  xmlns:MMR="http://localhost/MetaModelRules\#">
  <MMR:Class rdf:ID="Safe">
    <MMR:minLimit rdf:datatype="&xsd;nonNegativeInteger">0</MMR:minLimit>
    <MMR:maxLimit rdf:datatype="&xsd;positiveInteger">50</MMR:maxLimit>
  </MMR:Class>
  <MMR:Class rdf:ID="UnSafe">
    <MMR:minLimit rdf:datatype="&xsd;positiveInteger">50</MMR:minLimit>
    <MMR:maxLimit rdf:datatype="&xsd;positiveInteger">1200</MMR:maxLimit>
  </MMR:Class>
  <MMR:Value rdf:ID="oldValue"/>
  <MMR:Value rdf:ID="currentValue"/>
  <MMR:Attribute rdf:ID="attribut">
    <MMR:hasOldValue rdf:resource="#oldValue"/>
    <MMR:hasValue rdf:resource="#currentValue"/>
  </MMR:Attribute>
  <MMR:Concept rdf:ID="CO">
    <MMT:hasAttribut rdf:resource="#attribut"/>
  </MMR:Concept>
  <MMR:ClassificationRule rdf:ID="CRuleCO1">
    <MMR:about rdf:resource="#CO"/>
    <MMR:applyOn rdf:resource="#attribut"/>
  </MMR:ClassificationRule>
  <MMR:ClassificationComparaison rdf:ID="ClassificationComp">
    <MMR:usedBy rdf:resource="#CRuleCO1"/>
    <MMR:use rdf:resource="#Safe"/>
    ...
  </MMR:ClassificationComparaison>
  ...
</rdf:RDF>
```

to create an RDF document which contains the instances of the defined concepts and their values as well as their links. It is worth to mention that at this level of instantiation, certain property values (attributes and links) are not yet defined, for example, the 'val' and 'isSignificant' attributes in the instances of the 'Value' concept, namely 'oldValue' and 'currentValue', and also the 'inClass' link between these two instances and instances of the class 'Class'. The values of this kind of properties will be defined at the level of the gateway where are the sources of these values (i.e. sensors). In our approach, we have called this an instantiation of the rule (of the rule model), as we will show in the following section.

4.2   Platform Specific Model for the Gateway Level

At the gateway level, the concepts of domain ontologies and rules are instantiated. The choice of concepts and rules is based on the mission of the gateway, i.e. based on the types of data to be collected by the sensors. In this step we need, then, to use the description of the sensors using ontologies like SSN. Moreover, the data obtained by the sensors will be annotated using (i.e. instantiation of) the domain ontologies.

We instantiate the concepts and connect these instances to the sensors (to update their values). We can then apply the rules on these instances (i.e. instantiation of the rules). To this end, we have defined a mapping between the different used models so that we can link these instances, as shown in Fig. 4.

The sign '≡' denotes the equivalence relation. More specifically, the value captured by the sensor is assigned in the instance whose concept (defined by rdfs: instanceOf or rdf: type) is the same as the sensor observes (SSN: observes). And in the same way we apply on this instance the rules having the value of "MMR: about" as the concept of the domain concept instance. The knowledge PIM models are customized and instantiated for each gateway (i.e. the sensors connected to the gateway). Therefore, we designate them as platform specific models (PSM) for the gateway level.

Table 4, shows an example of instantiation of the gas domain ontology (its namespace is GasO). It describes an instance of the CO concept (CO_inst1) having a value of 60PPM.

Table 5 shows an instantiation of the model of the "CRuleCO1" rule presented in Table 3. As discussed earlier, this instantiation is to define and update the elements related to the platform (gateway), like the new value "currentValue" and its meaning "isSignificant", and the addition of link "inClass" between the instances of classes "Value" and "Class".

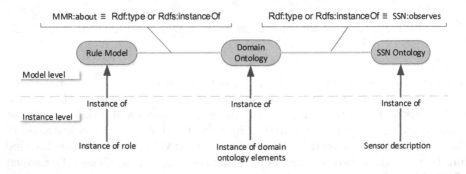

Fig. 4. Models mapping

Table 4. Example of instantiation of domain concept

```
<rdf:RDF
  xmlns:rdf="http://www.w3.org/1999/02/22-rdf-syntax-ns#"
  xmlns:GasO="http://localhost/GasOntology#">

  <rdf:Description rdf:ID="CO_inst1">
    <rdf:type rdf:ressource="GasO:CO"/>
    <GasO:MeasureUnit rdf:datatype="&xsd;string">PPM</GasO:MeasureUnit>
    <GasO:hasValue rdf:datatype="&xsd;positiveInteger">60</GasO:hasValue>
  </rdf:Description>
  ...
</rdf:RDF>
```

Table 5. Example of rule instantiation

```
<rdf:RDF
  xmlns:rdf="http://www.w3.org/1999/02/22-rdf-syntax-ns#"
  xmlns:GasO="http://localhost/GasOntology#"
  xmlns:MMR="http://localhost/MetaModelRules#">
  ...
  <MMR:Value rdf:ID="oldValue">
    <MMR:val rdf:datatype="&xsd;positiveInteger">40</MMR:val>
    <MMR:inClass rdf:resource="#Safe"/>
  </MMR:Value>

  <MMR:Value rdf:ID="currentValue">
    <MMR:val rdf:datatype="\&xsd;positiveInteger">60</MMR:val>
    <MMR:inClass rdf:resource="#UnSafe"/>
    <MMR:isSignificant rdf:datatype="&xsd;boolean">true</MMR:isSignificant>
  </MMR:Value>
  ...
  <MMR:ClassificationComparaison rdf:ID="ClassificationComp">
    <MMR:usedBy rdf:resource="#CRuleCO1"/>
    ...
    <MMR:classChanged rdf:datatype="&xsd;boolean">true</MMR:classChanged>
  </MMR: ClassificationComparaison>
  ...
</rdf:RDF>
```

5 Implementation and Evaluation of the Proposed Approach

In this section we present the prototype implementation and evaluation of the proposed approach. To test our approach, we have launched a set of experimentations using a test bed consists of three parts: sensor nodes, middleware, and the gateway.

We have created set of virtual electrochemical sensors (60 sensors) for gas detection such as CO, NH3, and NO2. These sensors are configured to periodically (after each 1 ms) send data to the implemented middleware. The middleware is intended to perform the data filtering process following the architecture presented in Fig. 1. We have used Java JDK 1.8.0_2 for implementing the prototype. For parsing the semantic documents, the infrastructure Jena 2.12.1 is used. The prototype is tested under Raspbian a lightweight Linux-based OS deployed on Raspberry pi3 model B which has a Quad-core 1.2 GHz Cortex-A53 CPU, 1 GB RAM, and 16 GB SD card.

We performed our experimentations to process sensor data in two cases namely: Without data filtering rules, and with data filtering rules. Two test criteria are considered as follows:

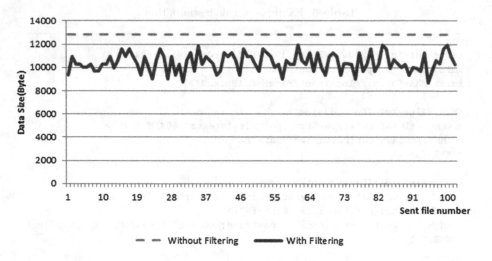

Fig. 5. Result of data size experimentation

– *Data size:* we measure the overall size of data generated in both aforementioned cases. The goal of this test is to identify how much data have been reduced using our rule-based filter module. Reducing the data size implies that our approach contributes at reducing the network traffic between the gateway and the cloud. Figure 5 depicts the size measurement of data to be sent to cloud using the data filter module (filtering) (in solid line) versus the data sending without filtering (in dashed line) where the X-axis represents sending file numbers (this number is incremented after each data file generation) and the Y-axis the size of data file in bytes. This result shows the obtained gain in information size when we use our filter based on rules. In this experiment, we have obtained 2850 KB as a total gap (the difference between the sum of the sizes of the data files) was obtained between the two above mentioned cases after 20 min of execution. This gap of data size increases if

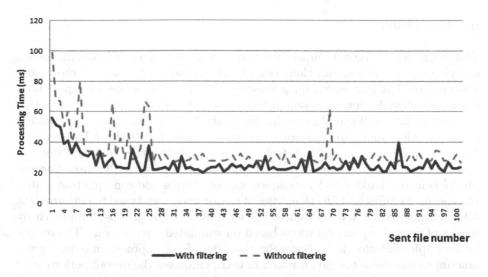

Fig. 6. Result of time consumption experimentation

more sensors are used, i.e. more raw data are generated. Figure 5 depicts the size measurement of data to be sent to cloud using the data filter module (filtering) (in solid line) versus the data sending without filtering (in dashed line) where the X-axis represents sending file numbers (this number is incremented after each data file generation) and the Y-axis the size of data file in bytes. This result shows the obtained gain in information size when we use our filter based on rules. In this experiment, we have obtained 2850 kbytes as a total gap (the difference between the sum of the sizes of the data files) was obtained between the two above mentioned cases after 20 min of execution. This gap of data size increases if more sensors are used, i.e. more raw data are generated.

- *Processing time:* In this category, we evaluate time needed for data filtering process. More specifically, we measure the response time starting from generating the raw data from sensors till receiving a response from the gateway that the data file is ready to send. This category of experimentation has been imposed by the addition of our filtering module. So we seek to identify until when this raw data filtering can influence the total execution time of the data collection. Figure 6 shows the results of these experimentation. The X-axis is, like in the previous test criterion, sent file number while the Y-axis is the time in milliseconds. We notice that the whole time with filtering is, in most cases, better than without filtering. This is explained by the time gained for the data generation process (due to data minimization) recover the time lost in the filtering process.

6   Conclusion

The delegation of the data processing task to the edge of an IoT system enables carrying out intelligent functions close to the sensor sinks such as processing semantic models and undertaking reasoning. In this paper, we have presented our approach which leverages semantic models and rules to enable being selective in sending only significant data to the cloud side. To facilitate sharing and reusing semantic rules among IoT gateways, we have proposed a Platform Independent Model, based on semantic web technologies, to define the rules and domain concepts at the cloud level. While at the gateway level, a Platform Specific Model is instantiated, which encompasses a set of rules and concepts that match the specific features and functionalities of sensor nodes, and used to perform data filtering process. We have evaluated the feasibility of the proposed approach by means of several experimentations based on simulated environment. The results of the implementation have shown the potential of our approach in reducing the amount of data sent the cloud, which in turn, enhances the overall performance of the system, and reduce the cost in terms of resources required to process and store data on the cloud. As future perspective, we plan to enrich our meta-model rule to support other aspects such as security, performance and maintenance. Moreover, we will consider studying the load balancing issue to manage the distribution of edge computing tasks based on resources available at the gateway level.

Acknowledgements. This work is partially supported the Nature Sciences and Engineering Research Council of Canada (NSERC).

References

1. Evans, D.: The internet of things: how the next evolution of the internet is changing everything. CISCO (2015)
2. Manyika, J., Michael, C., Peter, B., Jonathan, W., Richard, D., Jacques, B., Dan, A.: The internet of things: mapping the value beyond the hype. McKinsey Global Institute (2015)
3. Borgia, E.: The internet of things vision: key features, applications and open issues. Comput. Commun. **54**, 1–31 (2014)
4. Dillon, T., Chang, E., Singh, J., Hussain, O.: Semantics of cyber-physical systems. In: Shi, Z., Leake, D., Vadera, S. (eds.) IIP 2012. IAICT, vol. 385, pp. 3–12. Springer, Heidelberg (2012). doi:10.1007/978-3-642-32891-6_3
5. Aggarwal, C.C., Ashish, N., Sheth, A.: The internet of things: a survey from the data-centric perspective. In: Aggarwal, C. (ed.) Managing and Mining Sensor Data. Springer, Boston (2013). doi:10.1007/978-1-4614-6309-2_12
6. Li, P.: Semantic reasoning on the edge of internet of things (2016)
7. Gyrard, A.: An architecture to aggregate heterogeneous and semantic sensed data. In: Cimiano, P., Corcho, O., Presutti, V., Hollink, L., Rudolph, S. (eds.) ESWC 2013. LNCS, vol. 7882, pp. 697–701. Springer, Heidelberg (2013). doi:10.1007/978-3-642-38288-8_54

8. Khan, I., Jafrin, R., Errounda, F.Z., Glitho, R., Crespi, N., Morrow, M., Polakos, P.: A data annotation architecture for semantic applications in virtualized wireless sensor networks. In: 2015 IFIP/IEEE International Symposium on Integrated Network Management (IM), pp. 27–35. IEEE (2015)
9. Compton, M., Barnaghi, P., Bermudez, L., García-Castro, R., Corcho, O., Cox, S., Graybeal, J., Hauswirth, M., Henson, C., Herzog, A., et al.: The SSN ontology of the W3C semantic sensor network incubator group. Web Semant. Sci. Serv. Agents World Wide Web **17**, 25–32 (2012)
10. Buchmayr, M., Kurschl, W., Küng, J.: A rule based approach for mapping sensor data to ontological models in AAL environments. In: Castano, S., Vassiliadis, P., Lakshmanan, L.V., Lee, M.L. (eds.) ER 2012. LNCS, vol. 7518, pp. 3–12. Springer, Heidelberg (2012). doi:10.1007/978-3-642-33999-8_2
11. Tao, M., Ota, K., Dong, M.: Ontology-based data semantic management and application in IoT-and cloud-enabled smart homes. Future Gener. Comput. Syst. **76**, 528–539 (2016)
12. Ian, H., Peter, F.P.S., Harold, B., Said, T., Benjamin, G., Mike, D.: SWRL: a semantic web rule language combining OWL and RuleML. https://www.w3.org/Submission/SWRL/. Accessed 30 October 2010
13. Callan: CO Poison line. http://hazmatcentral.com/. Accessed 30 October 2010
14. Uschold, M., Gruninger, M.: Ontologies: principles, methods and applications. Knowl. Eng. Rev. **11**(02), 93–136 (1996)
15. Ruiz, F., Hilera, J.R.: Using ontologies in software engineering and technology. In: Calero, C., Ruiz, F., Piattini, M. (eds.) Ontologies for Software Engineering and Software Technology. Springer, Heidelberg (2006). doi:10.1007/3-540-34518-3_2
16. Henderson-Sellers, B.: Bridging metamodels and ontologies in software engineering. J. Syst. Softw. **84**(2), 301–313 (2011)
17. Saeki, M., Kaiya, H.: On relationships among models, meta models and ontologies. In: Proceedings of the Proceedings of the 6th OOPSLA Workshop on Domain-Specific Modeling (DSM 2006) (2006)
18. Guizzardi, G.: Ontological foundations for structural conceptual models. CTIT, Centre for Telematics and Information Technology (2005)
19. Fensel, D.: Ontologies: A Silver Bullet for Knowledge Management and Electronic-Commerce. Springer, Heidelberg (2004). doi:10.1007/978-3-662-09083-1

Model-Driven Engineering of an OpenCypher Engine: Using Graph Queries to Compile Graph Queries

József Marton[1]([✉]) [iD], Gábor Szárnyas[2,3] [iD], and Márton Búr[2,3] [iD]

[1] Database Laboratory, Budapest University of Technology and Economics,
Budapest, Hungary
marton@db.bme.hu
[2] Fault Tolerant Systems Research Group,
Budapest University of Technology and Economics, Budapest, Hungary
[3] MTA-BME Lendület Research Group on Cyber-Physical Systems,
Budapest, Hungary
{szarnyas,bur}@mit.bme.hu

Abstract. Graph database systems are increasingly adapted for storing and processing heterogeneous network-like datasets. Many challenging applications with near real-time requirements—such as financial fraud detection, on-the-fly model validation and root cause analysis—can be formalised as graph problems and tackled with graph databases efficiently. However, as no standard graph query language has yet emerged, users are subjected to the possibility of vendor lock-in.

The openCypher group aims to define an open specification for a declarative graph query language. However, creating an openCypher-compatible query engine requires significant research and engineering efforts. Meanwhile, model-driven language workbenches support the creation of domain-specific languages by providing high-level tools to create parsers, editors and compilers. In this paper, we present an approach to build a compiler and optimizer for openCypher using model-driven technologies, which allows developers to define declarative optimization rules.

1 Introduction

Context. Graphs provide an intuitive formalism for modelling real-world scenarios, as the human mind tends to interpret the world in terms of objects (*vertices*) and their respective relationships to one another (*edges*) [30].

The *property graph* data model [33] extends graphs by adding labels/types and properties for vertices and edges. This gives a rich set of features for users to model their specific domain in a natural way. Graph databases are able to store property graphs and query their contents by matching complex graph patterns, which would otherwise be cumbersome to define and/or inefficient to evaluate on traditional relational databases [39].

Neo4j, a popular NoSQL property graph database, offers the Cypher query language to specify graph queries. Cypher is a high-level declarative query language, detached from the query execution plan, which allows the query engine

T. Csöndes et al. (Eds.): SDL 2017, LNCS 10567, pp. 80–98, 2017.
DOI: 10.1007/978-3-319-68015-6_6

to use sophisticated optimisation techniques. The openCypher project [25] aims to deliver an open specification of Cypher.

Problem and Objectives. Even though the openCypher specification was released more than 1.5 years ago, there are very few open implementations available and even those offer limited support for the more advanced language constructs. Besides the novelty of the openCypher specification, the primary reason for the lack of open implementations is the complexity of the language. Even with the artifacts provided by the openCypher project—including the specification, the language grammar and a set of test cases—implementing a compiler is a non-trivial task and requires significant engineering efforts. Our goal is to deliver a reusable compiler that can be extended with transformation rules for query optimisation.

Contributions. In this paper, we use graph queries defined on a cyber-physical system to demonstrate the key challenges in compiling openCypher queries. We present an approach for implementing an openCypher query compiler including a model-based parser generator and a set of model transformation rules built on a modern language workbench based on Eclipse technologies. We released the compiler as part of the open-source ingraph project, where it is used as part of an incremental graph query engine, released under the commercially-friendly Eclipse Public License.[1]

Structure of the Paper. We first introduce the running example in Sect. 2 and the concepts of graph queries and model transformations in Sect. 3. We give an overview of the compiler in Sect. 4 and use example queries to elaborate the details of query compilation in Sect. 5. We discuss related research in Sect. 6 and conclude the paper in Sect. 7.

2 Running Example

To demonstrate our approach, we use a cyber-physical system demonstrator, MoDeS3 [7], which stands for Model-Based Demonstrator for Smart and Safe Systems. It is an educational platform of a model railway system that prevents trains from collision and derailment using runtime verification techniques based on safety monitors. The railway track is instrumented with several sensors, such as *cameras* and *shunt detectors* capable of sensing trains on a particular segment of a track, connected to computing units. In addition to collecting data, these computing units also control the trains to guarantee safe operation. In this paper, we will only introduce a small self-contained fragment of the demonstrator in order to keep the example compact.

---

[1] Available at http://docs.inf.mit.bme.hu/ingraph/.

Figure 1(a) depicts a snapshot of the simplified system in operation, where trains are located at different parts of the railway. The railway network itself consists of two types of railway elements: *segments* and *turnouts*. Segments are selected tracks of the railway network with one entry and exit points individually, they are approximately of same lengths, and they have no intermediate branches between the entry and exit points. As opposed to segments, turnouts allow trains to change tracks. A turnout can either be in *divergent* or *straight* state. A *station* can represent a railway station with an arbitrary purpose, and they can include any number of railway elements.

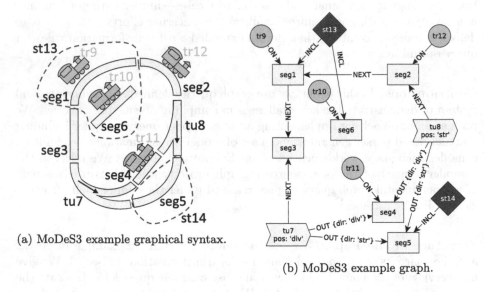

(a) MoDeS3 example graphical syntax.

(b) MoDeS3 example graph.

Fig. 1. The running example.

We introduce the following example *monitoring objectives* that are evaluated continuously by graph queries:

- *Close proximity* identifies trains on consecutive segments with only a limited distance between each other (train **tr9** on **seg1** and **tr12** on **seg2** in the example).
- *Station with free track* monitoring objective finds stations that have at least one free track available (station **st14** in the example).
- *Busy station* identifies stations with at least two trains residing on its corresponding tracks (station **st13** in the example).

3   Preliminaries

In this section, we present the theoretical and practical foundations for compiling openCypher queries. This includes the notion of property graphs, a brief description of the openCypher language and the relational algebraic foundations for formalising graph queries. We also discuss model-driven engineering (MDE) along with the MDE tools used in our work.

3.1 Property Graphs and the OpenCypher Query Language

The *property graph* data model [32] extends typed graphs with properties on the vertices and edges. This data model is used in NoSQL graph database systems such as Neo4j [24], OrientDB [27], SparkSee [36], and Titan [40]. Graph databases provide no or weak metamodeling capabilities. Hence, models can either be stored in a weakly typed manner or the metamodel must be included in the graph (on the same metalevel as the instance model). The property graph of the running example is shown in Fig. 1(b).

Cypher is a high-level declarative graph query language used in the Neo4j graph database [29]. It allows users to specify graph patterns with a syntax resembling an actual graph, which makes the queries easy to comprehend. The goal of the openCypher project [25] is to provide a standardised specification of the Cypher language.

Listing 3.1 shows a query that returns all tr, seg pairs, where a particular train tr is ON a particular segment seg.

```
1 MATCH (tr:Train)-[:ON]->(seg:Segment)
2 RETURN tr, seg
```

Listing 3.1. Example openCypher query.

3.2 Relational Graph Algebra

We gave a formal specification for the core subset of the openCypher language in [23] using relational graph algebra, which extends relational algebra with graph-specific operators. Here, we give a brief summary of the operators in relational graph algebra, which operates on multisets (bags) [15] of tuples, that form *graph relations*. We refer to named elements of a tuple as *attributes*.

Notation. Graph relations, schemas and attributes are typeset in *italic* (r, R, A_1), variable names set in monospace (x1), while labels, types and constants are set in sans-serif (min, l_1, t_k). The NULL value is represented as ε.

Nullary Operators. The *get-vertices* [18] nullary operator $\bigcirc_{(v:l_1 \wedge \ldots \wedge l_n)}$ returns a graph relation of a single attribute v that contains vertices that have *all* of labels $l_1, \ldots, l_n$.

Additionally to our previous work, we introduce *Dual*, which is a relation with no columns and a single (empty) tuple, i.e. $Dual = \{\langle\rangle\}$.[2] The *Dual* relation is

---

[2] The *Dual* relation is inspired by the DUAL table in the Oracle database [6].

the identity element of the Cartesian product and the natural join operators. We also introduce *Singular*, which denotes the empty relation {} and is the zero element of the Cartesian product and the natural join operators.

Unary Operators. The *projection* operator π keeps the specified set of attributes of the relation: $\pi_{A_1,...,A_n}(r)$. The projection operator can also rename attributes, e.g. $\pi_{\text{x1}\rightarrow\text{x2}}(r)$ renames x1 to x2. Note that tuples are not deduplicated, i.e. the result has the same number of tuples as the input relation r.

As relational graph algebra operates on multisets, there is a bespoke operator for removing duplicate tuples. The *duplicate-elimination* operator δ takes a multiset of tuples on its input, performs deduplication and returns a set of tuples.

The *selection* operator σ filters the incoming relation according to some criteria: $\sigma_\theta(r)$, where predicate θ is a propositional formula. The operator selects all tuples in r for which θ holds.

The *expand-out* unary operator $\uparrow \, {}^{(w:l_1 \wedge ... \wedge l_n)}_{(v)} [e : t_1 \vee ... \vee t_k](r)$ adds new attributes e and w to each tuple iff there is an outgoing edge e from v to w, where e has *any* of types $t_1, ..., t_k$, while w has *all* labels $l_1, ..., l_n$. Similarly, the *expand-in* operator $\downarrow$ uses incoming edges, while the *expand-both* operator $\updownarrow$ uses both incoming and outgoing edges. An extended version of this operator, $\uparrow \, {}^{(w)}_{(v)} [e*^{max}_{min}]$ may use any number of hops between min and max.

Binary Operators. The result of the *natural join* operator $\bowtie$ is determined by creating the Cartesian product of the relations, then filtering for those tuples which are equal on the attributes that share a common name. The combined tuples are projected: for input relations r and s (with schemas R and S, respectively), we only keep the attributes in r and drop the ones in s. Hence,

$$r \bowtie s = \pi_{R \cup S} \, \sigma_{(r.A_1=s.A_1 \wedge ... \wedge r.A_n=s.A_n)}(r \times s),$$

where $\{A_1, ..., A_n\} = R \cap S$ is the set of attributes that occur both in R and S.

The *antijoin* operator $\triangleright$ (also known as *left anti semijoin*) collects the tuples from the left relation r that have no matching pair in the right relation s:

$$r \triangleright s = r \setminus \pi_R(r \bowtie s),$$

where π_R denotes a projection operation, which only keeps the attributes of the schema over relation r.

The *left outer join* $\bowtie$ pads tuples from the left relation that did not match any from the right relation with ε values and adds them to the result of the natural join [35].

Table 1 shows a concise set of rules for mapping openCypher expressions to relational graph algebra [23].

3.3   Model-Driven Engineering

Model-driven engineering (MDE) is a development paradigm, used in many areas of software and system engineering, such as designing safety-critical systems.

Table 1. Mapping from openCypher constructs to relational algebra [23]. Variables, labels, types and literals are typeset as «v». The notation (|p|) represents patterns resulting in a relation p, while [|r|] denotes previous query fragment resulting in a relation r. To avoid confusion with the ".." language construct (used for ranges), we use $\cdots$ to denote omitted query fragments.

Language construct	Relational algebra expression
Vertices and patterns. (|p|) denotes a pattern that contains a vertex «v».	
`(«v»:«l1»:…:«ln»)`	$\bigcirc_{(v:l1\wedge\cdots\wedge ln)}$
`(|p|)<-[«e»:«t1»|…|«tk»]->(«w»)`	$\updownarrow^{(w)}_{(v)}[e:t1\vee\cdots\vee tk]\,(p)$, where e is an edge
`(|p|)-[«e»*«min»..«max»]->(«w»)`	$\uparrow^{(w)}_{(v)}[e*^{max}_{min}]\,(p)$, where e is a list of edges
Combining and filtering pattern matches	
`MATCH (|p1|), (|p2|), …`	$\neq_{\text{edges of } p1,\ p2,\ …}(p1\bowtie p2\bowtie\cdots)$
`MATCH (|p1|)` `MATCH (|p2|)`	$\neq_{\text{edges of } p1}(p1)\bowtie\neq_{\text{edges of } p2}(p2)$
`OPTIONAL MATCH (|p|) WHERE (|condition|)`	$Dual\ ⟕_{condition}\ \neq_{\text{edges of } p}(p)$
`[r] OPTIONAL MATCH (|p|)`	$\neq_{\text{edges of } r}(r)\ ⟕\ \neq_{\text{edges of } p}(p)$
`[r] WHERE «condition»`	$\sigma_{condition}(r)$
`[r] WHERE (|p|)`	$r\bowtie p$
Result and subresult operations. Rules for `RETURN` also apply to `WITH`.	
`[r] RETURN «x1» AS «y1», …`	$\pi_{x1\to y1,…}(r)$
`[r] RETURN «x1», «aggr»(«x2»)`	$\gamma^{x1}_{x1,aggr(x2)}(r)$
`[r] WITH «x1»` `[s] RETURN «x2»`	$\pi_{x2}\Big(\big(\pi_{x1}(r)\big)\bowtie s\Big)$

MDE focuses on creating and analyzing models at different levels of abstraction during the engineering process. *Model transformations* are used to process models, e.g. to convert models between different modeling languages and to generate code.

Domain-Specific Languages. While there are some extensible formalisms intended as a general-purpose way of representing models (such as UML), industrial practice often prefers domain-specific languages (DSLs) for describing modeling languages instead. These can be designed and modified to the needs of application domains and actual design processes. On the other hand, developing such a DSL (and providing tool support) is an expensive task.

The Eclipse Modeling Framework (EMF) is a domain-specific modeling technology, built on the Eclipse platform. A DSL development process with EMF starts with the definition of a metamodel, from which several components of the modeling tool can be automatically derived. The metamodel is defined in Ecore, the metamodeling language of EMF [37].

Language Workbenches. Model-driven language workbenches [13] support the creation of domain-specific languages by providing high-level tools to create parsers, editors and compilers. Xtext [14] is an EMF-based framework for development of programming languages and DSLs. Xtend is a general-purpose programming language (implemented with an Xtext-based parser), which is transpiled to Java source code. Xcore [12] is an extended textual syntax for Ecore and provides an Xtext-based language for defining EMF metamodels.

Model Transformations. VIATRA [43] is an open-source Eclipse project written in Java and Xtend [11]. VIATRA builds on the Eclipse Modeling Framework and provides the following main features:

- The VIATRA Query Language, a declarative language for writing queries over models, which are evaluated once or incrementally upon each model change.
- An internal domain-specific language over the Xtend language to specify both batch and event-driven, reactive transformations.
- A rule-based design space exploration framework [17] to explore design candidates with transformation rules where the design candidates must satisfy multiple criteria.

4   Overview of the Approach

The high-level workflow of our openCypher query engine is shown in Fig. 2. A domain expert first formulates the *query* using the openCypher language, which serves as the input for our engine. The query is then parsed and transformed into the *query syntax graph* using the openCypher grammar (created by the Slizaa project[3]). It is then compiled to our relational graph algebra model. This produces a canonical relational graph algebra representation to keep compiler code simple. The relational graph algebra representation is modified by the relational algebra optimizer. The resulting relational algebra model is then passed on to the query execution engine.

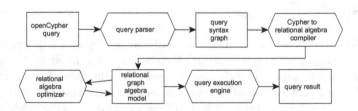

Fig. 2. Workflow of the query engine: compiler and execution engine.

---

[3] https://github.com/slizaa/slizaa-opencypher-xtext, released under EPL v1.0.

Relational Graph Algebra Metamodel. The metamodel of the relational graph algebra operators introduced in Sect. 3.2 is shown in Fig. 3. An openCypher query is represented by a *rooted tree* having nullary operators as its leaves and unary or binary operators as its non-leaf nodes.

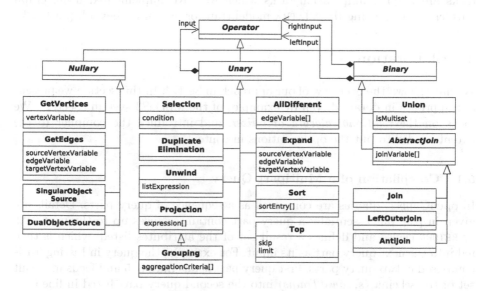

Fig. 3. Operator metamodel of the relational graph algebra.

Nullary operators. The GetVertices and GetEdges operators retrieve vertices and edges of the graph, respectively. SingularObjectSource and DualObjectSource emit the *Singular* and the *Dual* relation, respectively.

Unary operators. Projection and Selection work as given in Sect. 3.2. Exact semantics of the other unary operators are given in [23]. DuplicateElimination, Grouping, Sort and Top operators work like their corresponding SQL clauses.[4] Expand is a graph-specific operation to traverse one or a sequence of edges from a source to a given target vertex, while AllDifferent is specific to openCypher's edge uniqueness semantics. The Unwind operator is the inverse of the list-constructing collect() aggregation function.

Binary operators. The Union operator creates the set or multiset union of its inputs. Join, LeftOuterJoin and AntiJoin operators, based on the joinVariable list declared in AbtractJoin creates the natural join, antijoin and left outer join operations on their inputs, respectively, as given in Sect. 3.2.

---

[4] In the order of appearance: DISTINCT, GROUP BY, ORDER BY and SKIP ... LIMIT ....

Relational Algebra Optimizer. The relational algebra optimizer has two main tasks. It removes idempotent operations from the relational graph algebra model and identifies combinations of operations that could be expressed using advanced operations. The relational graph algebra model is also a graph, so both of these tasks are graph manipulation tasks which we have implemented using graph pattern matches using the VIATRA model transformation framework (Sect. 3.3).

5   Elaboration

We have shown the overview of our approach in Sect. 4. In this section we present our approach in detail, driven by examples of the MoDeS3 system (Sect. 2). We focus on the *relational algebra optimizer*, and introduce the compiler to the extent needed to put the optimizations in context.

5.1   Compilation of a Multipart Query

In openCypher, queries are composed as a sequence of query parts. Details are given in [23], but essentially a query part contains clauses up to the next WITH or RETURN clause and defines a result set of the attributes listed, which is then fed into the next query part as its input. For example, the query in Listing 5.1 is composed of two query parts: first query part spans lines 3–5 and feeds its result set of the schema $\langle s, countTrains \rangle$ into the second query part listed in line 6.

Variable chaining refers to the fact that attributes of the resulting schema are available in the subsequent query part, i.e. s and countTrains are available.

```
1 // identifies stations with at least two trains residing on its
2 // corresponding tracks
3 MATCH (s:Station)-[:INCL]->(:Element)<-[:ON]-(tr:Train)
4 WITH s, count(tr) AS countTrains
5 WHERE countTrains >= 2
6 RETURN s
```

Listing 5.1. Busy station.

Compilation of each query part starts from the *Dual* relation. Each pattern given in a MATCH clause is then compiled and joined to the previous patterns: for MATCH clauses we use the natural join operator and for OPTIONAL MATCH, we use left outer join. Possible projection, grouping and duplicate-elimination operators are appended above as required by the WITH or RETURN clauses.

Query parts are compiled one by one and combined together using the natural join operator as follows. The natural join is injected into the compiled form of the current query part just below the possible projection, grouping and duplicate-elimination operators populating its right input with the descendants. Its left input is the compiled form of the query parts processed so far.

Each query part that begins with a non-optional MATCH clause, like the first query part in Listing 5.1 is joined with *Dual*. As the second query part has no patterns, its inputs are the first query part's result set and the *Dual* relation. The raw compiled form of this query is shown in Fig. 4(a), which contains two joins having *Dual*, its identity operand as one of its operands. Thus these natural join operations along with *Dual* should be removed, which we implemented using a VIATRA graph transformation rule (see Sect. 5.4). Applying this transformation, we get the simplified form shown in Fig. 4(b).

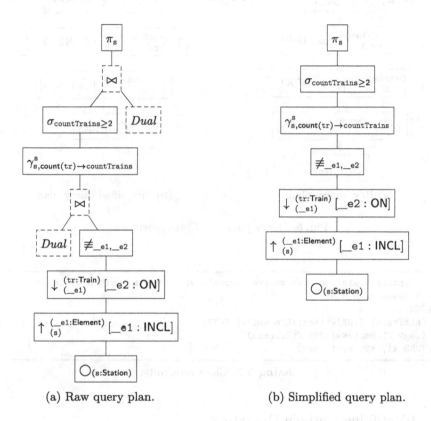

(a) Raw query plan.   (b) Simplified query plan.

Fig. 4. Query plans for *Busy station*.

5.2 Compilation of Variable Length Path Patterns

The query in Listing 5.2 features a variable length path pattern stating that two segments, seg1 and seg2 are connected through one to two edges of type NEXT. A variable length path pattern is compiled to an expand-both operator given in Sect. 3.2. The raw compiled form of this query is shown in Fig. 5(a), which is simplified to Fig. 5(b) using the transformation rule described in Sect. 5.1 to remove a join having *Dual* on one of its inputs.

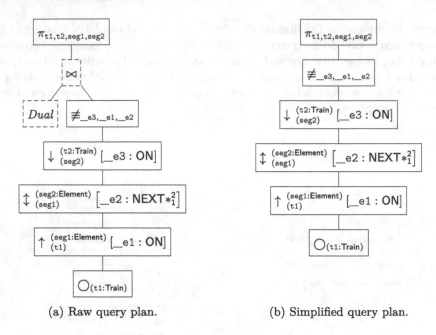

(a) Raw query plan.   (b) Simplified query plan.

Fig. 5. Query plans for *Close proximity*.

```
1  // identify trains on consecutive segments with only a limited distance
2  // between each other
3  MATCH
4    (t1:Train)-[:ON]->(seg1:Element)-[:NEXT*1..2]-
5    (seg2:Element)<-[:ON]-(t2:Train)
6  RETURN t1, t2, seg1, seg2
```

Listing 5.2. Close proximity.

5.3 Identifying Antijoin Operators

The query in Listing 5.3 uses negative pattern match on line 4 to express that track element **re** does not have a train on it. This is essentially an antijoin operation. In order to keep compiler simple, the query is compiled in the raw form to the left outer join of the two pattern matches and a negated selection stating that edge and vertex variables of the pattern condition are all non-null ($\neq \varepsilon$). We highlighted the corresponding operator nodes with dotted lines in the raw compiled form of this query, shown in Fig. 6(a). These are transformed by an other VIATRA rule to the antijoin operator, also highlighted using dotted lines in Fig. 6(b).

```
1  // monitoring objective finds stations that have at least one free track
2  // available
3  MATCH (s:Station)-[:INCL]->(re:Element)
4  WHERE NOT (re)<-[:ON]-(:Train)
5  RETURN DISTINCT s
```

Listing 5.3. Station with free track.

The simplification of this query again shows the removal of an unused join (in dashed lines). The dash-dotted box in Fig. 6(a) shows the all-different operator which states that the listed edge variables match unique edges. This is specified by openCypher's edge uniqueness semantics. As a single edge is always unique, we added another transformation rule to remove this operator from the tree.

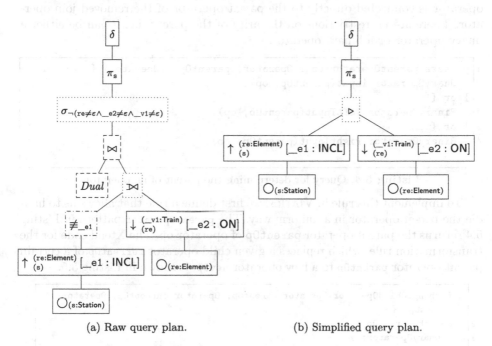

(a) Raw query plan.   (b) Simplified query plan.

Fig. 6. Query plans for *Station with free track*.

5.4   Formalisation as Graph Transformation Rules

Based on the previous examples, we introduce generic transformation rules for query optimization.

Removing Unnecessary Joins. Figure 7 shows the transformation rule for detecting and removing unnecessary join operators. It looks for *natural join* operators that have a *Dual* operator on one of their inputs and another child

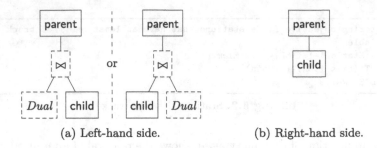

(a) Left-hand side.   (b) Right-hand side.

Fig. 7. Transformation for removing unnecessary join operators.

operator on their other inputs. If a match is found, it is removed and the child operator is connected directly to the parent operator of the removed join operator. There are no restrictions on the arity of the parent, i.e. it can be either a unary operator or a binary operator.

```
1  pattern parentOperator(op : Operator, parentOp : Operator) {
2    UnaryOperator.input(parentOp, op);
3  } or {
4    BinaryOperator.leftInput(parentOp, op);
5  } or {
6    BinaryOperator.rightInput(parentOp, op);
7  }
```

Listing 5.4. Query for determining the parent of an operator.

To implement this rule in VIATRA, we first define a rule that allows us to handle the parent operator in a uniform way. The parentOperator pattern in Listing 5.4 returns the parent operator parentOp of operator op. The Xtend code for the transformation rule, which replaces a given child operator currentOp of a certain parent operator parentOp to a new operator newOp, is shown in Listing 5.5.

```
1  def changeChildOperator(Operator parentOp, Operator currentOp, Operator
      newOp) {
2    switch parentOp {
3      UnaryOperator:
4        parentOp.input = newOp
5      BinaryOperator: {
6        if (parentOp.getLeftInput.equals(currentOp))
7          parentOp.leftInput = newOp
8        if (parentOp.getRightInput.equals(currentOp))
9          parentOp.rightInput = newOp
10     }
11   }
12 }
```

Listing 5.5. Change child operator.

```
1  pattern unnecessaryJoin(childOp: Operator, joinOp: JoinOperator, parentOp:
       Operator) {
2    find parentOperator(joinOp, parentOp);
3    DualObjectSourceOperator(dualOp);
4    JoinOperator.leftInput(joinOp, dualOp);
5    JoinOperator.rightInput(joinOp, childOp);
6  } or {
7    find parentOperator(joinOp, parentOp);
8    DualObjectSourceOperator(dualOp);
9    JoinOperator.leftInput(joinOp, childOp);
10   JoinOperator.rightInput(joinOp, dualOp);
11 }
```

Listing 5.6. Determine unnecessary joins. The `parentOperator` pattern is defined in Listing 5.4.

```
1  def removeUnnecessaryJoinOperator() {
2    createRule()
3      .precondition(UnnecessaryJoinMatcher.querySpecification)
4      .action [
5        changeChildOperator(parentOp, joinOp, otherInputOp)
6      ].build
7  }
```

Listing 5.7. Rule for removing unnecessary joins.

The `unnecessaryJoin` pattern in Listing 5.6 uses the `parentOperator` rule to find the parent operator of a certain join operator, checks whether there is a DualObjectSource operator on either the left or the right input of the join operator. The VIATRA transformation rule for removing unnecessary joins is shown in Listing 5.7.

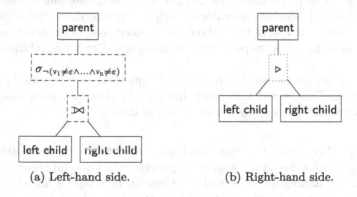

(a) Left-hand side.   (b) Right-hand side.

Fig. 8. Transformation for introducing antijoin operators.

Introducing Antijoins. In order to evaluate negative conditions efficiently, the optimizer tries to introduce *antijoin* operators where possible. Figure 8 shows the transformation rule for detecting antijoins. The rule looks for *left outer join* operators that:

- have a *selection* operator as their parent, which defines a condition that is satisfied iff $\neg (v_1 \neq \varepsilon \wedge \ldots \wedge v_n \neq \varepsilon)$ and
- $v_1, \ldots, v_n$ are the variables of the right input of the left outer join operator (see Sect. 5.3).

If there is a match, the *left outer join* operator is replaced by a single antijoin operator (shown in dotted lines) and the selection operator is removed.

6   Related Work

6.1   Graph Query Languages

As graph queries are increasingly used in industry, graph query languages are available across different technological spaces. Here, we discuss related query languages and compilers.

Property Graphs. The Cypher language was originally designed as the primary query language of the Neo4j graph database system [24,29]. The grammar specification and the language behaviour of openCypher was defined to match those of Neo4j. Consequently, the compiler and query engine of Neo4j form the most complete openCypher implementation available, and is dual licensed (GPLv3/AGPLv3 for compatible projects and custom licensing for commercial applications).

The authors of [18] studied the Cypher query language and defined graph-specific relational algebra operators, such as get-vertices and expand-out (Sect. 3.2). While their work focused on optimisation, our work aims to provide a mapping and compilation steps for transforming openCypher to relational graph algebra.

In [19], graph queries were defined in a Cypher-like language and evaluated in the Apache Flink-based GRADOOP framework. However, formalisation and compilation of the queries was not discussed in detail.

TinkerPop. The TinkerPop framework aims to define a standard data model for property graphs. For graph queries, it provides the Gremlin Structure API, a low-level programming interface and the Gremlin language, a high-level imperative graph traversal language [31]. The latter is implemented as a Groovy DSL [20].

EMF. Eclipse Modeling Framework (Sect. 3.3) is an object-oriented modelling framework widely used in model-driven engineering. Henshin [3] provides a visual language for defining patterns, while Epsilon [21] and VIATRA Query [5] provide high-level declarative (textual) query languages, the Epsilon Pattern Language and the VIATRA Query Language (Sect. 3.3), respectively. VIATRA Query supports both incremental and search-based queries [9].

RDF. Widely used in semantic technologies, SPARQL is a standardised declarative graph pattern language for querying RDF [47] graphs. SPARQL bears close similarity to Cypher queries, but targets a different data model and requires users to specify the query as triples instead of graph vertices/edges. A formal definition of the language is given in [28]. Apache Jena ARQ [2] and Eclipse RDF4J [10] are open-source compilers and query engines for the SPARQL language.

Comparing Graph Query Engines. The Train Benchmark is a framework for comparing graph query frameworks across different technological spaces, such as property graphs, EMF, RDF and SQL [39].

6.2   Query Compilation in Graph Transformation Systems

The authors of [8] adapted the Rete algorithm originally developed in the domain of production rule systems for pattern matching in a GT engine. The presented solution supported a simple core graph pattern language.

The Fujaba [26] graph transformation tool fixes a single, breadth-first traversal strategy at compile-time, using simple heuristics, e.g. that navigation along an edge with an at most one multiplicity constraint precedes navigations along edges with arbitrary multiplicity. PROGRES [34] uses a sophisticated cost model for basic operations and generates the search plan at compile-time by a greedy algorithm.

An algorithm to produce a high-quality (e.g. compact) Rete network from a pattern specification was proposed in [44]. Paper [45] presented an algorithm to define efficient search plans on EMF models. These approaches are used in the eMoflon system [22]. The approach of [46] uses both metamodel- and instance model-level information to adaptively optimize graph queries based on statistical data collected from the current instance model. GrGen.NET provides a dynamic, runtime optimization engine, which uses a mix of heuristical and cost-based techniques [16].

The first VIATRA prototype, which was capable of generating Prolog code from metamodels and model transformations defined in XMI (XML Metadata Interchange) format, was presented in [42].

The INCQUERY-D [38] system is an incremental graph query engine, built on top of the components of the VIATRA Query framework [43] (later known as EMF-INCQUERY [41]). INCQUERY-D reused the query parser and compiler of EMF-INCQUERY, but used a different query engine, tailored for scalable distributed query evaluation and operating on RDF data sets.

7   Conclusion and Future Work

In this paper, we presented an approach to design and implement a query engine for the openCypher graph query language. We implemented this approach based on a language workbench built on EMF-based technologies, such as Xcore, Xtext, Xtend and VIATRA. The resulting prototype is part of the ingraph project, an openCypher-compatible incremental graph query engine.

In the future, we plan to enhance a query optimizer. A possible approach is to use *search-based optimization techniques using model transformations*, also known as *planning by rewriting* [1]. As our solution already utilizes the VIA-TRA query engine, the optimizer can be based on the VIATRA-DSE design-space exploration framework [17] without a significant integration overhead. Another feasible approach is to use Catalyst, a state-of-the-art extensible optimizer framework developed as part of the Apache Spark SQL project [4].

Acknowledgements. The second and third authors of this work were partially supported by the MTA-BME Lendület Research Group on Cyber-Physical Systems. We would like to thank János Maginecz and Dávid Szakállas for their contributions to the relational graph algebra model. We are also grateful to András Vörös and Gábor Bergmann for their suggestions and comments on the draft of this paper.

References

1. Ambite, J.L., Knoblock, C.A.: Planning by rewriting. J. Artif. Intell. Res. **15**, 207–261 (2001)
2. Apache Software Foundation. Apache Jena. https://jena.apache.org/
3. Arendt, T., Biermann, E., Jurack, S., Krause, C., Taentzer, G.: Henshin: advanced concepts and tools for in-place EMF model transformations. In: Petriu, D.C., Rouquette, N., Haugen, Ø. (eds.) MODELS 2010. LNCS, vol. 6394, pp. 121–135. Springer, Heidelberg (2010). doi:10.1007/978-3-642-16145-2_9
4. Armbrust, M., et al.: Spark SQL: relational data processing in Spark. In: SIGMOD, pp. 1383–1394 (2015)
5. Bergmann, G., Horváth, Á., Ráth, I., Varró, D., Balogh, A., Balogh, Z., Ökrös, A.: Incremental evaluation of model queries over EMF models. In: Petriu, D.C., Rouquette, N., Haugen, Ø. (eds.) MODELS 2010. LNCS, vol. 6394, pp. 76–90. Springer, Heidelberg (2010). doi:10.1007/978-3-642-16145-2_6
6. Bryla, B., Loney, K.: Oracle Database 12C The Complete Reference, 1st edn. McGraw-Hill Osborne Media, USA (2013)
7. Budapest University of Technology and Economics, Department of Measurement and Information Systems. Model-based Demonstrator for Smart and Safe Systems (2015). https://modes3.inf.mit.bme.hu/
8. Bunke, H., Glauser, T., Tran, T.-H.: An efficient implementation of graph grammars based on the RETE matching algorithm. In: Ehrig, H., Kreowski, H.-J., Rozenberg, G. (eds.) Graph Grammars 1990. LNCS, vol. 532, pp. 174–189. Springer, Heidelberg (1991). doi:10.1007/BFb0017389
9. Búr, M., Ujhelyi, Z., Horváth, Á., Varró, D.: Local search-based pattern matching features in EMF-INCQUERY. In: Parisi-Presicce, F., Westfechtel, B. (eds.) ICGT 2015. LNCS, vol. 9151, pp. 275–282. Springer, Cham (2015). doi:10.1007/978-3-319-21145-9_18

10. Eclipse Foundation. RDF4J. http://rdf4j.org/
11. Eclipse Foundation. Xtend - Modernized Java. https://www.eclipse.org/xtend/
12. Eclipse Foundation. Xcore (2017). http://wiki.eclipse.org/Xcore
13. Erdweg, S., et al.: The state of the art in language workbenches - conclusions from the language workbench challenge. In: Erwig, M., Paige, R.F., Wyk, E. (eds.) SLE 2013. LNCS, vol. 8225, pp. 197–217. Springer, Cham (2013). doi:10.1007/978-3-319-02654-1_11
14. Eysholdt, M., Behrens, H.: Xtext: implement your language faster than the quick and dirty way. In: SIGPLAN, SPLASH/OOPSLA, pp. 307–309 (2010)
15. Garcia-Molina, H., Ullman, J.D., Widom, J.: Database Systems - The Complete Book, 2nd edn. Pearson Education, London (2009)
16. Geiß, R., Batz, G.V., Grund, D., Hack, S., Szalkowski, A.: GrGen: a fast SPO-based graph rewriting tool. In: Corradini, A., Ehrig, H., Montanari, U., Ribeiro, L., Rozenberg, G. (eds.) ICGT 2006. LNCS, vol. 4178, pp. 383–397. Springer, Heidelberg (2006). doi:10.1007/11841883_27
17. Hegedüs, Á., Horváth, Á., Varró, D.: A model-driven framework for guided design space exploration. Autom. Softw. Eng. **22**(3), 399–436 (2015)
18. Hölsch, J., Grossniklaus, M.: An algebra and equivalences to transform graph patterns in Neo4j. In: GraphQ at EDBT/ICDT (2016)
19. Junghanns, M., et al.: Cypher-based graph pattern matching in Gradoop. In: GRADES at SIGMOD (2017)
20. Koenig, D., Glover, A., King, P., Laforge, G., Skeet, J.: Groovy in Action. Manning Publications Co., Greenwich (2007)
21. Kolovos, D.S., Paige, R.F., Polack, F.A.C.: The epsilon transformation language. In: Vallecillo, A., Gray, J., Pierantonio, A. (eds.) ICMT 2008. LNCS, vol. 5063, pp. 46–60. Springer, Heidelberg (2008). doi:10.1007/978-3-540-69927-9_4
22. Leblebici, E., Anjorin, A., Schürr, A.: Developing eMoflon with eMoflon. In: Ruscio, D., Varró, D. (eds.) ICMT 2014. LNCS, vol. 8568, pp. 138–145. Springer, Cham (2014). doi:10.1007/978-3-319-08789-4_10
23. Marton, J., Szárnyas, G., Varró, D.: Formalising openCypher graph queries in relational algebra. In: Martite, K., Kjetil, N., George, A.P. (eds.) Advances in Databases and Information Systems: 21st European Conference on Advances in Databases and Information Systems. Conference location and date: Nicosia, Ciprus, 2017-09-24-2017-09-27. LNCS. Springer (2017). http://dx.doi.org/10.1007/978-3-319-66917-5_13. ISBN: 978-3-319-66916-8
24. Neo Technology. Neo4j. http://neo4j.org/
25. Neo Technology. openCypher project (2017). http://www.opencypher.org/
26. Nickel, U., Niere, J., Zündorf, A.: The FUJABA environment. In: ICSE, pp. 742–745. ACM (2000)
27. OrientDB LTD. OrientDB graph-document NoSQL DBMS. http://www.orientdb.org/
28. Pérez, J., et al.: Semantics and complexity of SPARQL. ACM TODS **34**(3), 16 (2009)
29. Robinson, I., Webber, J., Eifrém, E.: Graph Databases, 2nd edn. O'Reilly Media, Sebastopol (2015)
30. Rodriguez, M.A.: A collectively generated model of the world. In: Collective Intelligence: Creating a Prosperous World at Peace, pp. 261–264 (2008)
31. Rodriguez, M.A.: The Gremlin graph traversal machine and language (invited talk). In: DBPL, pp. 1–10 (2015)
32. Rodriguez, M.A., Neubauer, P.: Constructions from dots and lines. Bull. Am. Soc. Inform. Sci. Technol. **36**(6), 35–41 (2010)

33. Rodriguez, M.A., Neubauer, P.: The graph traversal pattern. In: Graph Data Management: Techniques and Applications, pp. 29–46 (2011)
34. Schürr, A., et al.: Handbook of graph grammars and computing by graph transformation, pp. 487–550. World Scientific Publishing Co., Inc. (1999)
35. Silberschatz, A., Korth, H.F., Sudarshan, S.: Database System Concepts, 5th edn. McGraw-Hill Book Company, Boston (2005)
36. Sparsity-technologies. Sparksee high-performance graph database. http://www.sparsity-technologies.com/
37. Steinberg, D., Budinsky, F., Paternostro, M., Merks, E.: EMF: Eclipse Modeling Framework 2.0, 2nd edn. Addison-Wesley Professional, Amsterdam (2009)
38. Szárnyas, G., Izsó, B., Ráth, I., Harmath, D., Bergmann, G., Varró, D.: IncQuery-D: a distributed incremental model query framework in the cloud. In: Dingel, J., Schulte, W., Ramos, I., Abrahão, S., Insfran, E. (eds.) MODELS 2014. LNCS, vol. 8767, pp. 653–669. Springer, Cham (2014). doi:10.1007/978-3-319-11653-2_40
39. Szárnyas, G., et al.: The Train Benchmark: Cross-technology performance evaluation of continuous model validation. Softw. Syst. Model. (2017). https://link.springer.com/article/10.1007/s10270-016-0571-8
40. ThinkAurelius. Titan. https://github.com/thinkaurelius/titan
41. Ujhelyi, Z., et al.: EMF-IncQuery: an integrated development environment for live model queries. Sci. Comput. Program. **98**, 80–99 (2015)
42. Varró, D.: Automated program generation for and by model transformation systems. In: AGT, pp. 161–174 (2002)
43. Varró, D., et al.: Road to a reactive and incremental model transformation platform: three generations of the VIATRA framework. Softw. Syst. Model. **15**(3), 609–629 (2016)
44. Varró, G., Deckwerth, F.: A rete network construction algorithm for incremental pattern matching. In: Duddy, K., Kappel, G. (eds.) ICMT 2013. LNCS, vol. 7909, pp. 125–140. Springer, Heidelberg (2013). doi:10.1007/978-3-642-38883-5_13
45. Varró, G., et al.: An algorithm for generating model-sensitive search plans for pattern matching on EMF models. Softw. Syst. Model. **14**(2), 597–621 (2015)
46. Varró, G., Friedl, K., Varró, D.: Adaptive graph pattern matching for model transformations using model-sensitive search plans. Electron. Notes Theor. Comput. Sci. **152**, 191–205 (2006)
47. W3C. Resource Description Framework (2014). https://www.w3.org/RDF/

A Model-Driven Process Enactment Approach for Network Service Design

Sadaf Mustafiz[1], Navid Nazarzadeoghaz[1], Guillaume Dupont[1],
Ferhat Khendek[1(✉)], and Maria Toeroe[2]

[1] ECE, Concordia University, Montreal, Canada
{sadaf.mustafiz,ferhat.khendek}@concordia.ca,
{n_nazarz,gdupont}@encs.concordia.ca
[2] Ericsson Inc., Montreal, Canada
maria.toeroe@ericsson.com

Abstract. The development of the Network Functions Virtualisation (NFV) paradigm has made way for the rapid deployment and management of network services. The European Telecommunications Standards Institute (ETSI) has been actively defining the NFV framework, which includes functional blocks and artifacts at different levels of abstraction. As part of the artifacts, various deployment templates have been defined to drive the deployment and the management of network services (NS) and Virtual Networks Functions (VNFs). The design of an NS is a complex activity that aims at selecting appropriate VNFs, creating the VNF forwarding graph (VNFFG), and all the necessary templates for the NS deployment and management, on the basis of the tenant's requirements and existing VNFs. Automating the NS design activity as well as the NS management process itself is highly desirable and beneficial for NFV systems. Continuous deployment for NFV with model-driven orchestration means has been recently advocated.

In this paper, we propose a model-driven process for the design of network services which covers the automatic generation of the NS deployment template and the associated templates. The core of the process involves the decomposition of the NS requirements with the help of an ontology, and the selection of proper network functions based on a catalogue of existing VNFs. Moreover, we provide support for automated process execution with a model-driven process enactment approach. The process is modelled as a UML activity diagram. All the artifacts are models of defined metamodels. Enactment of the NS design process is carried out by mapping the process model to a model transformation chain, and executing the chain.

1 Introduction

Network Functions Virtualisation (NFV) is an emerging paradigm that builds on cloud computing and the virtualisation technology to eliminate the drawbacks of traditional physical network infrastructure and enables rapid provisioning of network services (NSs) [11,18]. The use of NFV reduces capital and operating

© Springer International Publishing AG 2017
T. Csöndes et al. (Eds.): SDL 2017, LNCS 10567, pp. 99–118, 2017.
DOI: 10.1007/978-3-319-68015-6_7

expenses, since it does not require a wide range of network equipments to be deployed. The physical devices are remodelled into virtual entities implemented as software packages, referred to as Virtual Network Functions (VNFs) [18].

The NFV reference architectural framework standardized by ETSI [18] and adopted by TOSCA [29], defines various functional blocks playing different roles in the different phases of NS and VNF lifecycle management, from on-boarding to deployment and management. The ETSI standard specifies the NFV reference framework, its functional blocks, their roles, their interfaces, and some NS and VNF-related operational flows [17–19]. An NS and VNF deployment and management process is implied from these, however the workflow as such is not defined. Previously, we have proposed a model-based process for network service design and deployment [28]. The proposed workflow is compliant with the NFV reference framework. We had also proposed the network service design activity (which is outside the scope of the standard) as part of the process. NS design entails the generation of new NS deployment templates, namely NS Descriptors (NSD [17]), based on the tenant's NS requirements and the provider's VNF catalogue [19]. Network service requirements (NSReq) consist of functional and non-functional characteristics of a service requested by a tenant. Examples of NSs being requested include VoLTE or VoIP, for instance, with some specific non-functional characteristics.

This workflow is a first step towards the necessary automation of the NS design and deployment process for NFV systems. Automating NS management, in other words, automating the execution of the workflow or process for NS management without manual intervention is highly desirable in the NFV domain and remains a major challenge [10,27]. The application of model-driven engineering (MDE) methods and tools is essential to further such developments in the NFV domain [6]. MDE advocates the use of models as first class citizens in the engineering process. The models are manipulated with model transformations which form the backbone for automation in MDE. ETSI has recently released an information model for NFV [21]. Leveraging these models can substantially benefit the NFV systems by reducing their development and management efforts. Moreover, explicit modelling of the process not only allows the automation of the NS management process but also paves the way for streamlining or optimizing the process to ultimately speed up deployment time. Such a process model (PM) can potentially be mapped to model transformation chains hence enabling NS management and orchestration via model-driven process enactment [5,15,34].

We propose an approach for model-driven enactment of the NS design, deployment and management process. In this paper, we focus on applying our approach to the NS design activity only. We model the internal behavior of the NS design activity by outlining a set of actions that need to be taken to come up with a deployment template for network services (NSD). The enactment of the NS design process allows for automatic generation of the NSD. We adapt the Papyrus [14] environment to provide tool support for process enactment.

This paper is structured as follows: Sect. 2 gives a brief background on the NFV reference framework and the NFV artifacts. Section 3 proposes a process model for NS design. Section 4 presents our enactment approach. In Sect. 5, we review the related work. Finally, Sect. 6 concludes with some future work.

2   Background

This section provides a brief introduction to network services and some of the artifacts and functional blocks in the NFV reference architecture as proposed in the ETSI standard [16–18].

As stated in [17], a *network service (NS)* is a composition of network functions (NF) arranged as a set of functions with unspecified connectivity between them or according to one or more forwarding graphs. ETSI defines the NF forwarding graph as a graph of logical links connecting NF nodes for the purpose of describing traffic flow between these network functions [16]. It is essentially the end-to-end sequence of NFs that packets traverse. *Virtualised Network Functions (VNFs)* are the building blocks of an NS in NFV. VNFs are software pieces which may have the same functionality as their corresponding physical network functions, *e.g.*, a virtual firewall (vFW) *vs.* a traditional firewall device. A VNF can be composed of multiple internal components (VNFC). The description of the deployment behaviour along with the non-functional characteristics of a VNFC is defined as a Virtual Deployment Unit (VDU) [16]. *Virtual links* (VLs) are used to connect VNFs to form a network topology. These are referred to as external VLs, whereas internal VLs are the links which connect VNFCs within a VNF. A *Connection Point* (CP) is the port that an NF exposes to connect to another NF component via VLs (similar to the ports in a physical network module, such as a switch). The connection point for an NS to link to the environment is defined as a *Service Access Point* (SAP), every *VNF Forwarding Graph* (VNFFG) is associated with one or more pool(s) of connection points (CpPool). The sequence of connection points inside a VNFFG is referred to as the *Network Forwarding Path* (NFP) which is required when different traffic flows exist.

During the lifetime of an NS, various artifacts at various levels of abstractions are used and produced. The deployment templates, referred to as **descriptors**, describe the deployment requirements, operational behaviour, and policies required by the NSs or VNFs. ETSI defines the Network Service Descriptor (NSD) as a deployment template which consists of information used by the NFV Orchestrator (NFVO) for lifecycle management of an NS [17]. Descriptors also exist for VNFs (VNFD) VLs (VLD), and VNFFGs (VNFFGD) among others. The constituent elements of an NSD are shown are Fig. 1.

Catalogues are defined in the NFV architecture which are part of the NFV data repositories. The **NS Catalogue** contains all the on-boarded NSDs, VNF-FGDs, and VLDs. The **VNF Catalogue** contains all the on-boarded VNFDs.

Nested NS and Physical Network Functions (PNF) are outside the scope of this paper. In our process, the artifacts are all considered to be models (instances which conform to existing meta-models).

The main functional module in the architecture is the NFV Management and Orchestration (NFV-MANO), which is in charge of deployment, management,

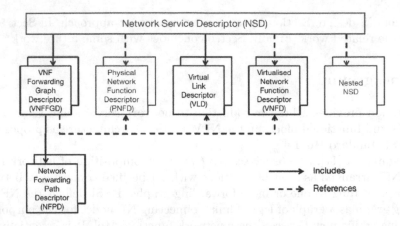

Fig. 1. NSD Overview (from ETSI NFV IFA014 [17])

and orchestration of NSs. The NS orchestration and lifecycle management which include onboarding and instantiation of NS is taken care of by the NFV Orchestrator (NFVO). NFV-MANO also includes managers which are responsible for the VNFs and the infrastructure, namely VNFM and VIM. Operations Support Systems and Business Support Systems (OSS/BSS) refer to the operator's proprietary systems and management applications supporting their business. The OSS/BSS systems exchange a lot of information with NFV-MANO functional blocks to provide the desired network service. For details on all the functional blocks in the NFV framework, the reader can refer to [18].

3   Network Service Design

The NS design entails the definition of deployment templates (namely NSD, VNFFGD, and VLD). These descriptors include static information elements related to an NS. The NSD is used by the orchestrator as a template for instantiating the NS.

We propose a method for NS design by taking inspiration from [1]. A tenant may request a new NS by specifying the NS Requirements (NSReq), which consist of functional and non-functional requirements possibly with some initial decomposition targeting specific functions. There is a big gap between the information provided by the tenant and the network service to be deployed. The tenant has limited knowledge regarding the details of this target network service, and hence this gap needs to be filled. The knowledge to help in filling this gap comes from the various architectures and standards existing in the telecommunications and network service domain. It is essential for this knowledge to be captured and retained for use later when a new network service is required. In our approach, we propose to define and retain this knowledge in a Network Function Ontology (NF Ontology). With each new NS design, information about new architectures and functionalities is gained and this is used to enrich the ontology.

NFOntology captures standard network function (de)compositions as defined by different standardisation bodies such as 3GPP as well as knowledge and experience from previous decompositions, architectures and network service designers.

In our work, we assume that the OSS/BSS of an NFV provider gets the NSReq and generates the NSD based on the provider's VNF Catalogue. The NS design method involves the decomposition of the NSReq and the selection of proper network functions, e.g., VNFs (and/or PNFs) from the VNF Catalogue. The NSReq decomposition is guided by a NFOntology. The NFOntology captures the decomposition of network functionalities to some level of granularity where each functionality can be mapped onto some VNF provided functionality. When the decomposition reaches that level, VNFs from the VNF Catalogue are matched and selected to compose the network service. During this activity, the VNF forwarding graph descriptor (VNFFGD) and the virtual link descriptors (VLD) are also generated. The design phase also takes into account the non-functional requirements and refines the NSD accordingly by adding deployment flavours and associating VNF profiles to the NS. *It should be noted that our NS design method does not address the concept of nested NS as yet.*

3.1   NS Design Languages

As part of our process, we propose languages for modelling the NSReq and the NFOntology which are required inputs for the process. We also define a VNF Catalogue metamodel for modelling a catalogue containing VNF packages (defined by ETSI in [21]).

NSReq and NFOntology. We have defined an abstract syntax as well as a concrete syntax for the NSReq and NFOntology languages.

The NSReq contains the hierarchy of requirements for a network service according to the needs of the tenant. The metamodel of the NSReq language is shown in Fig. 2. As shown in the figure, an NSReq consists of the main functional requirement which is the highest level functionality of the network service. Each functional requirement (identified with an unique name in FunctionalRequirement) can be decomposed into lower-level functional requirements, and this builds a hierarchy of NS requirements. A functional requirement can be associated with various non-functional requirements (Non-FunctionalRequirement), such as availability, reliability, and throughput.

The proposed NFOntology language for NFV is an extended variant of a feature diagram [24]. The metamodel is shown in Fig. 3. The ontology language has two main components: Functionalities and Architectural Blocks. The *Functionality* part of the Ontology is modelled as a variant of a feature diagram. The *ArchitecturalBlock* part has specific syntax and semantics in addition. Essentially, the NFOntology is a hierarchy of (unique) functionalities in the network service domain where a functionality can have zero to many decompositions. As in feature diagrams, decomposition relationships between a functionality and lower-level functionalities can be categorized as: *mandatory, optional, alternative*, and *OR*. A functionality can be dependent on another functionality.

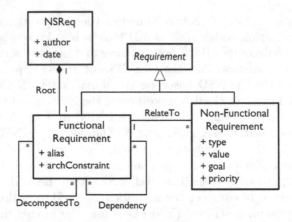

Fig. 2. NS requirements metamodel

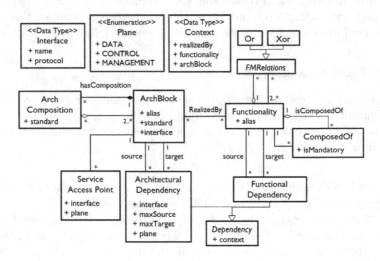

Fig. 3. Network function ontology metamodel

The architecture defines possible ways of realizing the functionalities with established architectures for network services. The architectural blocks in the ontology are unique blocks detailing specific architectural designs with well-defined interfaces and protocols. Dependency relationships may exist between architectural blocks. On the basis of the functionality and the architectural blocks, a good decomposition of the network service requirements can be achieved. For example, VoIP service is an essential NS nowadays. While capturing the details required to create such a service can be quite difficult, having such architectures like IMS (IP Multimedia Subsystem) to cover most of the requirements for providing VoIP can be very helpful. IMS has a well known architecture and well known functional components. There is a high possibility of finding VNFs which have been developed for implementing such architectures. IMS blocks include components such as P/S/I-CSCF, HSS, AS. Adding them to the ontology allows new NS designs (e.g., VoIP service) to reuse these components.

VNFD and NSD (Part of the ETSI Defined Information Model). The VNFCatalogue includes Onboarded VNF Packages (OnboardedVngPkgInfo as defined in [21]) which includes references to VNF deployment templates (VNFD). The metamodel is trivial and is not shown here for space reasons. The VNFD and NSD metamodels, as well as the metamodels of the other descriptors (VLD, VNFFGD, SAPD), are defined by ETSI and are available in [21]. For clarity, simplified VNFD and NSD metamodels are shown in Figs. 4 and 5 which present the main elements in the descriptors.

3.2 NS Design Process

The high-level NS design and deployment Process Model (PM) was presented in [28], in which the NS design was shown as a black-box activity. In this paper, we refine the process and model its behaviour with a UML 2.0 Activity Diagram. The NS Design PM is shown in Fig. 6.

During the process, we make use of an intermediate model, namely SolutionMap which conforms to the SolutionMap metamodel (not shown here

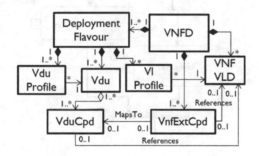

Fig. 4. Simplified VNFD metamodel (adapted from ETSI NFV IFA015 [21])

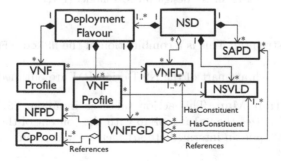

Fig. 5. Simplified NSD metamodel (adapted from ETSI NFV IFA015 [21])

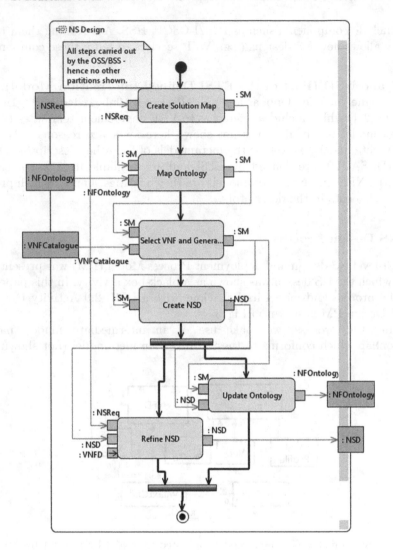

Fig. 6. NS design process model (PM)

due to space constraints). This is a combination of the NSReq, NFOntology, and VNFD metamodels.

The actions which are part of the NS Design PM are outlined here.

- **Create Solution Map.** This action takes as input an NSReq model (see Fig. 7) and initializes the SolutionMap with the content of the source model. The SolutionMap is an intermediate artifact created to aid in the NSD generation process.
- **Map Ontology.** This action takes as input the SolutionMap model created in the first step and an existing NFOntology model (see Fig. 8). For each functionality in the SolutionMap, the ontology is traversed to find any existing

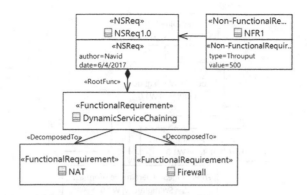

Fig. 7. NSReq model

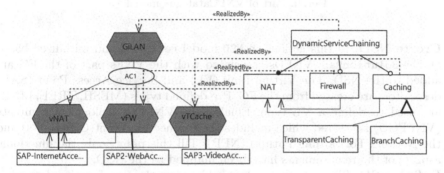

Fig. 8. NFOntology model

knowledge about its composition and dependencies. When a match is found in the ontology, all the details not available in the SolutionMap are added, including the architectural blocks and their dependencies. Unmatched functionalities, architectural blocks, and dependency relationships are tagged in the SolutionMap, and may be used to enrich the ontology later.

– **Select VNF and Generate FG.** This action takes as input the refined SolutionMap and the VNFCatalogue (see Fig. 9). With the SolutionMap as a guide, a proper set of VNFs is selected for creating the NS. The functionalities of the VNFs found in the catalogue are matched with the architectural blocks and the functionalities in the SolutionMap. The VNFD (see Fig. 10) of each of the selected VNFs are added to the SolutionMap. Next, the proper combination of a set of functionalities is derived, leading to the combination of a set of architectural blocks, and ultimately to the combination of a set of VNFs which fulfill the NS requirements. For this purpose, an initial forwarding graph (FG) is created which contains the VNFDs, their sequence, and the details of the interfaces and service access points (SAP). This FG contains only dependencies but no real virtual links. The created FG becomes part of the refined SolutionMap.

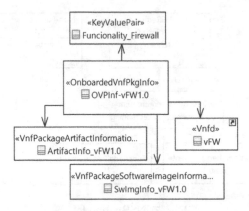

Fig. 9. Part of VNFCatalogue model

- **Create NSD.** In this action, an NSD model is created and initialized based on the `SolutionMap`. VNFDs associated with the VNFs part of the FG are added to the NSD. The Virtual Link (VL) and Service Access Point (SAP) descriptors are created from the FG. Pre-defined types (MESH, TREE, LINE) are used to define a VL type. Finally, the VNFFG deployment template (VNFFGD) is created which includes the Connection Point(CP) pool(s) and the Network Forwarding Path(s) (NFP). Till this point, only the functional aspects of the requirements have been mapped to the NSD.
- **Refine NSD.** This action involves addressing the non-functional requirements in the `NSReq` and adding to the NSD the relevant details, such as the deployment flavours and the VNF Profiles. The non-functional requirements are available in the `SolutionMap` and so it is used as input here. The other input is the `VNFDs` for the VNFs selected from the `VNFCatalogue` earlier in the process (see Fig. 10). NS-specific VNF Profiles are defined for the VNFDs at this stage. This step completes the NSD generation process. This NSD (see Fig. 11) then can be sent to the NFVO for onboarding.
- **Update Ontology.** Once an NSD has been successfully generated, the ontology is enriched if applicable. If the `NSReq` includes functionalities and/or their decompositions which do not exist in the ontology yet, i.e. those that were marked as unmatched, these elements are added to the `NFOntology` as new functionalities based on the `SolutionMap`.
- **Set Thresholds.** This action involves creating initial threshold models, `NSCapacityThreshold` and `NSPerformanceThreshold`, based on the `SolutionMap` to define the capacity and performance related thresholds of an NS.

Each action in the PM is mapped to a model transformation written in the ATL transformation language.

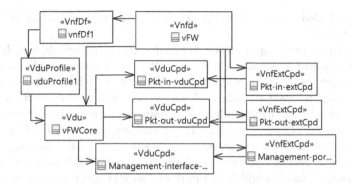

Fig. 10. VNFD model of a firewall

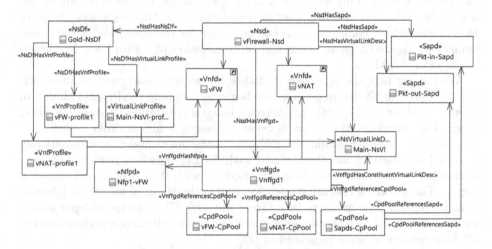

Fig. 11. Generated NSD model

4   Process Enactment

In this section, we present our approach for model-driven enactment of the NS design process. Our goal is to provide tool support for process execution by integrating enactment means with the Papyrus Activity Diagram environment leading to an integrated environment for process modelling and enactment.

4.1   Enactment Approach

In our approach, process enactment is carried out with the use of transformation chain orchestration in combination with model management means. Transformation chaining is the preferred technique for modelling the orchestration of different model transformations [8]. Orchestration languages are used for the composition of the transformations in order to model the chain as sequential steps of transformations. Complex chains can incorporate conditional branches

and loops, and also can model composite chains (a chain including other transformation chains).

Model management approaches typically use megamodels which provide
structures to avoid the so-called 'meta-muddle' [7]. A megamodel contains artifacts (which are models), relations between them (which may be transformations), and other relevant metadata. A megamodel can be seen as a map to find
and link together all involved models. A megamodel forms a repository of models
and transformations (and even tools). It can be used to enforce conformance and
compatibility checks between the various models and transformations. It is also
useful for reusing and composing transformations in transformation chains. The
input and output models which are part of the PM are typed by metamodels
residing in the megamodel. The transformation models that are associated with
the actions in the PM are also known in the megamodel. In case of a transformation chain with a heterogeneous set of transformations, the megamodel helps in
determining which transformation engine to use for the execution of the transformation. Figure 12 shows the visual representation of a simplified NS design
megamodel (MgM).

We present here the approach we follow for process enactment to automatically execute the NS design process. We begin by mapping the Process Model (in
essence a subset of the UML 2.0 Activity Diagram) to a model transformation
chain. The transformation chain is generated using a higher order transformation [36] in a manner similar to [26]. An initial megamodel is automatically
derived from the PM and then refined with further details if required. Orchestration of the transformation chain is carried out with the use of an orchestration
engine. The workflow execution engine executes the chain of model transformations to generate the artifacts (the target models). The enactment approach is
outlined in Fig. 13. We intend to apply the method to ultimately orchestrate the
NS Management process presented in [28].

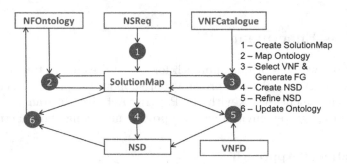

Fig. 12. NS design megamodel

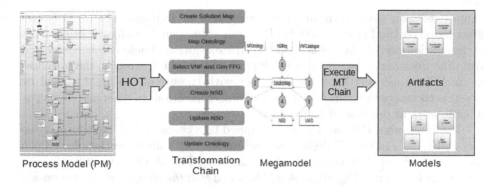

Fig. 13. Process enactment approach

4.2 Tool Support in Papyrus

We use Papyrus for both process modelling and enactment. Papyrus is NFV's tool of choice. The NFV information model [21] released uses Papyrus as the modelling tool. We have extended the activity diagram environment in Papyrus to incorporate enactment means. The activity diagram contextual menu was adapted to include the *Enactment* option as shown in Fig. 14. The user has the option of choosing the transformation chain to execute (via run configurations) or the default chain gets executed.

The execution is carried out in the backend with a workflow execution engine. We use MoDISCO [9] for orchestrating the transformation chain. MoDISCO is a framework for model-driven reverse engineering which supports transformation

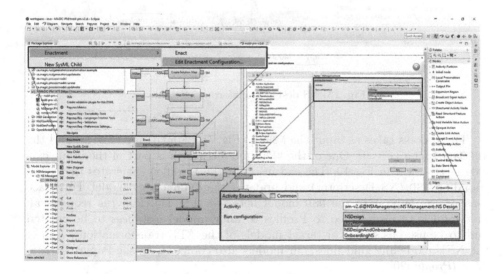

Fig. 14. Papyrus process enactment environment

chain execution along with automated discovery of artifacts. The MgM is created based on the Papyrus Activity Diagram. The launch configurations for the orchestration need to be defined prior to the execution. These can be generated from the information available in the PM and the MgM. Currently, the workflow is an ATL transformation chain. However with the use of the MgM, it will be possible to support execution of a chain of transformations in different languages. This is work in progress at the moment.

The NS Design PM (see Fig. 6) is mapped to a chain of ATL transformations (see in Fig. 15). In the NS design case, all underlying transformations have been modelled with the ATL transformation language. The MoDisco workflow for the NS design is shown in Fig. 16. *It should be noted that the chain and the megamodel does not include the transformation for initializing the threshold models (Set Threshold action in PM), which is currently work in progress.*

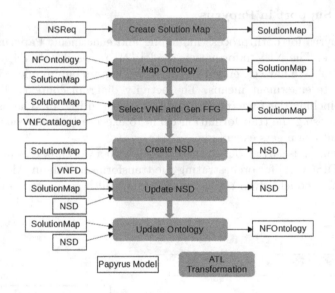

Fig. 15. NS design transformation chain

The process takes as input the NSReq (Fig. 7), NFOntology (Fig. 8), and the VNFCatalogue (Fig. 9). One of the VNFD models which is part of the input catalogue is shown in Fig. 10. The execution of the workflow generates the corresponding NSD (NS Descriptor) and updates the NFOntology model. For space reasons, we only show the NSD model here (see Fig. 11). Papyrus requires all metamodels to be mapped to Profiles to allow model instances to be created and to be used as source or target models of the ATL transformations. As per the NFV modelling guidelines, our models also comply with the Papyrus *Open-ModelProfile* [20].

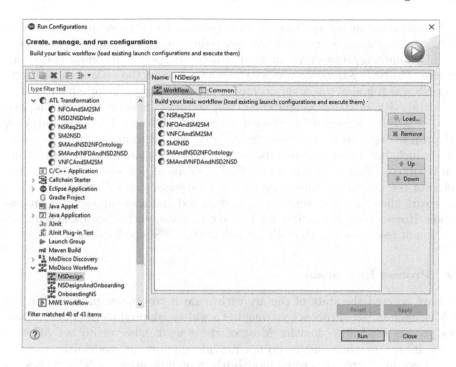

Fig. 16. NS design chain in MoDisco

5   Related Work

5.1   NS Design

While there exists work in the literature on service composition and decompositions, the notion of decomposing network service requirements for NFV systems has not been proposed to the best of our knowledge. We discuss here some related work on requirements and service (de)composition. Czarnecki et al. [13] presents an approach for carrying out staged configuration using specialization and multi-level configurations of cardinality-based feature models. At an abstract level, this is similar in concept to our NS requirements decomposition method. However, their work is applicable for feature models only and the decomposition technique is not automated. Web service composition is an area where extensive work has been done on decompositions of goals and functionalities [12,32,33]. These approaches however mostly deploy formal methods and are not model-driven in nature like our work.

Lin et al. [25] propose using an ontology as part of a requirements management process to capture design knowledge to help in concurrent engineering. Bartsch et al. [4] handles a component service replacement problem in the IT service domain with the help of ontologies. They do not address decomposition of user requirements.

As mentioned earlier, our work takes inspiration from the method proposed in [1]. In a similar manner, we carry out user requirements decomposition with the help of an ontology. However, our approach caters specifically towards network services. The NSD generation needs to take into account the various constituents of an NS which makes this a very complex method applicable for NFV systems.

In the NFV domain, Sahhaf et al. [35] consider different service compositions, i.e., VNFs arranged in different ways with different VNFFGs and VLs, and propose algorithms to select the optimal composition according to some criteria including resource demands, quality-of-service, and available infrastructure resources. This work focuses on VNF placement while our concern is the design of the network service. The *Oracle Communications Design Studio* [31] framework allows network services to be designed and also supports NS orchestration. However, the NS design requires to create various framework-specific NS constituent resources and they do not follow the ETSI specifications.

5.2 Process Enactment

We have covered the state of the art with regards to process modelling in the NFV domain in [28]. Process enactment is a widely adopted method in the business process modelling domain. Most of these work however do not follow a model-driven approach and/or do not provide support for model-driven enactment. Berezin [6] promotes using model-driven orchestration for NFV orchestration and talks about why this is a more robust method than business process workflows. BPMN-like workflows are in general implementations of specific task-oriented cases which are appropriate for immutable business processes as stated in [6]. In software defined environments which evolve rapidly, such workflows bring about difficulties and risks.

There has been a lot of work on megamodelling [2,7], transformation chaining [15,30,34,38], and a combination of both [23,37] in the MDE community. A few MDE-based continuous integration and deployment methods and tools have been proposed with cloud applications as the target domain [3,22]. While model-based approaches exist in the NFV domain [10,29], the application of such advanced MDE techniques is minimal for NFV systems.

6 Conclusion

The two main contributions of this paper are the following: (1) a high-level process for creating network service deployment templates (referred to as NSD by ETSI) based on requirements from the tenant, and (2) an integrated environment for automatically generating the NSD using model-driven process enactment means.

The process for NS design proposes the use of a network function ontology to decompose the NS requirements and to select appropriate VNFs for the NS (from a VNF catalogue or repository). Based on this decomposition and selection, deployment templates (NSD, VNFFGD, and VLD) are generated. The generation of the descriptors after the receipt of a tenant's requirements is automated using a model-driven enactment approach. The process is modelled in Papyrus as a UML 2.0 Activity Diagram, and can be automatically executed within Papyrus by orchestrating the workflow. The Process Model is mapped to a chain of ATL transformations for this purpose. As part of the process, several domain-specific languages have been proposed to model the associated artifacts: NS Requirements (NSReq), Network Function Ontology (NFOntology), and VNF Catalogue. We have built modelling environments in Papyrus that allow users to create model instances. The NFV descriptors (NSD, VNF-FGD, and VLD) have meta-models defined by ETSI [21]. In our process, the generated models conform to the ETSI-defined meta-models.

This work sets the basis for the enactment of the entire NS design, deployment and management process. Each activity in the NS life-cycle involves a complex chain of tasks. We are currently working on modelling the internals of the other activities, such as *NS Instantiation* and *VNF Instantiation*, and writing model transformations. The entire Process Model can then be mapped on to a composite chain of transformations along with an extended mega-model to allow for automated deployment and management of network services.

As future work, we intend to extend our transformation chain orchestration means to support different transformation languages (such as QVT). Moreover, we plan on integrating further model management techniques (using the mega-model) with process enactment. This will allow us to enforce conformance and compatibility checks between the various models and transformations, and will also aid in providing end-to-end traceability support.

Acknowledgment. This work is partly funded by NSERC and Ericsson, and carried out within NSERC/Ericsson Industrial Research Chair in Model Based Software Management.

References

1. Abbasipour, M., Sackmann, M., Khendek, F., Toeroe, M.: A model-based approach for user requirements decomposition and component selection. In: Bouabana-Tebibel, T., Rubin, S.H. (eds.) Formalisms for Reuse and Systems Integration. AISC, vol. 346, pp. 173–202. Springer, Cham (2015). doi:10.1007/978-3-319-16577-6_8
2. Allilaire, F., Bézivin, J., Brunelière, H., Jouault, F.: Global Model Management in Eclipse GMT/AM3. In: Eclipse Technology eXchange Workshop (eTX) - A ECOOP 2006 Satellite Event. Nantes, France, July 2006
3. Artač, M., Borovšak, T., Di Nitto, E., Guerriero, M., Tamburri, D.A.: Model-driven continuous deployment for quality DevOps. In: Proceedings of the 2nd International Workshop on Quality-Aware DevOps. QUDOS 2016, pp. 40–41. ACM (2016)
4. Bartsch, C., Shwartz, L., Ward, C., Grabarnik, G., Buco, M.J.: Decomposition of IT service processes and alternative service identification using ontologies. In: NOMS 2008–2008 IEEE Network Operations and Management Symposium, pp. 714–717, April 2008

5. Basciani, F., Ruscio, D., Iovino, L., Pierantonio, A.: Automated chaining of model transformations with incompatible metamodels. In: Dingel, J., Schulte, W., Ramos, I., Abrahão, S., Insfran, E. (eds.) MODELS 2014. LNCS, vol. 8767, pp. 602–618. Springer, Cham (2014). doi:10.1007/978-3-319-11653-2_37

6. Berezin, A.: Utilizing Declarative Model-Driven TOSCA Orchestration for NFV. DZone, March 2017. https://dzone.com/articles/utilizing-declarative-model-driven-tosca-orchestration-for-nfv

7. Bézivin, J., Jouault, F., Rosenthal, P., Valduriez, P.: Modeling in the large and modeling in the small. In: Aßmann, U., Aksit, M., Rensink, A. (eds.) MDAFA 2003-2004. LNCS, vol. 3599, pp. 33–46. Springer, Heidelberg (2005). doi:10.1007/11538097_3

8. Brambilla, M., Cabot, J., Wimmer, M.: Model-Driven Software Engineering in Practice, 1st edn. Morgan & Claypool Publishers, San Rafael (2012)

9. Brunelière, H., Cabot, J., Dupé, G., Madiot, F.: MoDisco: a model driven reverse engineering framework. Inf. Softw. Technol. 56(8), 1012–1032 (2014)

10. Chen, Y., Qin, Y., Lambe, M., Chu, W.: Realizing network function virtualization management and orchestration with model-based open architecture. In: 11th International Conference on Network and Service Management (CNSM 2015), pp. 410–418. IEEE (2015)

11. Chiosi, M., Clarke, D., Willis, P., Reid, A., Feger, J., Bugenhagen, M., Khan, W., Fargano, M., Cui, C., Deng, H., et al.: Network functions virtualisation: an introduction, benefits, enablers, challenges and call for action. In: SDN and OpenFlow World Congress, pp. 22–24 (2012)

12. Chung, L., Ma, W., Cooper, K.: Requirements elicitation through model-driven evaluation of software components. In: Fifth International Conference on Commercial-off-the-Shelf (COTS)-Based Software Systems, pp. 1–10. IEEE (2006)

13. Czarnecki, K., Helsen, S., Eisenecker, U.W.: Staged configuration through specialization and multilevel configuration of feature models. Software Process Improv. Pract. 10(2), 143–169 (2005)

14. Papyrus, 16 June 2017. https://eclipse.org/papyrus/

15. Etien, A., Aranega, V., Blanc, X., Paige, R.F.: Chaining model transformations. In: Proceedings of the 1st Workshop on the Analysis of Model Transformations. AMT 2012, pp. 9–14. ACM (2012)

16. ETSI: Network Functions Virtualisation (NFV); Terminology for Main Concepts in NFV: ETSI GS NFV 003 V1.2.1, December 2014

17. ETSI: Network Functions Virtualisation; Management and Orchestration; Network Service Templates Specification: ETSI GS NFV-IFA 014 V2.1.1, October 2016

18. ETSI: Network Functions Virtualisation; Management and Orchestration; Report on Architectural Options: ETSI GS NFV-IFA 009 V1.1.1, July 2016

19. ETSI: Network Functions Virtualisation; Management and Orchestration; VNF Packaging Specification: ETSI GS NFV-IFA 011 V2.1.1, October 2016

20. ETSI: Network Functions Virtualisation (NFV) Release 2; Information Modeling; Papyrus Guidelines: ETSI GR NFV-IFA 016 V2.1.1, March 2017

21. ETSI: Network Functions Virtualisation (NFV) Release 2; Management and Orchestration; Report on NFV Information Model: ETSI GR NFV-IFA 015 V2.1.1, January 2017

22. Ferry, N., Song, H., Rossini, A., Chauvel, F., Solberg, A.: CloudMF: applying MDE to tame the complexity of managing multi-cloud applications. In: 2014 IEEE/ACM 7th International Conference on Utility and Cloud Computing, pp. 269–277, December 2014

23. Fritzsche, M., Gilani, W.: Model transformation chains and model management for end-to-end performance decision support. In: Fernandes, J.M., Lämmel, R., Visser, J., Saraiva, J. (eds.) GTTSE 2009. LNCS, vol. 6491, pp. 345–363. Springer, Heidelberg (2011). doi:10.1007/978-3-642-18023-1_9

24. Kang, K.C., Cohen, S.G., Hess, J.A., Novak, W.E., Peterson, A.S.: Feature-Oriented Domain Analysis (FODA) Feasibility Study. Technical report CMU/SEI-90-TR-021, SEI, arnegie Mellon University, November 1990

25. Lin, J., Fox, M.S., Bilgic, T.: A requirement ontology for engineering design. Concurrent Eng. **4**(3), 279–291 (1996)

26. Lúcio, L., Mustafiz, S., Denil, J., Vangheluwe, H., Jukss, M.: FTG+PM: an integrated framework for investigating model transformation chains. In: Khendek, F., Toeroe, M., Gherbi, A., Reed, R. (eds.) SDL 2013. LNCS, vol. 7916, pp. 182–202. Springer, Heidelberg (2013). doi:10.1007/978-3-642-38911-5_11

27. Mijumbi, R., Serrat, J., Gorricho, J.L., Latre, S., Charalambides, M., Lopez, D.: Management and orchestration challenges in network functions virtualization. IEEE Commun. Mag. **54**(1), 98–105 (2016)

28. Mustafiz, S., Palma, F., Khendek, F., Toeroe, M.: A network service design and deployment process for NFV systems. In: IEEE NCA16: The 15th IEEE International Symposium on Network Computing and Applications, pp. 131–139. IEEE, October 2016

29. OASIS: TOSCA Simple Profile for Network Functions Virtualization (NFV) Version 1.0, March 2016. http://docs.oasis-open.org/tosca/tosca-nfv/v1.0/tosca-nfv-v1.0.html

30. Oldevik, J.: Transformation composition modelling framework. In: Kutvonen, L., Alonistioti, N. (eds.) DAIS 2005. LNCS, vol. 3543, pp. 108–114. Springer, Heidelberg (2005). doi:10.1007/11498094_10

31. Oracle: Oracle Communications Network Service Orchestration Solution Implementation Guide, Release 1.1. White Paper, July 2016. https://docs.oracle.com/cd/E71075_01/doc.11/e65331/toc.htm

32. Oster, Z.J., Santhanam, G.R., Basu, S.: Decomposing the service composition problem. In: 8th IEEE European Conference on Web Services, pp. 163–170, December 2010

33. Oster, Z.J., Santhanam, G.R., Basu, S.: Identifying optimal composite services by decomposing the service composition problem. In: IEEE International Conference on Web Services. ICWS 2011, pp. 267–274. IEEE Computer Society (2011)

34. Rivera, J.E., Ruiz-Gonzalez, D., Lopez-Romero, F., Bautista, J., Vallecillo, A.: Orchestrating ATL model transformations. In: Proceedings of MtATL 2009, pp. 34–46. Nantes, France, July 2009

35. Sahhaf, S., Tavernier, W., Colle, D., Pickavet, M.: Network service chaining with efficient network function mapping based on service decompositions. In: 1st IEEE Conference on Network Softwarization (NetSoft), pp. 1–5, April 2015

36. Tisi, M., Jouault, F., Fraternali, P., Ceri, S., Bézivin, J.: On the use of higher-order model transformations. In: Paige, R.F., Hartman, A., Rensink, A. (eds.) ECMDA-FA 2009. LNCS, vol. 5562, pp. 18–33. Springer, Heidelberg (2009). doi:10.1007/978-3-642-02674-4_3

37. Vanhooff, B., Ayed, D., Baelen, S., Joosen, W., Berbers, Y.: UniTI: a unified transformation infrastructure. In: Engels, G., Opdyke, B., Schmidt, D.C., Weil, F. (eds.) MODELS 2007. LNCS, vol. 4735, pp. 31–45. Springer, Heidelberg (2007). doi:10.1007/978-3-540-75209-7_3
38. Wagelaar, D.: Blackbox composition of model transformations using domain-specific modelling languages. In: 1st European Workshop on Composition of Model Transformations (CMT), pp. 15–19 (2006)

Model-Based Regression Testing
of Autonomous Robots

Dávid Honfi, Gábor Molnár, Zoltán Micskei$^{(\boxtimes)}$, and István Majzik

Department of Measurement and Information Systems,
Budapest University of Technology and Economics, Budapest, Hungary
{honfi,micskei,majzik}@mit.bme.hu

Abstract. Testing is a common technique to assess quality of systems. Regression testing comes into view, when changes are introduced to the system under test and re-running all tests is not practical. Numerous techniques have been introduced to select tests only relevant to a given set of changes. These are typically based on source code, however, model-based development projects use models as primary artifacts described in various domain-specific languages. Thus, regression test selection should be performed directly on these models. We present a method and a case study on how model-based regression testing can be achieved in the context of autonomous robots. The method uses information from several domain-specific languages for modeling the robot's context and configuration. Our approach is implemented in a prototype tool, and its scalability is evaluated on models from the case study.

1 Introduction

Nowadays quality is a crucial aspect of software systems development. The employment of different verification and validation techniques is a possible way of achieving higher quality. One of the most commonly used techniques is testing, which intends to evaluate whether the behavior of the system under test meets its requirements. As the system develops, changes are introduced, which may require re-testing functions of the system. In these cases regression testing could be used as a solution.

Regression testing is the "selective re-testing of a system or component to verify that modifications have not caused unintended effects and that the system or component still complies with its specified requirements" [22]. Regression testing can be performed on any testing level (i.e., module, integration, etc.), and it can cover both functional and non-functional requirements. Re-running every test after each modification is resource and time-consuming. Thus a trade-off must be made between the confidence gained from regression testing and resources used. For this reason, several techniques were proposed over the years, particularly to select only a subset of the test suite, what is relevant for the current change, or to identify those new parts of the system, which are not covered by existing tests. To discuss test selection and identification, in this paper we use the categorization of tests introduced by Leung and White [26]:

© Springer International Publishing AG 2017
T. Csöndes et al. (Eds.): SDL 2017, LNCS 10567, pp. 119–135, 2017.
DOI: 10.1007/978-3-319-68015-6_8

- *Re-usable* tests that exercise unmodified parts of the system.
- *Re-testable* tests that are changed or are able to cover changed parts in the system.
- *Obsolete* tests that cannot be used anymore due to changed specification or system structure.
- *New structure* tests that contribute to the overall coverage of the current, new system structure.
- *New specification* tests that verify new elements in the current specification.

Three common approaches exist for regression testing. *Test Prioritization* [27, 37] is usually applied, when the total execution time of tests is not relevant, however discoverable errors shall be highlighted as soon as possible. When using *Test Suite Minimization (TSM)* [20, 24] or *Regression Test Selection (RTS)* [21, 35] the goal is to reduce the number of executed tests, especially when re-testing the whole system requires significant amount of time. Moreover, RTS uses optimization for selecting the minimal subset of these tests that have maximal test coverage with a minimal associated execution cost. Our paper focuses on RTS, which uses the actual changes as an input to identify *re-testable* tests.

One testing criteria of RTS is reaching the maximal coverage possible. In the domain of RTS for source code, numerous approaches have been presented that define various coverage metrics: code executed by tests [1], dynamic slicing [2], graph-based representation [21]. Several tools exist implementing RTS for source code. For example, SoDA [40] is a tool for C/C++ repositories, while ChOPSJ [38] is available for code written in Java.

In the past decade, the increasing adoption of models as development artifacts led to the birth of a new approach called *Model-Driven Development* (MDD). MDD is "a development paradigm that uses models as the primary artifact of the development process" [7]. These models are commonly composed using *domain-specific languages* (DSL). DSLs are special languages for a particular problem domain. The model artifacts describe the system itself and could also serve as inputs for the testing process. As MDD is conducted in an incremental manner, model artifacts – similarly to the source code – tend to change in time. The changes in the model artifacts influence the system functions and properties (as models drive the synthesis of software, hardware, configuration, parameterization etc. of the system), this way these changes can be used to trigger re-testing the influenced parts of the system. In an MDD setting, having the relation between (changed) model artifacts and system parts, regression test selection can be applied on model level rather than on the generated code.

We encountered this situation in the context of the *Reconfigurable ROS-based Resilient Reasoning Robotic Cooperating Systems* (R5-COP) project[1]. The project worked with several industrial demonstrators: autonomous robots that need to be re-tested after reconfigurations due to changes in their functionality or their components. We developed a model-based approach that uses several domain-specific languages to model the capabilities of the robots and their tests

---

[1] http://www.r5-cop.eu.

contexts, and created an RTS model to represent the artifacts of the regression testing domain, among others the tests, testables, and coverage relations. The specific input models and artifacts as well test elements (e.g., test cases, test setups) can be mapped to this representation, and the test classification and regression test selection algorithms can be implemented uniformly on the basis of this model. The approach was implemented in a prototype tool using the Eclipse framework and its various modeling components.

The rest of the paper is structured as follows. Section 2 details the autonomous robot case study. Section 3 presents the approach that was developed to support regression test selection. Section 4 presents the implementation of the approach in a prototype tool. Section 5 evaluates the scalability of the approach and the implemented tool.

2   Presentation of the Case Study

An autonomous system can be defined as one that makes and executes decisions to achieve a goal without full, direct human control [12]. Notable characteristics shared by the different kinds of autonomous systems include reasoning, learning, adaptation and context-awareness. A typical example of an autonomous system is an autonomous robot, which is working in a real, uncontrolled environment, possibly in the presence of humans.

The autonomous robots case study was performed in the R5-COP project. The project focused on reconfigurable robots coping with quickly changing environments and conditions. The verification of autonomous robot systems is an essential part of their development process due to their safety-critical nature. Thus testing and regression testing arc crucial tasks during their development.

Testing autonomous systems is particularly challenging due to the facts that their behavior is highly context-aware and their context contains a large number of possible situations [39]. Full behavior specification can be impractical due to the complexity of the behavior and the diversity of the system environments. Therefore a typical solution is to specify high-level properties and scenarios and evaluate these to detect violations of (safety) requirements [18]. Robots are placed in different situations (either in physical test environment or simulator), and properties are checked at runtime using monitors or off-line via trace analysis.

One of the industrial demonstrators of the project was an emergency response robot, a special type of mobile robots that is capable of performing certain activities in an environment that may possess the risk of human injury (e.g., critical tasks in handling explosives). The verification process of the completely built robots is usually conducted in special test rooms. These rooms are able to pose challenges for different capabilities of the robot through different terrain and obstacle types. The rooms use standardized elements (e.g., alleys, ramps) [5,23,29] that can be assembled in different configurations, and several tasks can be performed on each element (just crossing it, crossing it by following a line, reading a sign, etc.).

The changes in the requirements of the robots may trigger modifications in the configuration (replacing a component) or the test rooms (using a new element for testing a new functionality). This is very similar to the maintenance of the test suites of software, hence regression testing could be applied also in this domain: the robot can be thought as the system under test, while a layout of test room or a particular element of a test room is a test case for the robot.

Our testing approach [28] used a model-based, system-level black-box testing method. We modeled both the capabilities of the robots and the test rooms. Based on the NIST guidelines [29], we defined the following main types of model elements for test rooms: (1) mobility terrain, (2) obstacle, (3) visual target. The capabilities of the robot are also captured in a model that describes both hardware and software elements and the dependencies amongst them. According to the model a robot has slots where hardware elements (e.g., sensor, actuator, motor) can be mounted. Robots also have several different software elements installed that control hardware elements. Due to space constraints the full meta-models are not included, but they can be found in the project's deliverables [33, 34].

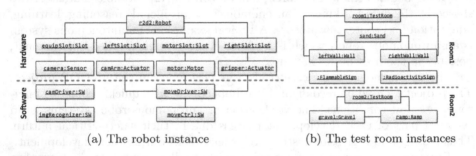

(a) The robot instance   (b) The test room instances

Fig. 1. Example instance models for robot configuration and test context

Figure 1a shows the simplified capability model of a sample robot, while Fig. 1b presents two sample test room instances. The robot model used in this example contains both hardware and software elements. The robot itself has four slots (left, right, motor, equipment). The motor slot is connected to the motor, which enables the robot to move. The right slot is connected to an arm that has a gripper to grasp objects. The left slot has an arm connected, which holds a camera. The camera is plugged into the equipment slot. Both actuators (camera arm, gripper) and the motor are controlled by a movement controller through a movement driver software. The camera has an image recognition software that communicates with the sensor using a special driver software. The terrain in the first room (*room*1) is sand, which is located between two walls (left and right). The left wall has a flammable warning sign, while the right one has a radioactivity sign on it. The second room (*room*2) has a gravel terrain and contains a ramp.

Let us consider the situation, when the specification of the robot is modified: a new `camera` is designed for the robot. Without any regression test selection, this change would trigger re-execution of all tests in both rooms. In a real scenario this may take high amount of time as the same room is used often with different layouts, thus would require multiple rearrangements. However, if only the camera is changed, it may be enough to the test the robot in *room*1.

To perform regression test selection it is crucial to have a mapping of coverage, which connects the test rooms with the capabilities of the robot. For example, the image recognizer component can be tested by the signs on the walls and the motor can be tested by the different terrain types. An RTS algorithm would be able to identify the minimal number of tests that are required to re-run to cover the modified parts of the system.

Selecting the right level of abstraction for the models and the goal of the testing was a non-trivial design decision. We performed multiple iterations with the industrial partners and designed several versions of the system and test models. Some models captured multiple possible configurations of the test rooms with different elements and selected tests based on which test room or which test room element is relevant for a given robot skill or component. Other models worked with a small, fixed number of test setups that were actually assembled at the partner's location, and varied what combinations of exercises should the robot perform in each test room. Therefore we needed an approach that can work with different input modeling languages and can be quickly adapted to new ones, without having to re-implement the whole regression testing algorithm.

The next section presents the approach we developed for the case study. Regression test selection was performed on similar domain-specific models by 1) defining an RTS model and 2) mapping the elements of the domain-specific inputs models to the elements of this RTS model. This approach was able to support regression testing in the presented setting.

3   Approach

RTS algorithms usually employ the following common concepts: (1) testable, (2) test and (3) coverage to handle the system under test (testables like elements of source code, model, etc.) and the tests that cover elements of the system. However, creating a compound representation is far from trivial and can be accomplished in various ways [43]. The forthcoming part of this section defines a representation that can be used for model-based regression test selection.

Several typical ways exist to define the coverage model. The most simple one is a binary matrix with program elements in its rows and tests in the columns. The matrix has 1 in cell (i, j) if the ith program element is covered by the jth test. However, if our inputs are DSL models and not just program lines or list of methods, a different, model-based representation is more suitable.

The main requirements of the RTS model were the followings. The RTS model shall (1) be easily extensible for different artifacts of various models and DSLs, and (2) separate the RTS algorithm from the core RTS concepts. To fulfill these requirements we developed an RTS model, which represents the generic concepts of RTS that can be mapped from the concrete artifacts (models and tests) of the input domain. The RTS model represents the data model that is required to conduct test selection for different models as input artifacts.

3.1   RTS Model

An RTS algorithm uses three main concepts: (1) elements in the system, (2) tests that exercise parts of the system and (3) a coverage relation that drives the selection process. Our proposed RTS metamodel contains four main concepts that is eligible to describe the underlying artifacts for the RTS algorithm.

- *Testable:* an abstract element that is verified by tests.
- *Component:* a type of *Testable* that supports dependencies; changing a component triggers all dependents to be re-tested.
- *Conditional:* a special type of *Testable* that represents a conditional element in the system (e.g., a branch or a condition in a decision), which requires individual handling during the RTS process (e.g., each value of the condition must be tested with a specific test case).
- *Test:* represents an executable test case in the system.

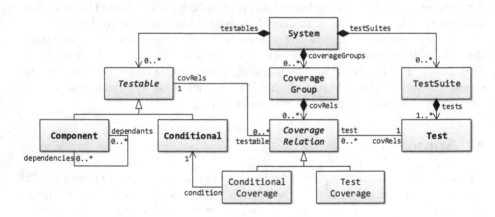

Fig. 2. The structure of the RTS metamodel

The full RTS metamodel is shown in Fig. 2. The main component of the model is the *system*. A system consists of *testables*, test suites and coverage groups. A testable instance could be a component or a conditional element, which were already presented. Components can depend on each other, thus there is a self-association defined. A test suite consists of *tests* connected to testables through coverage relations of coverage groups. A *coverage relation* connects a testable and a test (denoted with association). An instance of the coverage relation could be conditional coverage or simple test coverage. Simple test coverage defines no special conditions on the notion of coverage, thus can be fulfilled by simply covering an element. On the contrary, conditional coverage also covers elements but uses additionally a conditional element (marked with association), that requires individual handling of condition values during regression test selection (e.g., covering both the inclusion and the absences of an input model element in the tests). A coverage group holds together relations that have similar meaning in the domain being used, which alleviates their handling. Furthermore, testables, test suites, tests and coverage relations are modifiable meaning that they store whether the given element in the system has been changed since the last run or not. This change is represented in the RTS model using a special attribute.

3.2   Mapping of Input Models

In order to produce an instance of this metamodel a mapping is needed where the inputs are the system and test models, and the result is an instance of the RTS model itself. The transformations should use unique identifiers to trace back elements to the original models. These transformations are specific to the domain-specific models used as inputs. By using the mapping, the selection becomes independent from the input models. The implementation of the RTS is bound to the RTS model this way it is not necessary to (re-)implement it on the basis of the specific model artifacts and coverage models.

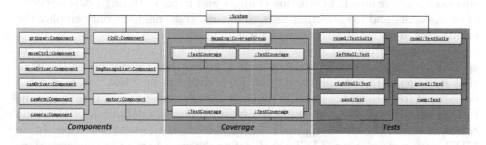

Fig. 3. The transformed sample RTS instance model

Notice that changes in the original models shall be represented in the RTS model. To tackle this question, our approach employs *checkpointing of models*, which is a common model versioning technique [4]. Hence, when a checkpoint during the model development is reached, the automatic mapping to the common RTS model is triggered with calculating the changes between checkpoints. These changes are applied to the RTS model incrementally and indicated on each modifiable element using the according attribute automatically.

Figure 3 depicts how this mapping was defined for the robot case study example presented on Fig. 1. One transformation was defined for the model of robot capabilities, which transformed every element into a *Component* in the optimization model. The approach supports dependencies between components, and these dependencies are used to find affected components transitively during the regression test selection for a given change. Additionally, the test rooms were transformed into test suites and tests. One may notice that we used *TestRooms* as test suites and elements as *Tests*, though they can be handled differently as the level of abstraction is changed (e.g., using the whole room as a test). Finally, a third, simple model (not shown on Fig. 3) was used to describe the mapping between robot capabilities and test room elements. This mapping model is translated into coverage elements in the RTS model.

Note that even the RTS model uses simple and compact concepts, these were enough to represent the regression testing problem in the current case study. For other case studies, the RTS model could be extended with other concepts.

3.3   Usage Scenarios

The approach can be used in two phases of an MDD development. First, the approach is intended to be used by *Test Engineers* during the development and maintenance phase of models as their common tasks are (1) identifying untested elements in the system, (2) performing impact analysis to identify the effects of particular changes, (3) re-testing the system after changes have been applied. Re-testing time should be reduced along with maintaining the same fault-detection capability of the test suite. This is where the presented approach emerges by (1) highlighting untested parts of the system calculated from the coverage relationships (2) detecting changes and impacts through dependencies of components and (3) selecting tests to re-run. Test engineers only employ the approach and do not develop or extend it.

Second, the presented approach shall also be used by developers of domain-specific languages as their tasks include (1) identifying elements of the DSL that correspond to tests and testables, (2) identifying how test coverage could be defined from elements and (3) implementing a transformation to a specific test model. These tasks are supported by providing the definition of the main concepts in the presented approach for generic regression test selection. In an MDD setting, developers of DSLs shall define the mappings and transformations to the RTS model, that can be used later by the test engineers.

4   Implementation

The approach is implemented in RTsMoT (Rts MOdeling Tool), a tool using the Eclipse Modeling Framework. To be able to handle several, different input models, the tool was given a layered architecture as shown in Fig. 4.

As the input models can be different domain-specific models, adapters are required for defining the mapping to the RTS model. A *Model Adapter* consists of transformations that map the domain models to the RTS model. RTsMoT provides interfaces for these transformations, hence only the knowledge of domain models is enough to implement them. For transformations, the adapters use VIATRA, a state-of-the-art incremental model transformation framework [6]. Using VIATRA requires the definition of patterns that can be matched to different domain model elements. Then, a transformation with VIATRA can be defined

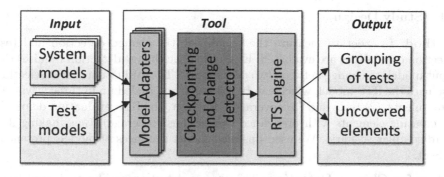

Fig. 4. Architecture and workflow of the prototype tool

for each match of the patterns, hence making able to map input model elements to new elements of the RTS model.

The model checkpointing technique, which is used in the presented approach demands for another layer in the architecture; the *Checkpointing and Change Detector* component provides the ability to create checkpoints during model development. At each checkpoint, this layer is also responsible for detecting changes in input models and indicating them on elements of the generic RTS model. The change detector marks all changes, i.e. all differences between the two versions of the model in the checkpoints. This process is performed with unique identifiers of elements that allows tracing between the input models and the generic RTS model. The prototype implementation currently uses the file system with time stamps for model versioning. However, this layer can be developed further to collaborate with well-known version control systems like Git and SVN.

The third layer of the RTsMoT tool is the *RTS engine*. This layer performs the actual test selection by using a replaceable algorithm subcomponent making the prototype tool more flexible. The algorithm yields the identification of elements in the RTS model, which are affected by changes in a checkpoint. Then, the algorithm selects test cases that are able to cover changed parts in the system. Also, the layer reports the uncoverable (but changed) and uncovered elements. The tool currently uses a simple greedy approximation algorithm for Minimal Set Cover as the problem of RTS can be reduced to this [19]. Further details of the implementation can be found in the project's deliverable [33].

5   Evaluation

We evaluated the applicability of the approach and the capabilities of RTsMoT to answer the following research question: *Could the prototype of the approach scale up to models found in the case study domain?*

5.1 Study Design

Method. In order to measure the scalability, the change detection and test selection capabilities are evaluated. Evaluating the change detection requires the input models to change between two checkpoints. The evaluation of test selection also uses the RTS model, which can be extended and scaled up in three ways: (1) components, (2) tests and (3) coverage. Moreover, the RTS evaluation demands for creating elements with predefined connections (coverage), thus making it a more complex scenario. We used upscaled model instances of models presented in Sect. 2.

Setup for Change Detection. The change detection can be evaluated from two aspects: (1) size of the input models to compare, (2) size of the change. Six different sizes of input models are defined for the evaluation: 16, 32, 64, 128, 256 and 512. These models were created by adding new component instances to the robot. Note that these sizes are the numbers of newly added components to the original robot instance model seen on Fig. 1a. Additionally sizes of the changes are defined in a smaller scale for this experiment: 1, 2, 4, 8, 16 and 32. According to the industrial partners in the R5-COP research project, these model sizes can be relevant in the autonomous robot domain. A significant aspect of the scalability is that how much time it takes to detect changes with different sizes of models and changes. Hence the evaluation addresses the following comparisons: (1) execution time with different sizes of inputs (number of changes here is 1), (2) execution time with different number of changes between checkpoints (size of input models here is set to 512).

Setup for RTS. The time that RTS takes during the test selection is a crucial part of the approach as it should not take unfeasible amount of time (e.g. running RTS and the selected tests should not take longer than re-running the whole test suite). Thus, the RTS model with 512 elements is used in this part of the evaluation with various amount of changes ranging from 1 to 512 on a logarithmic scale. Furthermore the number of dependencies to a changed component may affect the time required for running the RTS. This analysis also uses the model with 512 elements with the number of changes tied to one. However, the number of dependants to a single component is modified on a logarithmic scale from 1 to 512.

5.2 Results

The values presented in this section were obtained from executing RTsMoT on a notebook with a 2-core CPU running at 3.0 GHz and 8 GBs of RAM. During the evaluation, every measurement was repeated 30 times and the average values are presented here. Before each measurement a warm-up session was conducted in order to avoid outlier values caused by initialization processes in the Eclipse framework. The data analysis was performed using R [32], while execution times were measured by using stopwatches in code. In order to use statistical measures,

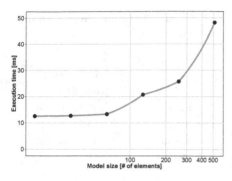

Fig. 5. Execution time of change detection with various model sizes

Table 1. Change detection times with different model sizes

Size [#]	Avg. time [ms]	CI
16	12.56	[10.3, 14.83]
32	12.7	[10.38, 15.02]
64	13.33	[11.48, 15.18]
128	20.73	[14.93, 26.53]
256	25.7	[22.3, 29.1]
512	48.23	[43.69, 52.78]

the normality of the results for each repetition was checked. All check yielded that the 30-times repeated results follows a normal distribution.

Figure 5 presents the relationship between the number of model elements on a logarithmic scale and the change detection time in milliseconds. The results show that as the size of the model is incremented, the detection time also increases. Table 1 summarizes these values including a confidence interval (CI) on 95% confidence level obtained using the one-sample t-test. The confidence intervals do not show large deviations, and the border values of the CIs grow with the average times. The presented change detection times may be thought feasible in the domain of the study. We also measured change detection time on larger models in order to determine the effects on practical applicability. We used two models containing 8192 and 16384 elements, from which the results were 5,59 and 22,02 s respectively, which are still convenient response times.

In terms of the relationship between the size of changes and the execution time of change detection, the results are promising. Figure 6 shows that there is a clear linear correlation between the number of changed elements and the related execution time. This is due to the linear search algorithm used in the background. Changing this algorithm to a model pattern detection-based technique may improve the performance.

Table 2 presents the results from the analysis of the relationship between the number of changes and the detection time. Note that the values are increasing linearly with the number of changes. Moreover the confidence intervals (CI) also show this relationship. The intervals were obtained again on 95% confidence level using the one-sample t-test. To sum up, these results show a clearly identifiable linear relationship between the number of changes and the change detection time. The maximum value was slightly more than one second even on the largest models used, thus can be thought as a promising and feasible result.

As mentioned earlier, the RTS execution time is also a crucial part of the process. To evaluate its performance the execution time was measured with different number of changes on a previously used model in the case study (containing 512 elements). Figure 7 depicts the results from this evaluation with the

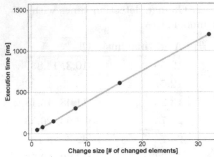

Fig. 6. Execution time of change detection with various number of changes

Table 2. Change detection times with different sizes of changes

Size [#]	Avg. time [ms]	CI
1	45.67	[41.70, 49.63]
2	78.53	[75.6, 81.46]
4	148.17	[144.82, 151.51]
8	304.27	[285.24, 323.3]
16	608.83	[584.84, 632.82]
32	1196.53	[1151.51, 1241.56]

sizes of changes on a logarithmic scale. It can be seen that no dependency exists between the number of changes and the RTS execution time because even when all the model elements were changed the time remained almost the same.

Table 3 reveals the details of this evaluation containing the average times and their confidence intervals (CI) with the previously used one-sample t-test on 95% level of confidence. The values are almost equal in all cases and do not show large deviations. However larger CIs exists, which is due to the first and second measurements that had longer execution times as the modeling framework did not cache the required model elements until the third run (though a warm-up run was conducted to avoid this effect). In brief, these execution times are acceptable for the domain of autonomous robots even on relatively large models.

As described in Sect. 5.1 we also analyzed how the RTS execution time is affected by the number of dependencies belonging to a changed component. Based on the results, the pattern-based dependency analysis that is implemented in RTsMoT turned out to be effective: the execution times were roughly the same that were presented in Table 3. Thus the execution time of RTS can be thought as independent from the number of dependencies to a component.

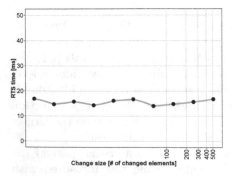

Fig. 7. Execution time of RTS with various number of changes

Table 3. RTS execution times with different sizes of changes

Size [#]	Avg. time [ms]	CI
1	16.9	[10.63, 23.17]
2	14.73	[10.78, 18.68]
8	14.33	[10.12, 18.55]
32	16.73	[12.1, 21.38]
128	14.87	[10.2, 19.53]
512	16.8	[9.12, 24.48]

The evaluation of these complex cases was performed to answer the RQ. The results produced by RTsMoT that implements the generic RTS approach are promising and scale up without significant increase of execution time even for these larger model sizes. Hence the presented approach and the prototype tool can scale to real models used in the autonomous robot domain.

6 Related Work

Regression test selection has a very broad area of research as it can be executed in numerous ways [17,36]. Engström et al. conducted a survey [13], where the regression test selection techniques for source code are gathered and assessed based on their evaluations. They had two conclusions to emphasize: (1) empirical evidence is not very strong on evaluating RTS techniques, (2) RTS techniques have to be tailored to the given context as no generic technique can be found.

Yoo et al. [43] also conducted a survey on regression test selection techniques, and identified new trends in the research of this area. According to them, model-based RTS techniques emerge for two reasons: (1) the higher level of regression testing and (2) the easier scalability. Some of these techniques use EFSM or UML, however some use other approaches like graphs or a specific internal model.

Methods Using EFSM. EFSMs add variables and conditional execution to the basic FSM semantics. This enables them to model software behavior better. Chen et al. [11] provide a way to use regression testing on EFSM models. The changes (elementary modifications) they cover are defined on a transition of the state machine; either addition, deletion or a change. Korel et al. also use the EFSM semantics in their work [24]. They also use the notion of elementary modification to describe changes on the input models. Vaysburg et al. presented a technique [41] that uses dependency analysis on EFSM system models. Their approach is able to capture various kind of interaction between elements, which is used as an input for the regression test selection process. Almasri et al. employed EFSMs to conduct impact analysis in model-based systems [3] in order to reduce maintenance costs and to identify critical parts of the system. They also defined model and data density metrics, which are found to be major influencing factors to the number of components involved in a change.

Methods using UML. Wu and Offut [42] provide an approach for regression testing component-based software based on their UML diagrams. The diagrams applied are class diagrams, collaboration diagrams and statecharts. Somewhat similarly Briand et al. [8,9] provide another approach that classifies test cases into the usual categorization; obsolete, re-testable or re-usable. They have also implemented a tool (RTSTool) to evaluate it. Farooq et al. propose an approach for UML state machines [15] and an Eclipse-based tool as well [14]. From these papers we have seen that UML diagrams are already used for regression testing purposes, there are even some tools implemented. Pilskalns et al. propose [31] an incremental test generation method for UML diagrams that transforms the input to a graph, on which then a test selection algorithm is run to identify re-testable test cases. Traon et al. [25] also use an internal model (test dependency graph) to represent the input towards the test selection algorithm. They are also mapping UML class diagrams to this graph. It is not clearly expressed, whether these techniques can be used for another model inputs (apart from UML) as well. Chen et al. use [10] UML activity diagrams to identify test cases that are affected by the modifications in release of a software. They employ activity diagrams as the specification and only separate two different types of regression tests (targeted and safety) unlike other, more generic approaches.

Generic approaches. A closely related approach for model-based RTS is presented by Zech et al. in [44,45]. Their approach uses the generic MoVe model versioning platform and calculates deltas from changes between model versions. The difference between the approaches is that theirs employs a domain-specific model obtained from the expanded delta, while our approach uses a generic RTS model. Fourneret et al. presented a generalized model-based regression testing technique in [16]. They extract behavior from the input models to supply impact analysis during the RTS process. These behaviors are extracted from guards or actions when using state charts, and from Object Constraint Language constraints in case of class diagrams. This process is clearly similar to the approach presented by Zech, although behavioral extraction is made additionally. Orso et al. provides an approach [30] on how to use metadata from external components to supply regression test selection process both on code and model.

7   Conclusions

This paper presented a model-based regression test selection (RTS) approach that was developed for the system-level testing of reconfigurable, autonomous robots. This technique uses an RTS model to enable the handling of multiple input models specified in different domain-specific languages. In order to use the approach on different input domains, simple transformations are needed, which can be defined by the potential users of the approach. This includes test engineers and domain-specific language developers.

The paper also introduced the architecture of a prototype tool called RTSMoT that implements the approach using the Eclipse framework and its modeling platform EMF. The scalability of the approach was evaluated on models from the case study. The results showed that the tool can scale to larger models and even after several changes the test selection is performed quickly.

The developed approach was able to capture the regression testing problem of the case study. However, an important lesson was that it required numerous iterations with the industrial partners to find the right level of abstraction of the models representing the capabilities, context and test setups of the robots. Several versions of the input model languages were developed targeting different testing goals (e.g. testing using rooms with different configurations, testing using different exercises in a fixed test room). In these iterations the layered architecture of the tool and the usage of small model adapters that can be quickly developed proved to be a really useful design decision.

Future work includes several directions. For example, the approach is able identify elements in the models for which no test exists, but offers no solution for the user. We are working on to automatically generate test setups including the missing elements using search-based techniques.

Acknowledgment. This work was partially supported by the ARTEMIS JU and the Hungarian National Research, Development and Innovation Fund in the frame of the R5-COP project.

References

1. Aggrawal, K., Singh, Y., Kaur, A.: Code coverage based technique for prioritizing test cases for regression testing. ACM Softw. Eng. Notes **29**(5), 1–4 (2004)
2. Agrawal, H., Horgan, J.R., Krauser, E.W., London, S.: Incremental regression testing. Int. Conf. Softw. Maintenance **93**, 348–357 (1993)
3. Almasri, N., Tahat, L., Korel, B.: Toward automatically quantifying the impact of a change in systems. Softw. Qual. J., 1–40 (2016)
4. Altmanninger, K., Seidl, M., Wimmer, M.: A survey on model versioning approaches. Int. J. Web Inform. Syst. **5**(3), 271–304 (2009)
5. ASTM International: Standard Terminology for Evaluating Response Robot Capabilities E2521–16 (2016)
6. Bergmann, G., Dávid, I., Hegedüs, Á., Horváth, Á., Ráth, I., Ujhelyi, Z., Varró, D.: VIATRA 3: a reactive model transformation platform. In: Kolovos, D., Wimmer, M. (eds.) ICMT 2015. LNCS, vol. 9152, pp. 101–110. Springer, Cham (2015). doi:10. 1007/978 3 319-21155-8_8
7. Brambilla, M., Cabot, J., Wimmer, M.: Model-Driven Software Engineering in Practice, 1st edn. Morgan & Claypool Publishers, Williston (2012)
8. Briand, L., Labiche, Y., He, S.: Automating regression test selection based on UML designs. Inf. Softw. Technol. **51**(1), 16–30 (2009)
9. Briand, L., Labiche, Y., Soccar, G.: Automating impact analysis and regression test selection based on UML designs. In: International Conference on Software Maintenance, pp. 252–261 (2002)
10. Chen, Y., Probert, R.L., Sims, D.P.: Specification-based regression test selection with risk analysis. In: Conference of the Centre for Advanced Studies on Collaborative Research, pp. 1–14 (2002)
11. Chen, Y., Probert, R.L., Ural, H.: Regression test suite reduction using extended dependence analysis. In: 4th International Workshop on Software Quality Assurance, SOQUA 2007, pp. 62 69. ACM (2007)
12. Connelly, J., Hong, W., Mahoney, R., Sparrow, D.: Challenges in autonomous system development. In: Proceedings of Performance Metrics for Intelligent Systems Workshop (PerMIS 2006) (2006)
13. Engström, E., Runeson, P., Skoglund, M.: A systematic review on regression test selection techniques. Inf. Softw. Technol. **52**(1), 14–30 (2010)
14. Farooq, Q., Iqbal, M., Malik, Z., Riebisch, M.: A model-based regression testing approach for evolving software systems with flexible tool support. In: IEEE International Conference on Engineering of Computer Based Systems, pp. 41–49 (2010)

15. Farooq, Q.u.a., Iqbal, M.Z.Z., Malik, Z.I., Nadeem, A.: An approach for selective state machine based regression testing. In: Proceeding of the 3rd International Workshop on Advances in Model-based Testing, A-MOST, pp. 44–52. ACM (2007)

16. Fourneret, E., Cantenot, J., Bouquet, F., Legeard, B., Botella, J.: SeTGaM: generalized technique for regression testing based on UML/OCL models. In: International Conference on Software Security and Reliability, pp. 147–156. IEEE, US (2014)

17. Graves, T.L., Harrold, M.J., Kim, J.M., Porter, A., Rothermel, G.: An empirical study of regression test selection techniques. ACM TOSEM **10**(2), 184–208 (2001)

18. Guiochet, J., Machin, M., Waeselynck, H.: Safety-critical advanced robots: a survey. Robot. Auton. Syst. **94**, 43–52 (2017)

19. Harman, M.: Making the case for MORTO: multi objective regression test optimization. In: ICST Workshops, pp. 111–114 (2011)

20. Harrold, M.J., Gupta, R., Soffa, M.L.: A methodology for controlling the size of a test suite. ACM TOSEM **2**(3), 270–285 (1993)

21. Harrold, M.J., Jones, J.A., Li, T., Liang, D., Orso, A., Pennings, M., Sinha, S., Spoon, S.A., Gujarathi, A.: Regression test selection for Java software. ACM SIGPLAN Not. **36**(11), 312–326 (2001)

22. IEEE: Systems and software engineering - Vocabulary, standard 24765:2010 (2010)

23. Jacoff, A., Huang, H.M., Messina, E., Virts, A., Downs, A.: Comprehensive standard test suites for the performance evaluation of mobile robots. In: Proc of the 10th Performance Metrics for Intelligent Systems Workshop, PerMIS 2010, pp. 161–168. ACM (2010)

24. Korel, B., Tahat, L., Vaysburg, B.: Model based regression test reduction using dependence analysis. In: International Conference on Software Maintenance, pp. 214–223 (2002)

25. Le Traon, Y., Jeron, T., Jezequel, J., Morel, P.: Efficient object-oriented integration and regression testing. IEEE Tran. Reliab. **49**(1), 12–25 (2000)

26. Leung, H., White, L.: Insights into regression testing. In: International Conference on Software Maintenance, pp. 60–69, October 1989

27. Malishevsky, A.G., Ruthruff, J.R., Rothermel, G., Elbaum, S.: Cost-cognizant test case prioritization. Technical report, Department of Computer Science and Engineering, University of Nebraska-Lincoln (2006)

28. Micskei, Z., Szatmári, Z., Oláh, J., Majzik, I.: A concept for testing robustness and safety of the context-aware behaviour of autonomous systems. In: Jezic, G., Kusek, M., Nguyen, N.-T., Howlett, R.J., Jain, L.C. (eds.) KES-AMSTA 2012. LNCS, vol. 7327, pp. 504–513. Springer, Heidelberg (2012). doi:10.1007/978-3-642-30947-2_55

29. NIST: Guide for Evaluating, Purchasing, and Training with Response Robots using DHS-NIST-ASTM International Standard Test Methods (2014). https://www.nist.gov/el/intelligent-systems-division-73500/response-robots

30. Orso, A., Do, H., Rothermel, G., Harrold, M.J., Rosenblum, D.S.: Using component metadata to regression test component-based software. Softw. Testing Verification Reliab. **17**(2), 61–94 (2007)

31. Pilskalns, O., Uyan, G., Andrews, A.: Regression testing UML designs. In: International Conference on Software Maintenance, pp. 254–264 (2006)

32. R Core Team: R: A Language and Environment for Statistical Computing. R Foundation for Statistical Computing (2013). http://www.R-project.org/

33. R5-COP: Incremental testing of behaviour (2016). http://www.r5-cop.eu/media/cms_page_media/35/R5-COP_D34.20_v1.0_BME.pdf, d34.20 deliverable

34. R5-COP: Assessment of the On-line Verification and Incremental Testing (2017). http://www.r5-cop.eu/media/cms_page_media/35/R5-COP_D34.50_v1.1_BME.pdf, d34.50 deliverable
35. Rothermel, G., Harrold, M.J.: Selecting regression tests for object-oriented software. In: International Conference on Software Maintenance, pp. 14–25. IEEE (1994)
36. Rothermel, G., Harrold, M.J.: Analyzing regression test selection techniques. IEEE Tran. Softw. Eng. **22**(8), 529–551 (1996)
37. Rothermel, G., Untch, R.H., Chu, C., Harrold, M.J.: Prioritizing test cases for regression testing. IEEE Tran. Softw. Eng. **27**(10), 929–948 (2001)
38. Soetens, Q.D., Demeyer, S.: ChEOPSJ: change-based test optimization. In: European Conference on Software Maintenance and Reengineering, pp. 535–538 (2012)
39. de Sousa Santos, I., de Castro Andrade, R.M., Rocha, L.S., Matalonga, S., de Oliveira, K.M., Travassos, G.H.: Test case design for context-aware applications: are we there yet? Inf. Softw. Technol. **88**, 1–16 (2017)
40. Tengeri, D., Beszedes, A., Havas, D., Gyimothy, T.: Toolset and program repository for code coverage-based test suite analysis and manipulation. In: 14th IEEE International Working Conference on Source Code Analysis and Manipulation, pp. 47–52 (2014)
41. Vaysburg, B., Tahat, L.H., Korel, B.: Dependence analysis in reduction of requirement based test suites. In: Proceeding of the International Symposium on Software Testing and Analysis, pp. 107–111 (2002)
42. Wu, Y., Offutt, J.: Maintaining evolving component-based software with UML. In: European Conference on Software Maintenance and Reengineering, pp. 133–142 (2003)
43. Yoo, S., Harman, M.: Regression testing minimization, selection and prioritization: a survey. Softw. Testing Verification Reliab. **22**(2), 67–120 (2012)
44. Zech, P., Felderer, M., Kalb, P., Breu, R.: A generic platform for model-based regression testing. In: Margaria, T., Steffen, B. (eds.) ISoLA 2012. LNCS, vol. 7609, pp. 112–126. Springer, Heidelberg (2012). doi:10.1007/978-3-642-34026-0_9
45. Zech, P., Kalb, P., Felderer, M., Atkinson, C., Breu, R.: Model-based regression testing by OCL. Int. J. STTT **19**, 115–131 (2015)

Automated Tooling for the Evolving SDL Standard: From Metamodels to UML Profiles

Alexander Kraas[✉]

Software Technologies Research Group, University of Bamberg, Bamberg, Germany
`Alexander.Kraas@swt-bamberg.de`

Abstract. The past decade has seen much research on a model-based language development of the Specification and Description Language (SDL) and a corresponding Unified Modeling Language (UML) profile. However, as far it is still not possible to derive a UML profile for SDL automatically; instead it has to be created by hand, which is error-prone and time-consuming.

To remedy this limitation, we present a publicly available metamodel for SDL, which was semi-automatically generated based on SDL's syntax rules. In addition, we automatically derive a UML profile in a novel way so that SDL's static semantics is automatically transferred from the metamodel.

Keywords: Metamodel · SDL · UML · Profile · Transformation

1 Introduction

Over three decades, the *Specification and Description Language* (SDL) [9] is employed in the telecommunications sector for specifying communication protocols and distributed systems. With the increasing interest for *Model-Driven Engineering* (MDE) approaches, several activities have been started to specify a metamodel for SDL (e.g., [3,20]). Because a metamodel defines the syntax and semantics of a computer language, an existing SDL metamodel would be an important prerequisite for the model-driven language development of SDL. To the best of our knowledge, no publicly available metamodel that embraces all language features of SDL exists.

With the increasing popularity of the *Unified Modeling Language* (UML) [17], not only has the number of available UML tools but also the size of the community increased. In contrast to UML, however, only a small number of SDL tools exists. Thus, the possibility of using UML tools for modelling SDL specifications would be an asset. This can be realized by means of a so-called UML profile, which is a standardized extension mechanism of the UML. Accordingly, the first version of a *UML profile for SDL* (SDL-UML) was published by the *International Telecommunication Union* (ITU) as Rec. Z.109 already in 1999 [7]. This version only supported the specification of structural aspects, whereas the most recent version of the profile [10] also captures the modelling of behavioural aspects and a

© Springer International Publishing AG 2017
T. Csöndes et al. (Eds.): SDL 2017, LNCS 10567, pp. 136–156, 2017.
DOI: 10.1007/978-3-319-68015-6_9

dedicated action language. However, constraints that define the static semantics of the profile are specified in natural language only. Therefore, additional effort is required to specify them via the *Object Constraint Language* (OCL) [18], so as to enable an automatic validation of the static semantics. A further drawback of the SDL-UML profile is that *'Stereotypes'*[1] are only mapped to corresponding constructs of SDL's abstract syntax, but not to a corresponding metamodel. In addition, this mapping is only specified in natural language, too.

This paper presents a (semi-)automatically generated and publicly available metamodel for SDL so that a model-based language development of SDL becomes possible in the future. Apart from syntactic aspects, our metamodel also captures the static semantics of SDL and is based on the language concepts provided by the *Meta Object Facility* (MOF) [15]. Based on this foundation, we employ our recent approach [12] for automatically deriving a UML profile for SDL. Since the syntactic structure is preserved during profile derivation, OCL constructs of the metamodel are transferred to the derived profile without any manual rework. In addition, our approach can also derive *Model-to-Model* (M2M) transformations that transform a domain model to a corresponding UML model and visa versa. Hence, on the basis of our SDL metamodel we obtain, in a highly automated manner, a UML profile for SDL as well as associated M2M transformations, thus enabling model-based language development of SDL.

The remainder of this paper is structured as follows. The next section introduces our derivation approach at an abstract level, while its details are presented in Sects. 3 to 5. The results of our approach and related work are discussed in Sects. 6 and 7. Finally, our conclusions and suggestions for future work are given in Sect. 8.

2   Background: Derivation Approach in a Nutshell

We recently developed a new approach for the automatic derivation of UML profiles, additional metaclasses and model transformations based on a single metamodel [12]. Before we discuss the application of our approach to SDL, this section gives a brief overview of our overall approach.

The central artefact for all derivations is a MOF-based metamodel for SDL (MM_{SDL} in Fig. 1), which is generated in Step (A) based on SDL's abstract syntax rules. To reduce the effort for a manual refinement of MM_{SDL}, we reuse 'Abstract Concepts' defined by the metamodel MM_{AC}. These concepts define basic language features, for instance 'inheritance' and 'namespaces', so that they can be considered as common building blocks of many different computer languages. In contrast to [3], we use annotated syntax rules to generate the metamodel.

Since we create MOF-based metamodels, we define a dedicated annotation type for each language concept (e.g., *'Generalization'*) of the MOF, whereby each annotation triggers a specific mapping action when generating our metamodel.

---

[1] Names within quotation marks and written in italic style refer to UML elements or attributes as specified by the *UML Superstructure* [17].

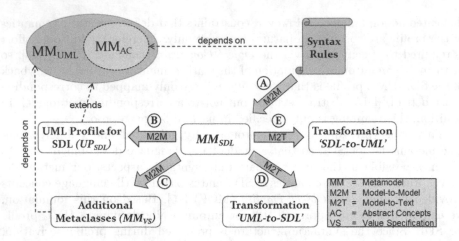

Fig. 1. Transformations and their derived artefacts.

Among other purposes, the annotations are employed for defining inheritance relationships to the 'Abstract Concepts', because each concept is represented by a particular metaclass of MM_{AC}. Thereby, we obtain more sophisticated metamodels when compared to pure syntax rules without any additional mapping information.

Before the generated MM_{SDL} can be used as input for Steps (B)–(E), it has to be manually refined. In particular, we have to specify OCL constraints to meet SDL's static semantics. Thereafter, we automatically derive the UML Profile for SDL (UP_{SDL}) and additional metaclasses (MM_{VS}) in Steps (B) and (C). The derivation of such metaclasses may be an option if stereotypes cannot be utilized due to their restrictions as defined by the UML [17]. We employ the additional metaclasses contained in MM_{VS} to represent SDL's expression and value specifications. In the present case, these kind of metaclasses extend the 'ValueSpecification' metaclass of UML. Since the input and output artefacts of Steps (B) and (C) are models, we realize both derivations by two *Model-to-Model* (M2M) transformations, which are implemented using the operational language of the *Query/View/Transformation* (QVT) specification [14].

In Steps (D) and (E), QVT operational code for the M2M transformations $T_{UML-to-SDL}$ and $T_{SDL-to-UML}$ is generated; this transforms a UML model to an SDL model and vice versa. We utilize two dedicated *Model-to-Text* (M2T) transformations that are implemented with the *MOF M2T Language* (MTL) [13] to generate the QVT code.

3   A New Metamodel for SDL

In this section, we explain the semi-automatic generation of a metamodel for SDL, which is a prerequisite for the derivation of a corresponding UML profile. This metamodel is generated based on the abstract syntax rules of SDL.

3.1   The 'Abstract Concepts' Used for the SDL Metamodel

The metamodel MM_{AC} holds a key role for our entire derivation approach, because generated metaclasses of MM_{SDL} inherit from the 'Abstract Concepts'. An important prerequisite for MM_{AC} is that it has to 'match' with a subset of MM_{UML}. Otherwise, a mapping of MM_{SDL} to a UML profile is impossible. We consider a metamodel MM_{AC} to be 'matching' with MM_{UML}, if for each meta-class of MM_{AC}, a corresponding UML metaclass is present. Furthermore, it is required that each attribute of a metaclass in MM_{AC} has a corresponding UML metaclass attribute. However, since we assume that only required features are employed to define a metamodel for a DSL of interest, an MM_{AC} metaclass can have an equal or lesser number of attributes than its matching UML counter-part. Our language-specific selection of MM_{AC} metaclasses and of their features prevents the creation of syntactically invalid models; for the same reason, the entire UML metamodel should never be used instead of a customized MM_{AC}.

Because MM_{AC} shall 'match' with MM_{UML}, we consider the creation of MM_{AC} from scratch to be too error-prone and expensive. Another option is to use the MOF or the *UML Infrastructure Library* [16]. As their metaclasses are primarily employed in MM_{UML} to define the 'Kernel' package, they could also be reused to create an MM_{AC} that only supports 'structural' language concepts. Because of SDL's different state machine types for the behavioural modelling, a generic concept for specifying state machines should be present as an 'Abstract Concept'. Hence, we considered the reuse of some metaclasses contained in MM_{UML} as the most appropriate option for manually creating MM_{AC} for SDL. Apart from this approach, the 'package merge' mechanism of UML could be utilized for an automatic generation. We have not employed this mechanism because not every feature of a UML metaclass is required for defining the SDL metamodel.

In our MM_{AC} for SDL, we reuse some metaclasses of the *'Classes'* package of MM_{UML} to support the modelling of structural aspects. In addition, we employ metaclasses of the *'State Machines'*, the *'Activities'* and the *'Common Behaviors'* packages of MM_{UML} to facilitate the specification of behavioural aspects. In total, we utilize 43 metaclasses of MM_{UML} to define the 'Abstract Concepts'.

An example of the employed 'Abstract Concepts' for SDL is given in Fig. 2, which shows a modified UML *'StateMachine'* in [17]. This 'Abstract Concept' specifies the basic language concepts required for defining the SDL Procedure-definition and Composite-statetype-definition. To obtain this *'StateMachine'* variant, we have removed all language features that are not required for SDL. An example for this is the metaclass AC_State, which has a lower number of features compared to its corresponding UML metaclass State. An SDL state only supports the invocation of an activity when it is entered or exited, but not when the state machine remains in the state. Thus, among other features, we have removed the doActivity feature from the AC_State metaclass.

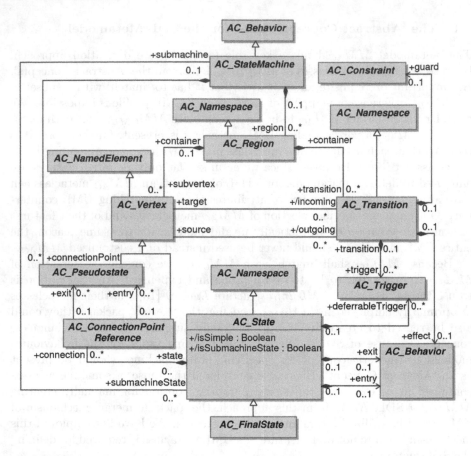

Fig. 2. The 'Abstract Concept' for a state machine in SDL. Details concerning attribute subsetting and redefinition are omitted here.

3.2   From Syntax Rules to an 'Initial' Metamodel

Because we use SDL's abstract syntax rules to generate an 'initial' metamodel, our employed notation for syntax rules is aligned to that specified in ITU-T Rec. Z.111 [8]. In addition, this notation is supplemented with particular annotations that are aligned to language concepts provided by the MOF [15]. The concrete syntax of our notation is shown in Fig. 3, where we distinguish between two different kinds of syntax rules: a `Definition-rule` defines a particular non-terminal node, whereas an `Equivalence-rule` is used to introduce an alias definition. If an `Equivalence-rule` is referenced on the right-hand side of another rule, this reference is replaced by the content of the `Equivalence-rule`. Apart from the `Name`, each `Rule` may consist of an `Expression` and a set of `Annotations`. A `RuleAnnotation` is applicable to syntax rules, whereas an `ExpAnnotation` can be employed to `Expression` nodes.

```
Grammar = Rule*
Rule = Definition-rule | Equivalence-rule
Definition-rule = Name "::" [ Annotations ] [Expression]
Equivalence-rule = Name "=" [Annotations] Expression
Expression = (Alternatives | Composition | Option | List | Set | Domain)
  [ Annotations ]
Alternatives = "(" Expression {"|" Expression }+ ")"
Composition = "{" Expression+ "}"
Option = "[" Expression "]"
List = Expression ( "*" | "+" )
Set = Expression ( "-set" | "+set" )
Domain = Non-terminal-domain | Elementary-domain | Enumeration-domain
Annotations = "annotations" "{" { Annotation ";" }+ "}"
Annotation = Documentation | RuleAnnotation | ExpAnnotation
RuleAnnotation = Constraint | AbstractClass | Generalization
ExpAnnotation = ReferencedRule | ReferencedType | CompositeType
  | Subsetted | Redefined | DerivedUnion | DerivedProperty | ReadOnly
...
```

Fig. 3. Concrete syntax of the syntax rule notation.

On a high level of abstraction, a `Rule` is mapped to a corresponding metaclass (i.e., *'Class'*) of a metamodel. The *'name'* of the metaclass is derived from the `Name` of a `Rule`. Furthermore, an `Expression` of a `Rule` is mapped to an *'ownedAttribute'* (i.e., a *'Property'*) of the generated metaclass. The *'type'* and the multiplicity of a *'Property'* depends on the employed `Expression` type. Apart from these mappings, also different kinds of `Annotations` are evaluated, because they trigger particular mapping actions during the metamodel generation.

To make our mapping more comprehensible, we illustrate it on the example of an annotated syntax rule for the SDL `Procedure-definition`. As shown in Fig. 4, this rule has a **'generalized class'** annotation, specifying that the generated metaclass shall inherit from `AC_StateMachine`. The two **'constraint'** annotations are mapped to corresponding *'Constraint'* elements of the generated metaclass `ProcedureDefinition`. Furthermore, all `Expression` items of the rule are mapped to corresponding *'ownedAttributes'* of the generated metaclass. Each `Expression` with a **'redefined property'** or **'subsetted property'** annotation is mapped to an *'ownedAttribute'* that redefines/subsets the attribute specified by the annotation. For instance, the mapped `procedureIdentifier` redefines the `superClass` attribute of `AC_Class`.

Although the *'type'* of an *'ownedAttribute'* depends on the `Expression`, this can explicitly be overridden by the **'compositetype'** and **'referenced rule'** annotations. Such an annotation is always required when an `Expression` represents an SDL identifier that refers to a type definition. This is because identifiers in SDL's abstract syntax are handled as simple strings, whereas they can be realized as references in metamodels.

```
Procedure-definition :: annotations {generalized class "AC_StateMachine";
  constraint name "Constraint_1" : body "The 'procedureGraph' of a 'Proce-
    dureDefinition' for an operation shall not contain a 'StateNode'";
  constraint name "Constraint_2" : body "All potentially instantiated
    procedures shall have a 'ProcedureStartNode'";
  ...}
{ Procedure-name annotations {redefined property "AC_NamedElement::name"}
  Procedure-formal-parameter* annotations { subsetted property
    "AC_Behavior::ownedParameter"; compositetype "SDL-MM::Parameter" }
  [Result] annotations { subsetted property
    "AC_Behavior::ownedParameter"; compositetype "SDL-MM::Parameter" }
  [Procedure-identifier] annotations { referenced rule
    Procedure-definition; redefined property "AC_Class::superClass" }
  Data-type-definition -set
    annotations { subsetted property "AC_Class::nestedClassifier" }
  Syntype-definition -set
    annotations { subsetted property "AC_Class::nestedClassifier" }
  Variable-definition -set
    annotations { subsetted property "AC_Namespace::ownedMember" }
  Composite-state-type-definition -set annotations { subsetted property
    "AC_BehavioredClassifier::ownedBehavior" }
  Procedure-definition -set annotations { subsetted property
    "AC_BehavioredClassifier::ownedBehavior" }
  Procedure-graph
    annotations {redefined property "AC_StateMachine::region"}
  [ ABSTRACT ] }
```

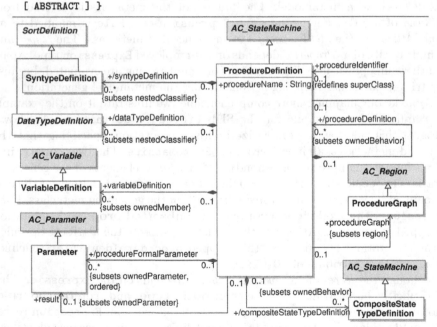

Fig. 4. Annotated abstract syntax rule of SDL's Procedure-definition and its corresponding metaclass in MM_{SDL}.

Based on 180 syntax rules of SDL, which consist of 93 `DefinitionRules` and 87 `EquivalenceRules`, we generated 102 metaclasses. The lower number of metaclasses in comparison to the number of syntax rules is caused by the fact that some `EquivalenceRules` only represent alias definitions that are removed automatically. Since not only generated metaclasses but also metaclasses of MM_{AC} are contained in MM_{SDL}, our SDL metamodel consists in total of 145 metaclasses.

3.3 Steps Towards the Final Metamodel

Although many aspects of a metamodel for SDL can be derived automatically by our approach, this does not apply for **'constraint'** annotations. This annotation type can only be specified in terms of plain text that is copied to a corresponding *'Constraint'* element. Hence, the OCL specification of a *'Constraint'* has to be implemented manually. In the case of SDL, the static semantics is defined in terms of a first-order predicate logic that can be translated manually to OCL as proposed in [20]. We employ a similar approach to implement the OCL *'Constraints'* for our SDL metamodel. However, a simplification of the OCL specifications can be achieved due to the use of inherited helper operations and attributes of the 'Abstract Concepts'. For instance, consider `Constraint_1` (see Fig. 4) that is translated to OCL as follows:

```
self.specification <> null implies
  self.allOwnedElements()->select(oclIsKindOf(StateNode))->isEmpty()
```

In the first line of the OCL constraint, we determine whether a `ProcedureDefinition` defines the behaviour of an SDL operation. Instead of a complex OCL expression, we can employ the inherited `specification` attribute for this purpose. Furthermore, we use the inherited operation `allOwnedElements()` to retrieve all elements owned by a `ProcedureDefinition`. Then, we only have to check whether these members do not contain any `StateNode`. In total, we have manually specified 204 OCL *'Constraints'* to capture the static semantics of SDL. According to the same approach, we have also implemented several OCL helper operations and the *'defaultValues'* of derived attributes.

Apart from OCL specifications, another refinement of the generated metamodel concerns the *'opposite'* feature of an *'ownedAttribute'* that is defined in terms of an *'Association'*. In this case, the *'opposite'* feature is derived from the opposite end of an *'Association'*. In case of an *'ownedAttribute'* redefines or subsets another *'Property'*, the *'opposite'* feature also has to redefine or subset another *'Property'* in an appropriate manner. Although this kind of refinement could be implemented by our approach, it is a design decision that a manual refinement shall be done in MM_{SDL}. Because in this case, we can utilize the build-in functionalities of a modelling tool to evaluate constraints of the MOF concerning *'Associations'*.

4   The Automatically Derived UML Profile for SDL

In this section, we discuss the application of our approach to automatically derive a UML profile for SDL based on our finalized SDL metamodel.

4.1   Enrichment of the SDL Metamodel

Our UML profile derivation of UP_{SDL} is based on the assumption that metaclasses of a source metamodel (MM_{SDL}) can be categorized into three disjoint sets of metaclasses. The first set consists of the 'Abstract Concept' metaclasses MC_{AC}, which can be identified by the common name prefix '`AC_`'. Because these metaclasses have a 'matching' counterpart in MM_{UML}, they are not mapped to any other kind of element during the profile derivation. The second set embraces all metaclasses that are mapped to 'Stereotypes' of UP_{SDL}, and which are marked with a «ToStereotype» stereotype. We use the term MC_{St} to refer to a metaclass of this set. Finally, the third set consists of all metaclasses that are mapped to 'additional metaclasses' contained in the derived metamodel MM_{VS}, and which have a «ToMetaclass» stereotype applied. We refer to a metaclass of this set by using the term MC_{AMC}.

After the classification, our metamodel MM_{SDL} is partitioned in 71 MC_{St}, 35 MC_{AMC} and 43 MC_{AC} metaclasses. We utilize the MC_{AMC} metaclasses to represent SDL's value and expression specifications. Even though stereotypes could be used for this purpose, we employ the same approach as applied in Z.109 [10] so as to preserve the comparability.

4.2   Automatic Derivation of the UML Profile

Stereotype derivation: According to our approach, each of the 71 MC_{St} metaclasses of MM_{SDL} is mapped to a corresponding 'Stereotype' contained in the UML profile UP_{SDL}. In addition, if an MC_{St} directly inherits from a MC_{AC}, we introduce an 'Extension' relationship between a derived 'Stereotype' and a metaclass of MM_{UML}. For example, see the `ProcedureDefinition` metaclass shown in Fig. 4 and its mapped «`ProcedureDefinition`» 'Stereotype' depicted in Fig. 5. When an MC_{St} inherits from another MC_{St}, we introduce a 'Generalization' instead of an 'Extension'. For example, see the `DataTypeDefinition` metaclass and its derived «`DataTypeDefinition`» 'Stereotype'.

Mapping of attributes: Each 'ownedAttribute' of an MC_{St} metaclass is mapped to a corresponding 'ownedAttribute' of a 'Stereotype'. During this mapping, the 'type' property of an attribute is recomputed so that it never refers to a 'Stereotype' of UP_{SDL}. Instead, the recomputed 'type' of a mapped attribute refers to a metaclass or data type contained in MM_{UML} or MM_{VS}. Hence, the 'type' properties of all 'ownedAttributes' of the «`ProcedureDefinition`» 'Stereotype' shown in Fig. 5 are recomputed. Apart from the 'type' property, all other properties of an 'ownedAttribute' of a MC_{ST} metaclass are usually mapped unchanged.

According to the UML [17], a *'Stereotype'* is not permitted to inherit from a UML metaclass. Therefore, *'ownedAttributes'* of a UML metaclass cannot be subsetted or redefined by *'Stereotype'* attributes. Hence, when the *'redefined-Property'* or *'subsettedProperty'* of an *'ownedAttribute'* of a MC_{ST} refers to an attribute of an MC_{AC}, we map this *'ownedAttribute'* to a read-only and derived *'ownedAttribute'* of a *'Stereotype'*. In addition, we generate OCL expressions that define the *'defaultValue'* properties of these attributes, so that their values can be computed at runtime. For instance, the `procedureIdentifier` and the `procedureDefinition` attributes of the «ProcedureDefinition» *'Stereotype'* shown in Fig. 5 are mapped in this way.

OCL Expressions: The generated OCL expressions for the *'defaultValue'* properties always consist of three different parts. The first part is used for navigating to the source attribute. Then, the required items are selected in the second part of the expression. Finally, we type-cast the selected items to match the *'type'* and the cardinality of a *'Stereotype'* attribute. For instance, the *'defaultValue'* of the «ProcedureDefinition» *'Stereotype'* is defined as follows:

```
self.base_StateMachine.ownedBehavior
  ->select(isStereotypedBy('SDLUML::ProcedureDefinition'))
  .oclAsType(UML::StateMachine)->asSet()
```

OCL Constraints: We introduce an OCL *'Constraint'* for each *'ownedAttribute'* of a UML metaclass that is used as source for a value computation, as discussed before. The aim is to ensure that the content of these attributes

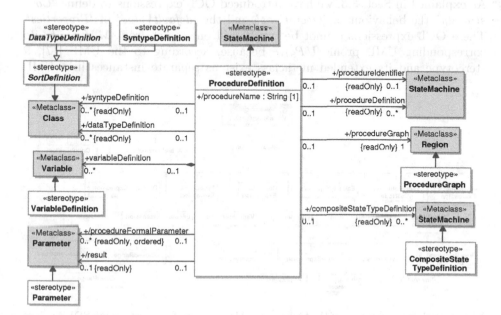

Fig. 5. The derived «ProcedureDefinition» stereotype.

is compliant to the static semantics as defined by the SDL metamodel. The first part of such a *'Constraint'* consists of a navigation to the attribute under consideration. In the second part, we test that only expected items can be contained in the attribute. For instance, the following *'Constraint'* ensures that the `ownedBehaviour` attribute of a `StateMachine` instance only contains «CompositeStateTypeDefinition» and «ProcedureDefinition» items.

```
self.base_StateMachine.ownedBehavior->notEmpty() implies
self.base_StateMachine.ownedBehavior->forAll(
  isStereotypedBy('SDLUML::CompositeStateTypeDefinition')
  or isStereotypedBy('SDLUML::ProcedureDefinition'))
```

In total, 139 OCL expressions for *'defaultValues'* and 73 additional *'Constraints'* are introduced during our derivation of the UML profile for SDL.

Additional metaclasses: In addition to the UML Profile for SDL, we also derive 'Additional Metaclasses' that are contained in the MM_{VS} metamodel. These metaclasses are derived based on the 35 MC_{AMC} metaclasses of the MM_{SDL} metamodel. A high-level overview of the derived metaclasses is given in Fig. 6. As shown, all metaclasses of MM_{VS} inherit from the UML `ValueSpecification` metaclass. The UML profile for SDL cannot be used without these metaclasses, because their instances are employed to specify concrete values and expressions.

4.3   Update of Existing OCL Expressions

As explained in Sect. 3.3, we have introduced OCL expressions to define *'Constraints'*, the behaviour of *'Operations'*, and the *'defaultValue'* of *'Properties'*. These OCL expressions cannot be transferred one-to-one from MM_{SDL} to its corresponding UML profile UP_{SDL} because, according to the UML [17], a stereotype and its extended metaclass exist as separate instances in a UML

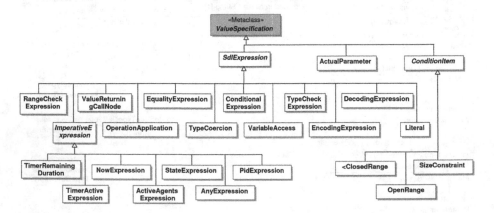

Fig. 6. High level overview of the 'Additional Metaclasses' for representing SDL's values and expressions.

model. Hence, the UML provides two implicitly defined properties to navigate between metaclass and stereotype instances: the *'extension_ <stereotype>'* property is used to navigate from a metaclass to an applied stereotype, whereas the *'base_ <metaclass>'* property is used for the opposite direction. Accordingly, OCL expressions of MM_{SDL} have to be updated before UP_{SDL} can be derived.

Since OCL expressions are only present as textual notations, they cannot be processed by the M2M-transformation that implements Step (B) of our overall approach. Instead, we implement the update by using an OCL parser and a pretty printer. Before UP_{SDL} is derived from MM_{SDL}, an Abstract Syntax Tree (AST) is generated by the parser for each OCL expression in MM_{SDL}. This AST consists of different types of nested OCL expressions, as specified in [18]. Every OCL expression of an AST is then visited by the pretty printer in order to perform the update. During this visit, the AST is converted back to its textual notation and the update is performed. Because OCL was specified by means of a metamodel, someone could argue that the 'update' of OCL expressions could also be realized by employing an M2M transformation. Before we implemented the current approach, we analysed such a solution, and evaluated it as infeasible. Due to an existing problem of OCL Pivot, parsed OCL expressions can be stored as an OCL model, but when this model is loaded afterwards, not all referenced classes and data types can be resolved; however, this is a prerequisite for processing models by an M2M transformation.

In the following, we explain the OCL update on the example of `Constraint_1` (see Sect. 3.3), which is introduced for the `ProcedureDefinition` metaclass of MM_{SDL}. After the profile derivation, the «ProcedureDefinition» stereotype extends the `StateMachine` of MM_{UML} as shown in Fig. 5. In addition, this stereotype owns the updated `Constraint_1`, and the `StateMachine` metaclass of MM_{UML} owns the `specification` attribute and the `allOwnedElements()` operation. Since the «ProcedureDefinition» stereotype does not inherit features of the `StateMachine` metaclass, the property navigation *'base_ StateMachine'* has to be introduced during the update. This is used to navigate from the stereotype instance to the metaclass instance. After the update, `Constraint_1` of the «ProcedureDefinition» stereotype is defined as follows:

```
self.base_StateMachine.specification <> null implies
self.base_StateMachine.allOwnedElements()
  ->select(isStereotypedBy('SDLUML::StateNode'))->isEmpty()
```

Apart from the additional navigations as argued above, also other OCL expression types have to be updated. In the last line of the constrained shown above, the `isStereotypedBy()` operation replaces the predefined OCL operation `oclIsKindOf()`. However, the update is only performed if the `oclIsKindOf()` operation is used to determine whether the result type of an OCL expression matches a given MC_{ST} metaclass, e.g., `StateNode`. In the same manner, we replace the `oclIsTypeOf()` operation with the `isStrictStereotypedBy()` operation. Because both introduced operations are custom-specific, they have to be implemented by the employed OCL tool.

5   Derivation of M2M Transformations

As argued in Sect. 2, we cannot only derive a UML profile for SDL but also M2M transformations that can be employed to transform an SDL model to a corresponding UML model ($T_{SDL\text{-}to\text{-}UML}$) and vice versa ($T_{UML\text{-}to\text{-}SDL}$). However, an important prerequisite is that MM_{SDL} is created by reusing 'Abstract Concepts'; otherwise, the transformations could not be derived based on a single metamodel. We utilize two M2T transformations to generate source code for QVT's operational language [14].

5.1   Common Concepts

In general, both derived transformations $T_{SDL\text{-}to\text{-}UML}$ and $T_{UML\text{-}to\text{-}SDL}$ shall implement a rewrite system so that an entire input model can be mapped to a corresponding output model. Therefore, based on each metaclass of MM_{SDL}, we generate a dedicated mapping operation for both transformations. In detail, the following kinds of mapping operations are introduced for each abstract and non-abstract metaclass:

- A disjunct mapping operation is introduced for each abstract metaclass. Such an operation consists of an ordered list of operation calls for all mapping operations introduced for subclasses of the abstract metaclass.
- A mapping operation with a specific operation body is generated for each non-abstract metaclass. The body contains the rules for the mapping of all owned and inherited metaclass attributes.

5.2   Transformation for Mapping a SDL to a UML Model

An important requirement for the mapping of elements of an SDL model (M_{SDL}) to corresponding elements of a UML model (M_{UML}) is that also *'Stereotypes'* have to be applied during the transformation. Therefore, we generate an operation that implements the mapping of a metaclass instance, and another operation that creates and applies a *'Stereotype'* instance (see Fig. 7).

Mapping to a UML element: Only a particular set of attributes is processed by a mapping operation that maps a model element of M_{SDL} to a corresponding element of M_{UML}. We determine this set (Att_{rel}) from the sets of inherited attributes (Att_{inh}) and owned attributes (Att_{Owned}) of an MC_{St} in MM_{SDL} as follows:

- Take those attributes of Att_{inh} that are not specified as 'read-only' and that are not redefined or subsetted by any other attribute.
- In addition, take those attributes of Att_{inh} that are redefined or subsetted by at least one attribute contained in Att_{Owned}.

We have to take into account the last mentioned attribute category for the element mapping, because these attributes are employed to compute the values

```
mapping SDLMM::ProcedureDefinition::toStateMachine() : UML::StateMachine {
    result.classifierBehavior := self.classifierBehavior.map toBehavior();
    result.connectionPoint += self.connectionPoint->map toPseudostate();
    result.general += self.general->map toClassifier();
    result.isAbstract := self.isAbstract;
    result.isActive := self.isActive;
    result.name := self.name;
    result.nestedClassifier += self.nestedClassifier->map toClassifier();
    result.ownedAttribute += self.ownedAttribute->map toProperty();
    result.ownedBehavior += self.ownedBehavior->map toBehavior();
    result.ownedComment += self.ownedComment->map toComment();
    result.ownedConnector += self.ownedConnector->map toConnector();
    result.ownedOperation += self.ownedOperation->map toOperation();
    result.ownedParameter += self.ownedParameter->map toParameter();
    result.ownedRule += self.ownedRule->map toConstraint();
    result.package := self.package.map toPackage();
    result.region += self.region->map toRegion();
    result.specification := self.specification.map toBehavioralFeature();
    result.submachineState += self.submachineState->map toState();
    result.superClass += self.superClass->map toClass();
}

mapping inout UML::StateMachine::applyStereotypeForProcedureDefinition()
    when { self.invresolveone(SDLMM::ProcedureDefinition)->notEmpty() } {
    // 1. Creation of the stereotype instance
    var srcElement := self.invresolveone(SDLMM::ProcedureDefinition);
    var stereotype := self.getApplicableStereotype('SDLUML::ProcedureDefinition');
    self.applyStereotype(stereotype);
    // 2. Value assignment to stereotype attributes
    var inst := self.getStereotypeApplication(stereotype)
        .oclAsType(SDLUML::ProcedureDefinition);
    inst.variableDefinition += srcElement.variableDefinition->map toVariable();
}
```

Fig. 7. Example mapping operations for mapping an SDL `ProcedureDefinition` to a UML *'StateMachine'* having applied the «ProcedureDefinition» stereotype.

of 'derived' stereotype attributes at runtime. After having determined Att_{rel} according to the above rules, an assignment statement in the operation body is generated for each attribute of Att_{rel}. An example of a generated mapping operation is given in Fig. 7. The shown `toStateMachine()` operation is used to map a `ProcedureDefinition` instance to a corresponding UML *'StateMachine'* instance.

Mapping to a *'Stereotype'*: Because most of the attributes of an element in M_{Domain} are processed by the mapping operations discussed before, only a small set of attributes remains. These attributes are mapped by a stereotype-specific mapping operation, because first a *'Stereotype'* instance has to be created before values can be assigned to stereotype attributes.

We determine the set of relevant attributes Att_{rel} based on the set of owned attributes Att_{Owned} of an MC_{St} metaclass in MM_{SDL}. As argued before, an attribute att' of a *'Stereotype'* is defined as 'read-only' and 'derived', if the corresponding attribute att of an MC_{St} redefines or subsets an attribute of an MC_{AC}. As no values can be assigned to 'read-only' attributes, such attributes have not to be regarded for the mapping of a *'Stereotype'* instance. Therefore, the Att_{rel} set only consists of Att_{Owned} attributes that do not redefine or subset any attribute of an MC_{St}.

The body of a mapping operation for a *'Stereotype'* comprises two parts, see the applyStereotypeForProcedureDefinition() operation of Fig. 7 as example. The first part is utilized to create the stereotype instance, while the second part consists of value assignments that are generated based on Att_{rel}. Because the derived «ProcedureDefinition» stereotype shown in Fig. 5 has only one 'read-only' attribute, exactly one attribute is mapped in the body of the applyStereotypeForProcedureDefinition() operation.

5.3   Transformation for Mapping a UML Model to a SDL Model

The common concepts discussed before also apply with regard to the generated transformation $T_{UML\text{-}to\text{-}SDL}$. However, an important difference to $T_{SDL\text{-}to\text{-}UML}$ is that only one mapping operation for a particular MC_{St} in MM_{SDL} is generated (see Fig. 8). This is because a *'Stereotype'* instance that is associated with a particular UML element instance already exists. Thus, both instances are directly accessible from the same mapping operation, which consists of the following two parts:

Mapping of stereotype attributes: The attribute values of a *'Stereotype'* instance are mapped in the first part of the mapping operation. The set of relevant attributes Att_{rel} is determined based on the set of owned attributes Att_{Owned} of an MC_{St} metaclass in MM_{SDL}. As a value assignment to 'read-only' attributes is impossible, we take only those attributes of Att_{Owned} that are not specified as 'read-only'. The generated code for Att_{rel} is shown in the upper part of Fig. 8, where all attributes of the «ProcedureDefinition» stereotype are mapped to their corresponding attributes of an SDL ProcedureDefinition.

Mapping of metaclass attributes: Attribute values of an element of M_{UML} towards a corresponding attribute of an element of M_{Domain} are processed in the second part of the mapping operation. We determine the set of relevant attributes Att_{rel} from the set of inherited attributes Att_{inh} of an MC_{St} in MM_{SDL} by taking only those attributes into account that are not mapped to attributes of a *'Stereotype'*. Then, all those attributes that are redefining or subsetting an MC_{St} attribute are removed from Att_{rel}, because these attributes are already processed in the first part of the mapping operation. Finally, an assignment statement is generated for each attribute in Att_{rel}.

---

mapping UML::StateMachine::toProcedureDefinition() : SDLMM::ProcedureDefinition
when { *self*.isStereotypedBy('SDLUML::ProcedureDefinition') } {
  // 1. Mapping of attributes of the applied stereotype
  var stereotype := *self*.getAppliedStereotype('SDLUML::ProcedureDefinition');
  var inst := *self*.getStereotypeApplication(stereotype)
    .*oclAsType*(SDLUML::ProcedureDefinition);
  result.compositeStateTypeDefinition += inst.compositeStateTypeDefinition
    −>*map* toCompositeStateTypeDefinition();
  result.dataTypeDefinition += inst.dataTypeDefinition−>*map* toDataTypeDefinition();
  result.procedureDefinition += inst.procedureDefinition−>*map* toProcedureDefinition();
  result.procedureFormalParameter += inst.procedureFormalParameter−>*map* toParameter();
  result.procedureGraph := inst.procedureGraph.*map* toProcedureGraph();
  result.procedureIdentifier := inst.procedureIdentifier.*map* toProcedureDefinition();
  result.procedureName := inst.procedureName;
  result._result := inst._result.*map* toParameter();
  result.syntypeDefinition += inst.syntypeDefinition−>*map* toSyntypeDefinition();
  result.variableDefinition += inst.variableDefinition−>*map* toVariableDefinition();
  // 2. Mapping of metaclass attributes
  result.isAbstract := *self*.isAbstract;
  result.isActive := *self*.isActive;
  result.ownedComment += *self*.ownedComment−>*map* toAC_Comment();
  result.package := *self*.package.*map* toAC_Package();
  result.specification := *self*.specification.*map* toAC_BehavioralFeature();
}

Fig. 8. Example operation that maps a UML *'StateMachine'* and its associated «ProcedureDefinition» instance to a corresponding SDL `ProcedureDefinition`.

6 Discussion

The above has discussed how to employ our most recent approach [12] to derive a metamodel and a corresponding UML profile for a computer language. Since the metamodel and the profile exist only in terms of UML class models, we cannot utilize them for a modelling tool without an implementation. Thanks to the code generation facilities of the *Model Development Tools (MDT)*[2] for Eclipse, we could generate the required code automatically. Thus, we have executable Eclipse plug-ins that provide a tree-based editor for SDL models and a runnable version of the UML profile. This profile can be applied to UML models that are created with the tree-based UML editor of Eclipse or with Papyrus[3], which is an Eclipse-based graphical UML modelling tool.

An example of the previously discussed SDL 'Procedure Definition' is given in Fig. 9. It shows the SDL model (Part A) and a corresponding UML model (Parts B/C). Although the presentation form is different, Parts B and C represent the same UML model. We have created the UML model with Papyrus in a graphical manner, and the outcome is represented by Part C. Due to the graphical representation, not all model parts can be displayed so that we additionally provide the tree-based representation, which is depicted as Part B in Fig. 9. Our

---

[2] https://eclipse.org/modeling/mdt/.
[3] https://eclipse.org/papyrus/.

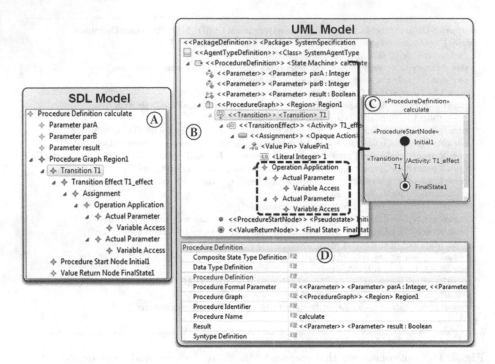

Fig. 9. SDL model and a corresponding UML model with applied UML profile for SDL. Both models represent the same SDL procedure definition.

example implements a trivial operation for accumulating two integer numbers. Thus, the procedure graph only consists of a 'Procedure Start Node' with a 'Transition' to a terminating 'Value Return Node'. The effect of the 'Transition' is an 'Assignment' statement, which assigns the calculated value to a result variable. Even though we are able to create an SDL specification by means of a UML model, the definition of expressions is currently tedious, because each expression instance has to be modelled explicitly. Hence, a dedicated textual notation would be much better suited for this purpose. An example for such an expression is the 'OperationApplication' shown in Part B of Fig. 9.

As discussed, we apply a particular mapping for redefined or subsetted meta-class attributes, so that the values for their corresponding stereotype attributes can be computed at runtime. For example, this applies for all attributes of the «ProcedureDefinition» stereotype shown in Part D of Fig. 9. Thanks to our automatic derivation approach, we can also transfer all OCL constraints and expressions of our SDL metamodel to the derived UML profile for SDL. Thus, we are able to directly validate the static semantics of an SDL specification with Papyrus or with the tree-based UML editor. Hence, we do not have to transform the UML model to a corresponding SDL model before it can be validated. Another advantage of our UML profile for SDL is that we do not have to implement SDL-specific diagrams, because we can use those of the UML. Even though we see advantages in a UML-based modelling of SDL specifications, this does not apply for the generation of executable code or the model export. In our point of view, this should always be based on SDL models, which could be obtained by applying the transformation $T_{UML\text{-}to\text{-}SDL}$ (see Sect. 5).

We have made the discussed SDL metamodel, the derived UML profile, the associated M2M transformations, and the components that implement our derivation approach publicly available [22]. Thus, these artefacts can serve as input for future standardization activities. Even though a SDL metamodel is not of interest, an automatic derivation of a future UML profile for SDL would be an asset for standardization, because it is less error-prone and much more efficient than a manual specification.

7   Related Work

In the first part of this section, related works concerning metamodels and UML profiles for SDL are discussed. Generic derivation approaches for UML profiles are treated in the second part.

Metamodels and UML profiles for SDL. The general relation between context-free grammars and metamodels is studied by Alanen and Porres in [1]. By applying their algorithm, an 'initial' metamodel can be automatically derived from the syntax rules of a computer language. The Text-to-Model transformation framework XText[4] implements a similar approach [2]. Yet another approach is introduced by Fischer et al. in [3,21], where 'Abstract Concepts' are employed to reduce the effort for a manual rework of the generated metamodel for SDL. However, the relations between 'Abstract Concepts' and generated metaclasses have to be modelled by hand. As points for further improvements, Fischer et al. identify the usage of concepts provided by the UML and of behavioural concepts, which we do here. Among other aspects, the static and dynamic semantics of a SDL metamodel is analysed by Prinz et al. [20] and by Scheidgen [21]. Both propose to define the static semantics in terms of OCL constraints, whereas the ASM formalism [20] or a dedicated action language [21] are used to formalize the dynamic semantics. Although many aspects are covered, the automatic derivation of a UML Profile for SDL is not considered in [20,21]. This gap is closed by our research.

A formalization of the existing UML profile for SDL, as specified in Z.109 [10], is analysed by Grammes in [6]. He proposes to create OCL constraints to capture the static semantics which is currently specified in natural language only. However, this approach does not ensure that the given descriptions match with the static semantics of SDL. Furthermore, Grammes proposes to formalize the relation between UML and SDL elements by a mapping to the abstract syntax of SDL. Because this is not based on a metamodel, standardized MDE technologies such as M2M transformations are not applicable. As an alternative to the standardized UML profile for SDL, the UML profile for 'communicating systems' is

---

[4] https://eclipse.org/Xtext/.

proposed by Werner in [23]. The static semantics of this UML profile is defined in terms of OCL constraints, and a mapping to the abstract syntax of SDL is specified by employing *eXtensible Stylesheet Language Transformations* (XSLT). However, the same restrictions as for [6] apply.

The identified limitations concerning the formalisation of a UML profile for SDL can be remedied by applying our derivation approach as presented here. Instead of manually creating a UML profile for SDL, we can automatically derive this profile. Based on this foundation, we can also automatically transfer the OCL-defined static semantics from the source metamodel to the derived UML profile. In addition, we can derive M2M transformations that transform an SDL domain model to a corresponding UML model and vice versa.

Generic approaches to deriving UML profiles. The most closely related approaches to ours are [4,5,19,24], which also derive a UML profile from an existing metamodel for a DSL. Their commonality is that, in addition to the metamodel, mapping rules have to be provided as input for the profile derivation. Depending on the approach, this is realized in terms of so called 'Integration Metamodels' or 'Mapping Models'. In contrast, our approach expects metamodels as input for the derivation of UML profiles, which enable the reuse of 'Abstract Concepts' as proposed in [3,21]. Since 'Abstract Concepts' are a subset of the metaclasses contained in the UML metamodel, not all aspects of a computer language have to be modelled from scratch. Furthermore, due to the correlation between 'Abstract Concepts' and UML metaclasses, no mapping rules must explicitly be defined in our approach. Equally important and in contrast to us, the related works do not treat the generation of OCL expressions and constraints for 'subsetted' or 'redefined' attributes, and do not address an automated transfer of the static semantics towards a UML profile.

8   Conclusions and Future Work

This paper presented our semi-automatically generated SDL metamodel and a corresponding automatically derived UML profile. Whereas we spent months to generate previous versions of SDL's UML profile by hand [10], our new and highly automated approach required only some weeks. Since our metamodel, UML profile and our employed tool-chain are publicly available [22], they can be used as input for future standardization activities so that a model-driven language development of SDL can finally become reality. Due to space constraints, we could not present more details concerning the derived M2M transformations here, but the interested reader can download them from [22], too.

Regarding future work we wish to use our SDL metamodel and UML profile for implementing a new version of our SDL-UML Modeling and Validation (SUMoVal) framework [11].

Acknowledgments. We thank Gerald Lüttgen of the Software Technologies Research Group at the University of Bamberg, Germany, for several discussions and comments on the paper's topic. Furthermore, we also thank the reviewers for their many valuable remarks.

References

1. Alanen, M., Porres, I.: A relation between context-free grammars and meta object facility metamodels, Turku Centre Comput. Sci., Finland, Technical report 606 (2004)
2. Efftinge, S., Völter, M.: oAW xText: a framework for textual DSLs. In: Modeling Symposium at Eclipse Summit, vol. 32, pp. 118–121 (2006). eclipsecon.org
3. Fischer, J., Piefel, M., Scheidgen, M.: A metamodel for SDL-2000 in the context of metamodelling ULF. In: Amyot, D., Williams, A.W. (eds.) SAM 2004. LNCS, vol. 3319, pp. 208–223. Springer, Heidelberg (2005). doi:10.1007/978-3-540-31810-1_14
4. Giachetti, G., Marín, B., Pastor, O.: Integration of domain-specific modelling languages and UML through UML profile extension mechanism. Int. J. Comput. Sci. Applicat. 6(5), 145–174 (2009)
5. Giachetti, G., Marín, B., Pastor, O.: Using UML as a domain-specific modeling language: a proposal for automatic generation of UML profiles. In: van Eck, P., Gordijn, J., Wieringa, R. (eds.) CAiSE 2009. LNCS, vol. 5565, pp. 110–124. Springer, Heidelberg (2009). doi:10.1007/978-3-642-02144-2_13
6. Grammes, R.: Syntactic and semantic modularisation of modelling languages. Ph.D. thesis, Department of Computer Science, TU Kaiserslautern, Germany (2007)
7. ITU-T: Recommendation Z.109: Specification and Description Language - SDL combined with UML. International Telecommunication Union (1999)
8. ITU-T: Recommendation Z.111: Notations and guidelines for the definition of ITU-T languages. International Telecommunication Union (2008)
9. ITU-T: Recommendation Z.100: Specification and Description Language - Overview of SDL-2010. International Telecommunication Union (2016)
10. ITU-T: Recommendation Z.109: Specification and Description Language - Unified Modeling Language profile for SDL-2010. International Telecommunication Union (2016)
11. Kraas, A.: Towards an extensible modeling and validation framework for SDL-UML. In: Amyot, D., Fonseca i Casas, P., Mussbacher, G. (eds.) SAM 2014. LNCS, vol. 8769, pp. 255–270. Springer, Cham (2014). doi:10.1007/978-3-319-11743-0_18
12. Kraas, A.: On the automated derivation of domain-specific UML profiles. In: Anjorin, A., Espinoza, H. (eds.) ECMFA 2017. LNCS, vol. 10376, pp. 3–19. Springer, Cham (2017). doi:10.1007/978-3-319-61482-3_1
13. OMG: MOF Model to Text Transformation Language - Version 1.0. Object Management Group (2008)
14. OMG: Meta Object Facility (MOF) 2.0 Query/View/Transformation Specification - Version 1.1. Object Management Group (2011)
15. OMG: OMG Meta Object Facility (MOF) Core Specification - Version 2.5. Object Management Group (2011)
16. OMG: OMG Unified Modeling Language (OMG UML), Infrastructure, Version 2.4.1. Object Management Group (2011)
17. OMG: OMG Unified Modeling Language (OMG UML), Superstructure, Version 2.4.1. Object Management Group (2011)
18. OMG: Object Constraint Language - Version 2.4. Object Management Group (2014)
19. Pastor, O., Giachetti, G., Marín, B., Valverde, F.: Automating the interoperability of conceptual models in specific development domains. Domain Engineering: Product Lines. Languages, and Conceptual Models, pp. 349–373. Springer, Heidelberg (2013). doi:10.1007/978-3-642-36654-3_14

20. Prinz, A., Scheidgen, M., Tveit, M.S.: A model-based standard for SDL. In: Gaudin, E., Najm, E., Reed, R. (eds.) SDL 2007. LNCS, vol. 4745, pp. 1–18. Springer, Heidelberg (2007). doi:10.1007/978-3-540-74984-4_1

21. Scheidgen, M.: Description of languages based on object-oriented meta-modelling. Ph.D. thesis, Math.-Natural Sci. Dept. II, HU Berlin, Germany (2009)

22. SDL-UML Modeling and Validation (SU-MoVal) framework homepage. http://www.su-moval.org/. Accessed 24 Feb 2017

23. Werner, C., Kraatz, S., Hogrefe, D.: A UML profile for communicating systems. In: Gotzhein, R., Reed, R. (eds.) SAM 2006. LNCS, vol. 4320, pp. 1–18. Springer, Heidelberg (2006). doi:10.1007/11951148_1

24. Wimmer, M.: A semi-automatic approach for bridging DSMLs with UML. Int. J. Web Inform. Sys. **5**(3), 372–404 (2009)

An Automated Change Impact Analysis Approach to GRL Models

Hasan Salim Alkaf[1], Jameleddine Hassine[1(✉)], Abdelwahab Hamou-Lhadj[2], and Luay Alawneh[3]

[1] Department of Information and Computer Science, King Fahd University of Petroleum and Minerals, Dahran, Saudi Arabia
{g201201840,jhassine}@kfupm.edu.sa
[2] Electrical and Computer Engineering Department, Concordia University, Montréal, Canada
abdelw@ece.concordia.ca
[3] Department of Software Engineering, Jordan University of Science and Technology, Irbid, Jordan
lmalawneh@just.edu.jo

Abstract. Goal-oriented approaches to requirements engineering have gained momentum with the development of many frameworks, methods, and tools. As stakeholders' needs evolve, goal models evolve quickly and undergo many changes in order to accommodate the rapid changes of stakeholders' goals, technologies, and business environments. Therefore, there is a need for mechanisms to identify and analyze the impact of changes in goal models. In this paper, we propose a Change Impact Analysis (CIA) approach to Goal-oriented Requirements Language (GRL), part of ITU-T's User Requirement Notation (URN) standard. Given a suggested modification within a given GRL model, our approach allows for the identification of all impacted GRL elements within the targeted model as well as across all GRL models that are linked to it through URN Links. Furthermore, the proposed approach allows for the identification of the potentially impacted GRL evaluation strategies. The developed GRL-based CIA approach is implemented as a feature within the Eclipse-based jUCMNav framework. We demonstrate the applicability of our approach using two real-world GRL specifications.

1 Introduction

Goal-oriented requirements engineering (GORE) is concerned with helping stakeholders understand, elaborate, analyze, and document their requirements. Goal modeling is becoming a popular way for describing and connecting stakeholders' intentions and goals with technical requirements. Goals are used to capture, at different levels of abstraction (ranging from high-level strategic mission statements to low-level operational tasks), the various objectives the system under development should accomplish or the concerns that stakeholders may have with it. The growing popularity of goal-oriented modeling, and its adoption by a large

© Springer International Publishing AG 2017
T. Csöndes et al. (Eds.): SDL 2017, LNCS 10567, pp. 157–172, 2017.
DOI: 10.1007/978-3-319-68015-6_10

international community, led to the development of many goal-oriented modeling languages and notations, e.g., i^* [1], TROPOS [2], and the Goal-oriented Requirements Language (GRL) [3], part of ITU-T's User Requirements Notation (URN) standard.

Although, goals are supposed to be more stable than the requirements that helped model them [4], due to continuous changes in the business environment and to the sustained technological advances, goal models are deemed to change accordingly. Commonly, when a change is made, there is often a ripple effect through the goal model. Hence, there is a need to trace such ripple effects across the goal model and identify the potential consequences of such impact on stakeholders' goals. Change Impact Analysis (CIA) is defined by Bohner and Arnold [5] as "identifying the potential consequences of a change, or estimating what needs to be modified to accomplish a change". Although change impact analysis techniques have been mostly used at lower levels of abstractions (e.g., code level [6]), many techniques have been developed to target other software artifacts, such as architectural models, software specifications, data sources, configuration files, etc.

The main motivation of this research is to apply change impact analysis to goal-oriented models. In particular, we are interested in understanding and capturing how changes propagate through GRL models. In this paper, we extend and build upon our preliminary work [7]. The paper serves the following purposes:

- It provides a GRL-based approach to Change Impact Analysis (CIA). The proposed CIA approach allows maintainers and analysts to understand how a change in a GRL model is propagated within the model itself (e.g., between actors of the model) and across other GRL models (i.e., GRL to GRL propagation) through URN Links. Furthermore, the proposed approach allows for the identification of the potentially impacted GRL evaluation strategies as a result of a proposed change.
- It provides a prototype tool that automates the proposed GRL-based change impact analysis approach. The prototype is implemented as a feature within the jUCMNav [8] tool and is publicly available.
- It demonstrates the applicability of our approach and tests our prototype tool, using two real-world GRL specifications presenting different constructs and features, namely, Adverse Event Management System (AEMS) and a commuting system.

The rest of this paper is organized as follows. Section 2 provides a brief overview of the Goal-Oriented Language (GRL). In Sect. 3, we present our proposed GRL-based Change Impact Analysis (CIA) approach along with the prototype tool. The applicability of the proposed approach is demonstrated in Sect. 4. A discussion of the related work, the benefits and limitations of our approach is provided in Sect. 5. Finally, conclusions and future work are presented in Sect. 6.

2   GRL in a Nutshell

The Goal-oriented Requirement Language (GRL) [3], part of ITU-T's User Requirement Notation (URN) standard, is a visual modeling notation that is used to model intentions, business goals, functional and non-functional requirements (NFR). A GRL goal model is a graph of intentional elements, that optionally reside within an actor. Actors (illustrated as ⬭Actor) are holders of intentions; they are the active entities in the system or its environment who want goals to be achieved, tasks to be performed, resources to be available, and softgoals to be satisfied [3]. Actor definitions are often used to represent stakeholders as well as systems. A GRL actor may contain intentional elements and indicators describing its intentions, capabilities and related measures.

Softgoals (illustrated as ⬭) differentiate themselves from goals (illustrated as ⬭) in that there is no clear, objective measure of satisfaction for a softgoal whereas a goal is quantifiable, often in a binary way. Tasks (illustrated as ⬭) represent solutions to (or operationalizations of) goals or softgoals. In order to be achieved or completed, softgoals, goals, and tasks may require resources (illustrated as ⬜) to be available. A GRL indicator (illustrated as ⬭) is a GRL element that is used to represent some real-world measurements. An indicator usually convert real-world values in user-defined units into GRL satisfaction values on a standard scale (e.g. [−100, 100]).

Various kinds of links connect the elements in a goal graph. Decomposition links (illustrated as ───+) allow an element to be decomposed into sub-elements (using AND, OR, or XOR). Contribution links (illustrated as ───→) indicate desired impacts of one element on another element. A contribution link has a qualitative contribution type (e.g., Make, Help, SomePositive, Unknown, SomeNegative, Break, Hurt) and/or a quantitative contribution (e.g., an integer value within [−100, 100]). Correlation links (illustrated as ------→) describe side effects rather than desired impacts. Dependency links (illustrated as ──▶──) model relationships between actors, where intentional elements inside actor definitions can be used as source and/or destination of a dependency link. In this research, we adopt the classification of GRL dependencies introduced in [9] that considers contributions, correlations and decompositions links as implicit dependencies, and dependency links as explicit dependencies.

Initial satisfaction levels, which can be quantitative (e.g., within [−100, 100]), or qualitative (e.g., Satisfied, Weakly Satisfied, Denied, Weakly Denied, etc.) of some of the intentional elements constitute a GRL strategy. These initial values (emanating from a contextual or a future situation) propagate to the other intentional elements of the model through the various model links, allowing for the assessment of how high-level goals are achieved and may reveal more appropriate alternative strategies. Finally, URN Links (illustrated as a black triangle symbol ▶ (source) ◀ (target)) are used to connect a source URN model element with a target URN model element. URN Links model user-defined relationships such as traceability, refinement, implementation, etc. For a detailed description of the GRL language, the reader is invited to consult [3].

3　GRL Change Impact Analysis (CIA) Approach

Figure 1 describes the proposed GRL-based change impact analysis approach. To identify the impact of a change in a GRL model under maintenance, an analyst may select a GRL construct (i.e., an intentional element, an indicator, or a link) to be changed, then specify the type of change (e.g., addition, modification, deletion). Next, the GRL Model Dependency Graph (GMDG) is constructed (see Sect. 3.1), then sliced according to the specified slicing criterion (see Sect. 3.2). GMDG impacted nodes are then identified, mapped back to the original GRL model, and marked with a different color. Finally, impacted evaluation strategies and impacted URN Links are displayed as a GRL Comment construct (see Sect. 3.5).

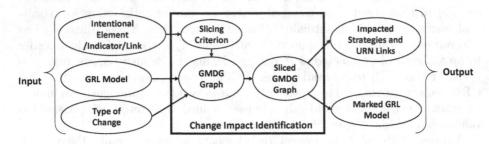

Fig. 1. GRL CIA approach

In what follows, we provide some necessary definitions (adopted and modified from [7]) that are used in the subsequent sections.

Definition 1 (GRL Model). *We assume that a GRL model GRLM is denoted by a 3-tuple: (Actors, Elements, Links), where:*

- Actors *is the set of actor references in the GRL model.*
- Elements *is the set of intentional elements (i.e., tasks, goals, softgoals, resources) and indicators in the GRL model.*
- Links *is the set of links in the GRL model.*

It is worth noting that we don't consider collapsed actors (although they are described in the URN standard [3]), since they are not supported in jUCMNav [8].

Definition 2 (GRL Link). *We define a GRL link as (type, src, dest): Link-Types × Elements × Elements, where LinkTypes = {contribution, correlation, dependency, decomposition}, src and dest are the source and destination of the link, respectively.*

Definition 3 (GRL Link Access Functions). *Let l = (type, src, dest) be a GRL link. We define the following access functions over GRL links:*

- TypeLink*: Links → LinkTypes, returns the link type (i.e., TypeLink(l) = type).*
- Source*: Links → Elements, returns the intentional element source of the link (i.e., Source(l) = src).*
- Destination*: Links → Elements, returns the intentional element destination of the link (i.e., Destination(l) = dest).*

3.1   GRL Model Dependency Graph (GMDG)

In this section, we define the GMDG graph and present the algorithm (Algorithm 1) to construct it.

Definition 4 (GRL Model Dependency Graph (GMDG)). *A GRL Model Dependency Graph (GMDG) is defined as a directed graph GMDG = (N, E), where:*

- *N is a set of nodes. Each GRL intentional element, indicator, or a link is mapped to a node* n ∈ N.
- *E is a set of directed edges. An edge* e ∈ E *represents a dependency between 2 nodes in GMDG and it is illustrated as a solid arrow (⟶).*

First, for each intentional element, indicator, or a link a new GMDG node is created. Next, depending on the type of the GRL links, GMDG dependency links are created between GMDG nodes (i.e., *CreateDependencyLinkGMDG (e1, e2)* creates a GMDG dependency link from e1 to e2).

Algorithm 1. Constructing a GRL Model Dependency Graph (GMDG)

Procedure Name: ConstructGMDG
Input   : A GRL Model: (Actors, Elements, Links)
Output: A GRL Model Dependency Graph (GMDG)
foreach *e ∈ Elements* **do**
   | n= createGMDGNode(e);
end
foreach *e ∈ Links* **do**
   | n= createGMDGNode(e);
   | **if** *(TypeLink(e) == contribution or TypeLink(e) == correlation or*
   | *TypeLink(e) == decomposition)* **then**
      | CreateDependencyLinkGMDG(Destination(e), Source(e)) ;
      | CreateDependencyLinkGMDG(Destination(e), n);
   | **else**
                     ▷ TypeLink(e) == Dependency
      | CreateDependencyLinkGMDG(Source(e), Destination(e)) ;
      | CreateDependencyLinkGMDG(Source(e), n);
   | **end**
end

Figure 2 illustrates a generic GRL model along with its corresponding GMDG graph. Each goal/contribution/decomposition/dependency is represented as a GMDG node. The satisfaction of *G2* depends on the satisfaction of *G5* and the contribution type (*help* in this case), hence, two GMDG links are created: (1) between *G2* and *G5* and (2) between *G2* and *Contrib-G5G2*. Since *G1* is decomposed into *G3* and *G4* (using AND-decomposition), four GMDG dependency links are created: (1) one between *G1* and *G3*, (2) one between *G1* and *G4*, (3) one between *G1* and *AND-Decomp-G3G1*, and (4) one between *G1* and *AND-Decomp-G4G1*. Finally, *G1* depends on *G2*, which is mapped as two GMDG links: (1) one between *G1* and *G2*, and (2) one between *G1* and *depend-G1G2*.

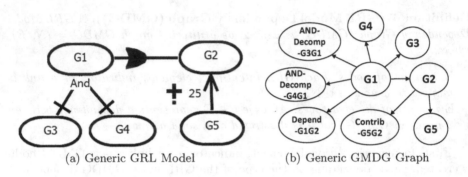

(a) Generic GRL Model   (b) Generic GMDG Graph

Fig. 2. A Generic GRL model and its corresponding GMDG

3.2   Slicing the GRL Model Dependency Graph

Program Slicing, introduced by Weiser [10] in the early 1980's, is a reduction technique used to decrease the size of a program source code by keeping only the lines within a program that are related to the execution of a specific slicing criterion specified by the user. In order to perform a change impact analysis on GRL models, we extend the concept of program slicing to GMDG graphs. In what follows, we introduce the notion of GRL slicing criterion, then we present the GMDG slicing algorithm (see Algorithm 2).

Definition 5 (GRL Slicing Criterion). *Let GRLM be a GRL model. A slicing criterion SC for GRLM may be either a GRL intentional element/Indicators or a GRL link.*

The slicing of the GMDG (see Algorithm 2) is based on a backward traversal of the GMDG. It requires as input the GMDG graph and the GMDG node that corresponds to the slicing criterion SC. The algorithm starts by adding the GMDG node (called *ImpactedGMDGNode*) to the set of impacted nodes (i.e., *SetGMDGImpactedNodes*). Next, it follows each incoming link leading to *ImpactedGMDGNode* and add its source to *SetGMDGImpactedNodes*. Finally, a recursive call is made by passing the GMDG and the new reached GMDG node.

Algorithm 2. GMDG Backward Slicing Algorithm

Function Name: SlicingGMDG
Input : A GMDG + GMDG node corresponding to SC
            (LocationInGMDG(SC))
Output: SetGMDGImpactedNodes
ImpactedGMDGNode = LocationInGMDG(SC);
if *ImpactedGMDGNode* ∉ *SetGMDGImpactedNodes* **then**
│   AddToImpactedNodes(ImpactedGMDGNode, SetGMDGImpactedNodes);
│   **if** *hasIncomingLinks(ImpactedGMDGNode)* **then**
│   │   **foreach** *incomingLink* **do**
│   │   │   AddToImpactedNodes(Source(incomingLink),
│   │   │   SetGMDGImpactedNodes);
│   │   │   GMDGslicingAlg(GMDG, ImpactedGMDGNode);
│   │   **end**
│   **end**
end

The resulting set of impacted GMDG nodes (i.e., *SetGMDGImpactedNodes*) is then mapped back to *SetGRLImpactedElements*, the set of the original GRL model elements. The elements within *SetGRLImpactedElements*, along with the impacted elements emanating from following the URN Links (see Sect. 3.3), are then marked in purple color (see examples in Sect. 4).

3.3   Impact Through URN Links

This step aims at identifying other potential GRL impacted elements by following existing URN Links. A URN Link is used to create a connection between any two URN elements, e.g., intentional element reference/definition, actor reference/definition, link, etc. A URN Link may be defined as follows:

Definition 6 (URN Links). *A URN Link is defined as urnl = (type, from, to), where (1)* type *denotes a user-defined URN Link type, (2)* from *denotes the ID of source URN element, and (2)* to *denotes the ID of the target URN element.*

Algorithm 3 iterates through the set of impacted elements (i.e., *SetGR-LImpactedElements*) and checks whether these elements are involved in any URN Link, as source (i.e., *from* field) or as a target (i.e., *to* field). Since an impacted element can serve as a source or a target in a URN Link and since one source element can be linked to many target elements and vice versa, we have used two search functions to retrieve the set of elements IDs depending whether we are looking for source or target IDs. (i.e., searchSourceURNLinks and searchTargetURNLinks). The new identified elements are then add to the set *SetGRLImpactedElements*.

Algorithm 3. Excerpt of the algorithm to identify impacted elements emanating from URN Links

Function Name: IdentificationOfOverallImpactedElements
Input : GRL Model + SetGRLImpactedElements
Output: SetGRLImpactedElements
URNLinksList = getAllURNLinks();
foreach $e \in SetGRLImpactedElements$ **do**
    ▷ Search for target elements IDs when e is defined as source;
    ToElementList = searchTargetURNLinks(e,from,URNLinksList);
    AddToGRLImpactedElements(ToElement, SetGRLImpactedElements);
    ▷ Search for source elements IDs when e is defined as target
    FromElementList = searchSourceURNLinks(e, URNLinksList);
    AddToGRLImpactedElements(FromElement, SetGRLImpactedElements);
end

3.4   Identification of the Impacted GRL Strategies

Once the set of impacted GRL model elements (i.e., *SetGRLImpactedElements*) is identified, we have to spot all impacted evaluation strategies. Algorithm 4 accepts as input a GRL model and the set of impacted GRL elements (*SetGRLImpactedElements* resulting from applying the GMDG slicing algorithm), and produces the set of impacted GRL strategies (i.e., *SetImpactedStrategies*).

Algorithm 4. Identification of the impacted GRL evaluation strategies

Function Name: IdentificationOfImpactedStrategies
Input : GRL Model + SetGRLImpactedElements
Output: SetImpactedStrategies
SetImpactedStrategies = $\emptyset$;
StrategiesList = getAllStrategies();
foreach $strategy \in StrategiesList$ **do**
    foreach $impactedElement \in SetGRLImpactedElements$ **do**
        if *PartOfStrategy(impactedElement, strategy)* **then**
            AddToImpactedStrategies(strategy, SetImpactedStrategies) ;
        end
    end
end

3.5   JUCMNav GRL-Based Change Impact Analysis Feature

Our proposed change impact analysis approach is implemented as a feature[1] within the jUCMNav framework [8], a full graphical editor and analysis tool for GRL models developed as an Eclipse-based plug-in.

---

[1] The CIA feature is publicly available and can be downloaded from https://github. com/JUCMNAV/projetseg/tree/grl.

To exercise this feature, the user starts by selecting a GRL intentional element, an indicator or a link, then right-clicks to choose from three sub-menu commands: *Addition*, *Deletion*, or *Modification* (see Fig. 3). For the addition option, it is required that the analyst adds the GRL construct first then call the feature. The deletion is provided as a separate option because there will be impacted elements due to the loss of connectivity caused by the deletion. It is worth noting that this CIA menu is activated for the supported GRL constructs only.

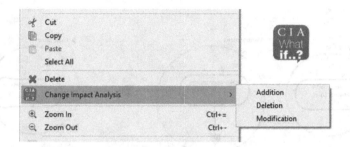

Fig. 3. GRL CIA included in command menu of jUCMNav framework (Color figure online)

If any of the impacted element (marked in purple color (see Fig. 6)), is part of a GRL evaluation strategy, the details of the impacted element will appear as a GRL Comment (in gray color) with its name, ID, and the name of strategies it belongs to (see Fig. 8(a)). Similarly, information about impacted URN Links, such as SourceID, TargetID, and Type, are also shown in the same GRL Comment box (see Fig. 7).

4   Experimental Evaluation

In this section, we evaluate our proposed GRL change impact analysis approach using two real-world GRL case studies of different sizes, complexity, and features. Table 1 provides some characteristics of the used case studies.

4.1   Case Study 1: Adverse Event Management System (AEMS)

This case study describes an adverse event management system (AEMS) for a hospital. Figure 4 illustrates one of the five GRL models constituting the case study.

The first CIA task aims to identify potential impacted elements if we modify softgoal *FastProcess* (i.e., the GMDG node corresponding to *FastProcess* is used as slicing criterion to execute Algorithm 2). The produced GMDG is shown in Fig. 5, while the impacted GRL elements are shown in Fig. 6. Since the goal

Table 1. Case studies characteristics

GRL Spec.	Nb. of GRL Models	Nb. of Intentional Elements	Nb. of GRL Links	Nb. of URN Links	Nb. of GRL Actors
Adverse event management system (AEMS)	5	30	27	6	9
Commuting system	4	19	37	10	3

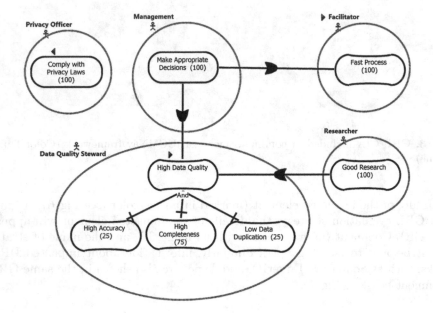

Fig. 4. AEMS GRL model

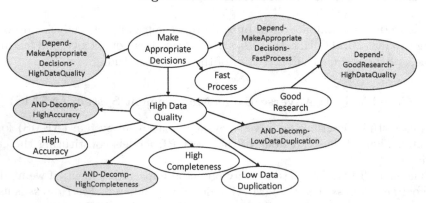

Fig. 5. GMDG graph corresponding to the AEMS GRL model of Fig. 4

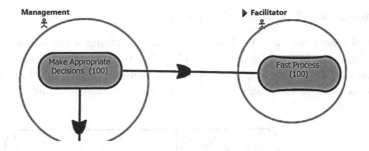

Fig. 6. Impacted elements of the first AEMS CIA task (Color figure online)

comply with Privacy Laws is only linked to the rest of the model through a URN Link, called *trace* (having its source at softgoal *High Data Quality*), there is no GMDG node associated with it.

The second CIA task aims to identify potential impacted elements once we modify the softgoal *High Data Quality*. Three elements are impacted (i.e., goal *Make Appropriate Decisions*, and softgoals *High Data Quality* and *Good Research*) as a result of slicing the GMDG graph with the GMDG node that corresponds to *High Data Quality* as slicing criterion. In addition, goal *Comply with Privacy Law* is impacted since it is the target of the URN Link *trace*, having its source at softgoal *High Data Quality*. Finally, one evaluation strategy is identified, called *AsIsAnalysis-Summer2010*, involving both softgoals *High Data Quality* and *Good Research*. Figure 7 illustrates the impacted elements.

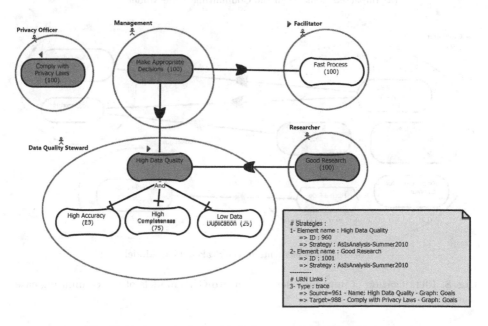

Fig. 7. Impacted elements of the second AEMS CIA task

4.2　Case Study 2: Commuting System

The second case study is a GRL specification describing a commuting system. Figure 8 shows the impact (in purple) of changing the task *Take own car*, on both models Commuting-Time (Fig. 8(a)) and Stakeholders (Fig. 8(b)). The impacted elements are part of a strategy, called *Take own car, Alarm, Stairs only*.

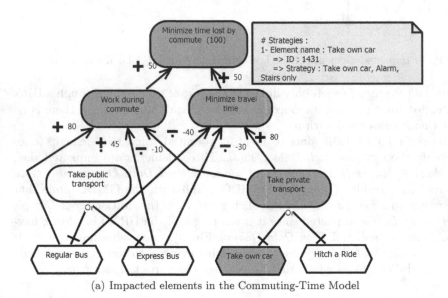

(a) Impacted elements in the Commuting-Time Model

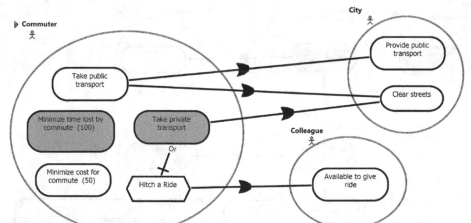

(b) Impacted elements in the Stakeholders Model

Fig. 8. Identification of impacted elements in two GRL models of the commuting case study

5   Discussion

In what follows, we discuss the benefits and limitations of the proposed approach, then we compare it with related work.

5.1   General Benefits of the GRL-based CIA Approach

The presented GRL-based change impact analysis approach presents the following advantages:

- It helps maintainers and analysts answer *"what if... ?"* questions, and assess the consequences of changes in GRL specifications. Indeed, our approach provides an insight into how changes propagate within a GRL model, and across models (i.e., from GRL to GRL) through URN Links. In addition, it allows for the identification of the impacted GRL strategies, if any. This would allow for reasoning about different alternatives, when it comes to implement changes in GRL models.
- Our approach is fully automated and covers the full GRL language constructs.
- We have chosen GRL as target language, given its status as an international standard, but our proposed approach can likely be adapted and applied to other goal-oriented languages such as i^* [1] and TROPOS [2].

5.2   Limitations

The proposed CIA approach is subject to the following limitations:

- Our approach supports the evaluation of the impact of a single change at a time. Assessing the impact of simultaneous changes is left for future work.
- We perform a single iteration to follow the involved URL links. The potentially impacted GRL elements are not used as a source/target to explore more URN connections, if any. However, we believe that implementing a transitive chain should take into account the semantics of the URN Links (i.e., there should be a strong dependency that justifies the capture of the full ripple effect). This is out of the scope of this research.
- The applicability of our approach was demonstrated using two case studies and a mock system (not presented in this paper) only. Bigger case studies should provide a better assessment of the effectiveness of our proposed approach.

5.3   Comparison with Related Work

Change impact analysis [5] techniques have focused mainly on source code level [6] in order to help developers understand and maintain their programs. Less work has been devoted to change impact analysis in other software artifacts such as requirements and design models [11]. In what follows, we survey and compare existing goal-oriented CIA techniques with our proposed approach.

In a closely related work, Hassine [7] proposed a preliminary (and manual) CIA approach based on slicing GRL Model Dependency Graphs (GMDG). In this paper, we extend the approach by considering inter model propagation, GRL evaluation strategies, and URN Links. We have also fully automated it. Cleland-Huang et al. [12] introduced a probabilistic approach for managing the impact of a change using a Softgoal Interdependency Graph (SIG) that describes non-functional requirements and their dependencies. This technique allows for the analysis of the impact of changes by retrieving links between classes affected by changes in the SIG graph. Our approach is bases on the GRL graph structure and does not distinguish between functional and non-functional requirements.

Tanabe et al. [13] introduced a change management technique in AGORA. The technique aims at detecting conflicts when a new goal is added and checks the satisfaction of the parent goal, when a goal is deleted. Semantic information, described as goal characteristics such as security or usability, should be attached to goals to allow for the detection of conflicts. Our approach considers structural change (both addition and deletion) propagation within the same model and across many models, regardless the semantic aspect of the impacted goals. Lee et al. [14] proposed a goal-driven traceability technique for analyzing requirements, which connects goals and use cases through three different traceability relations (evolution, dependency, and satisfaction), which are stored as a matrix. Impacted entities can then be identified by applying a reachability analysis on the matrix. Our GRL-based approach builds a GRL model dependency graph (GMDG) to represent explicit and implicit, e.g., contribution, dependencies between model elements. In addition, our approach identifies the potential changes in other model elements that are linked through user-defined URN Links.

Ernst et al. [15] proposed an approach to find suitable solutions (that minimize the effort required to implement new solutions) as requirements change. Their approach [15] explores a Requirements Engineering Knowledge Base (REKB), describing goals, tasks, refinements, and conflicts, in order to find new operations that are additionally required as a result of an unanticipated modification such as the addition of a new feature or the introduction of a new law. Our approach does simply spot potential impacted elements based on the GRL model structure and does not propose a solution to implement the change. In order to help developers identify where changes are required, Nakagawa et al. [16] proposed an approach based on the extraction of control loops, described as independent components that prevent the impact of a change from spreading outside them.

More recently, Grubb and Chechik [17] proposed an i*-based method to model the evolution of goal evaluations over time. Their proposed method integrates variability in intentions' satisfaction (using qualitative values) over time allowing the stakeholders to understand and consider alternatives over time. In a closely related work to [17], Aprajita and Mussbacher [18] introduced Timed-GRL, an extension of the GRL standard, allowing for the capture and analysis of a set of changes to a goal model over time (using quantitative values such as concrete dates). Both the goal model and the expected changes are represented in one model. However, both approaches described in [17,18] focus only on the evolution of satisfactions values (qualitative and quantitative) and they do not consider the evolution of the goal model structure over time.

6 Conclusions and Future Work

In this paper, we have presented an automated GRL-based approach to change impact analysis. The proposed CIA approach allows maintainers and analysts understand how a change is propagated within a GRL model and across related GRL models (i.e., from GRL to GRL), linked using URN Links. In addition, the approach allows for the identification of the potentially impacted GRL evaluation strategies. The approach has been implemented as a feature within the jUCMNav [8] tool.

As a future work, we plan to extend our approach to cover simultaneous GRL changes, and to assess the impact of such changes on related Use Case Maps (UCM) functional models.

Acknowledgment. The authors would like to acknowledge the support provided by the Deanship of Scientific Research at King Fahd University of Petroleum & Minerals for funding this work through project No. FT151004.

References

1. Yu, E.S.: Towards modelling and reasoning support for early-phase requirements engineering. In: Proceedings of the Third IEEE International Symposium on Engineering, Requirements, pp. 226–235. IEEE (1997)
2. Giorgini, P., Mylopoulos, J., Sebastiani, R.: Goal-oriented requirements analysis and reasoning in the tropos methodology. Eng. Appl. Artif. Intell. **18**, 159–171 (2005)
3. ITU-T: Recommendation Z.151 (10/12), User Requirements Notation (URN) language definition, Geneva, Switzerland (2012)
4. van Lamsweerde, A., Letier, E.: Handling obstacles in goal-oriented requirements engineering. IEEE Trans. Softw. Eng. **26**(10), 978–1005 (2000)
5. Bohner, S.A., Arnold, R.S.: Software Change Impact Analysis. IEEE Computer Society Press, Los Alamitos (1996)
6. Li, B., Sun, X., Leung, H., Zhang, S.: A survey of code-based change impact analysis techniques. Softw. Testing Verification Reliabil. **23**(8), 613–646 (2013)
7. Hassine, J.: Change impact analysis approach to GRL models. In: SOFTENG 2015: The First International Conference on Advances and Trends in Software Engineering, pp. 1–6. IARIA (2015)
8. jUCMNav v7.0.0: jUCMNav Project (tool, documentation, and meta-model) (2016). http://softwareengineering.ca/~jucmnav. Accessed June 2017
9. Hassine, J., Alshayeb, M.: Measurement of actor external dependencies in GRL models. In: Dalpiaz, F., Horkoff, J. (eds.) Proceedings of the Seventh International i* Workshop Co-Located with the 26th International Conference on Advanced Information Systems Engineering (CAiSE 2014), Thessaloniki, Greece, 16–17 June 2014, vol. 1157 of CEUR Workshop Proceedings, CEUR-WS.org (2014)

10. Weiser, M.: Program slicing. In: Proceedings of the 5th International Conference on Software Engineering (ICSE 1981), Piscataway, NJ, USA, pp. 439–449. IEEE Press (1981)
11. Lehnert, S.: A taxonomy for software change impact analysis. In: Proceedings of the 12th International Workshop on Principles of Software Evolution and the 7th Annual ERCIM Workshop on Software Evolution, pp. 41–50. ACM (2011)
12. Cleland-Huang, J., Settimi, R., BenKhadra, O., Berezhanskaya, E., Christina, S.: Goal-centric traceability for managing non-functional requirements. In: Proceedings of the 27th International Conference on Software Engineering, pp. 362–371. ACM (2005)
13. Tanabe, D., Uno, K., Akemine, K., Yoshikawa, T., Kaiya, H., Saeki, M.: Supporting requirements change management in goal oriented analysis. In: 16th IEEE International Requirements Engineering (RE 2008), pp. 3–12. IEEE (2008)
14. Lee, W.T., Deng, W.Y., Lee, J., Lee, S.J.: Change impact analysis with a goal-driven traceability-based approach. Int. J. Intell. Syst. 25(8), 878–908 (2010)
15. Ernst, N.A., Borgida, A., Jureta, I.: Finding incremental solutions for evolving requirements. In: 19th IEEE International Requirements Engineering Conference (RE 2011), pp. 15–24. IEEE (2011)
16. Nakagawa, H., Ohsuga, A., Honiden, S.: A goal model elaboration for localizing changes in software evolution. In: 21st IEEE International Requirements Engineering Conference (RE 2013), pp. 155–164. IEEE (2013)
17. Grubb, A.M., Chechik, M.: Looking into the crystal ball: requirements evolution over time. In: 24th IEEE International Requirements Engineering Conference (RE 2016), pp. 86–95, September 2016
18. Aprajita, M.G.: TimedGRL: specifying goal models over time. In: 24th IEEE International Requirements Engineering Conference Workshops (REW), pp. 125–134, September 2016

Author Index

Printed in the United States
By Bookmasters